FOTOFEST2006

THE EARTH • ARTISTS RESPONDING TO VIOLENCE

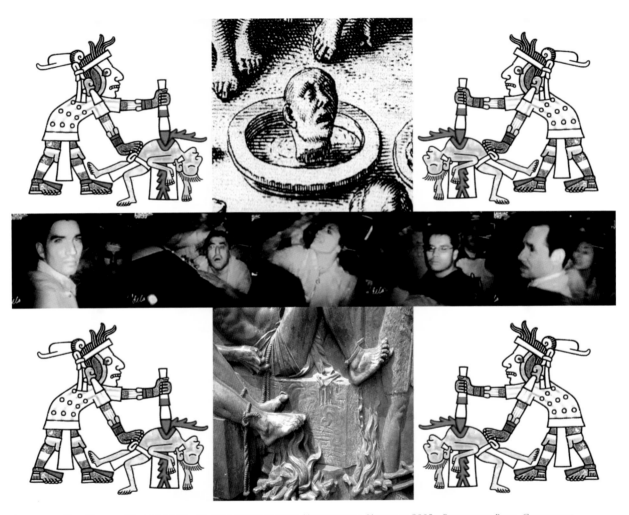

LISDEBERTUS (LUIS DELGADO QUALTHROUGH) · *TLAHUAC*, FROM THE SERIES *UNFATHOMABLE HUMANITY*, 2005 · PIGMENT ON PAPER, COURTESY OF
DE SANTOS GALLERY

AES+F · *Episode 1, No. 13*, from the series *Action Half Life*, 2003 · Digital Color Photograph Collage stretched on canvas · Courtesy of Multimedia Complex for Actual Arts, Moscow and Ruzicska Gallery, Salzburg

Doug and Mike Starn · *Structure of Thought #15*, 2001-2004 · MIS and Lysonic inkjet prints on Thai mulberry, gampi and tissue papers with wax

HARRI KALLIO · *RIVIERE DES ANGUILLES #3, MAURITIUS*, FROM THE SERIES *THE DODO AND MAURITIUS ISLAND, IMAGINARY ENCOUNTERS*, 2001 · ARCHIVAL INKJET PRINT

SPONSORS

MAJOR INSTITUTIONAL AND INDIVIDUAL SPONSORS

William Stamps Farish Foundation

The Brown Foundation Inc., Houston

Houston Endowment, Inc.

The Cullen Foundation

City of Houston through the Cultural Arts Council of Houston/Harris County

The Annenberg Foundation

National Endowment for the Arts

Houston Press

Axiom Design, Houston

JP Morgan Chase Foundation

Vine Street Studios–Margaret Regan and Fletcher Thorne-Thomson Jr.

The Doubletree Hotel Downtown, Houston

Hexagroup

Trust for Mutual Understanding

The Clayton Fund

Eleanor and Frank Freed Foundation

Judith and Gamble Baldwin

The Favrot Fund

Susan Vaughan Foundation

The Wortham Foundation

iland Internet Solutions

Grey Goose Vodka

Bombay Sapphire Gin

The Bruni Smothers Foundation

BOARD OF DIRECTORS

David Ayers, *President*

Frederick Baldwin, *Chairman*

Blair Bouchier

Michael A. Casey

Julie Crosswell

Susan Criner

Cabanne Gilbreath

Carola Herrin

Mavis P. Kelsey. Jr., *Vice President*

James C. Kempner, *Vice President*

Meg King Murray

Gregory M. Spier

Alice Thomas, *Secretary*

Anne Wilkes Tucker

Wendy Watriss, *Artistic Director*

SPECIAL SPONSORSHIP FOR THE FOTOFEST2006 CATALOGUE

Eleanor and Frank Freed Foundation

ADDITIONAL INSTITUTIONAL AND INDIVIDUAL SUPPORT

Texas Commission for the Arts

Houston Downtown District

The Kensan Trust

Continental Airlines

Weingarten Realty

Howard Maisel and Eve France

The Mellon Foundation

The Greentree Fund

American Society of Media Photographers (ASMP)

Museum of Fine Arts, Houston– Film Department

Sotheby's New York–Photography Department, Denise Bethel

New World Museum–Armando Palacios and Cinda Ward

De Santos Gallery–Luis and Gemma De Santos

Art League Houston

Spacetaker, Inc.

Williams Tower Gallery

DiverseWorks Artspace

Bering & James

Trizec Office Properties

Deborah Colton

McCord Development

David and Catherine Miller

Curry Glassell

MacKey Gallery

Mike and Mickey Marvins

Lawndale Art Center

Ceci and Michael Goldstone

Gremillion & Co. Fine Art, Inc.

The Samuels Foundation– Endowment Fund of the Jewish Community of Houston

Art League, Houston

The Wealth Group– Erie City Ironworks

Cita Cook

Kinzelman Art Consulting

KUHF 88.7 FM

IN HONOR OF DAPHNE WOOD GAWTHROP

FotoFest and FOTOFEST2006 are honoring a much respected colleague and close friend, Daphne Wood Gawthrop. Daphne worked with FotoFest first as a professional consultant and, later, as a member of the Board of Directors. Her spirit and energy helped sustain both the art and education programs of FotoFest for many years. She had enormous professional capacity and a fearless determination to achieve what she set out to do. Her activism in both the visual and performing arts extended from Texas to Washington DC and California —the Museum of Fine Arts, Houston, Houston Museum of Natural Science, the Houston Grand Opera and FotoFest, the Institute of Museum and Library Services and the National Endowment for the Arts in Washington D.C., and, more recently, the Sacramento Ballet and the California Arts Council. Her ability to understand the creative process and bridge the often disparate needs of artists, arts institutions, and art patrons was remarkable and effective. She moved gracefully between different classes and cultures. She was a very special person. Her vision and generosity of spirit are an enduring part of FotoFest and many other arts organizations. —Frederick Baldwin and Wendy Watriss, Co-founders, FotoFest

ART MEDIA PARTNERS

American Society of Media Photographers (ASMP)

Aperture Magazine

European Photography Magazine

Fotograf Magazine, International Magazine for Photography and Visual Culture

Pluk Magazine

Photo L.A.

FOTOFEST2006 FINE PRINT AUCTION SPONSORS AUCTION SPONSORS

The Doubletree Hotel-Downtown, Houston

Grey Goose

Houston Press

Sotheby's, Inc.

Bering & James Gallery

Gremillion & Co. Fine Art, Inc.

Sicardi Gallery

TABLE SPONSORS (AT TIME OF PRINTING)

PLATINUM

Bering & James Gallery / Kelly Gale Amén

Susie and Sanford Criner

Family of Daphne Gawthrop

Kathy and Harry Masterson / Hillary and Stan Stratton / Lisa and Will Mathis

SILVER GELATIN

Joan and Stanford Alexander

Shelley and Geoff Bracken

BG North America, LLC

Marita and Jonathan Fairbanks / Gretchen and Andrew McFarland

Judy and Bobby Gerry / Katherine and David Miller

Wendy and Mavis Kelsey

Sherry and Jim Kempner

Meg and Nelson Murray

Veronique and Michael Prentice

Alice Thomas and Julie Crosswell

TECHNICOLOR

Raymona and Bill Bomar / Erla and Harry Zuber

Janice and Blair Bouchier

Michael Casey

De Santos Gallery

Friends of Daphne Gawthrop / Greenwood Properties / Wells Design / Jerry Jeannard

Annie Hadow

Carola and John Herrin

Jenny and Jay Kempner / Ceci and Michael Goldstone

James Edward Maloney

Sicardi Gallery

Werner & Kerrigan LLP

Marion and Bim Wilcox

ORGANIZATION — **FOTOFEST2006**

BOARD OF DIRECTORS

ORGANIZERS

Frederick Baldwin and Wendy Watriss *Artistic Direction and General Management*

FOTOFEST STAFF

Angela Grace, *Director, Literacy Through Photography and Student Projects*

Frank Rose, Coordinator, *Press and Website*

Nan Stombaugh, *Co-coordinator, International Meeting Place and Workshops*

Marianne Stavenhagen, *Volunteer Coordinator, Office manager and Executive Assistant*

Jennifer Ward, *Exhibitions Coordinator, Biennial Map and Calendar Coordinator*

CONSULTANTS

Marta Sánchez Philippe, *Senior Coordinator, International Meeting Place, International Press and Special Projects*

Martha Skow, *Coordinator, Fine Print Auction*

Michele Stoll, *Coordinator, Opening Night Events, Special Biennial Projects, Media Sponsorship*

Wes Jonees, Axiom, *Graphic Design, 2006 Logo and Publications*

Lisa Lerch, Connect2Creative, *Production and Layout, Biennial Publications*

Ping Lau, Ping's Design Studio, *Design Biennial Exhibition Invitations*

Hexagroup, *FotoFest Website Design*

Jim Walker, Earthcolor, *Printing, Biennial Publications*

Dancie Ware Public Relations, *Media Coordination and Opening Night*

Blue Medium, *National and International Press*

Jon Bartosh, *Doubletree Hotel-Downtown*

Jim Kanan, *Kanan Construction, Biennial Production*

Keith Hollingsworth, Hollingsworth Art Services, *Producer, Exhibition Matting/Framing*

Mark Larson, *Facets, Supervisor, Exhibition Installation*

Todd Greenlaw, *Exhibition Installation*

Ruth Antonius, The Travel Solution, *Travel Coordinator*

John Abrash, Destination Houston, *Coordinator, Houston Transportation*

Jeff Johnson, Brilliant Computers, *Computer Manager*

Alex Kapadia, Brilliant Computers, *Computer Consultant*

Annick Dekiouk, *Exhibitions Assistant*

Marilia Fernandes, *Exhibitions Assistant*

Rattaya Nimibuter, *Publications Assistant for Map and Calendar*

Chason Chaffin, *Website Assistant*

Christina Miller, *Special Projects Assistant*

Karen Whitaker, *Assistant, Biennial Office Administration*

CATALOGUE

Wendy Watriss, *Editor and Art Director*

Wes Jones, Axiom, *Designer*

Lisa Lerch, *Director, Production and Layout*

Marianne Stavenhagen, *Coordination, Participating Spaces*

Jennifer Ward, *Coordination, FotoFest Exhibitions*

Earth Color, *Printing*

FINE PRINT AUCTION

Meg and Nelson Murray, *Chairs*

Martha Skow, *Action Coordinator*

Marta Sanchez Philippe, *Auction Catalogue Coordinator*

Denise Bethel, Sotheby's Inc., *Auctioneer*

Masterpiece Litho, *Catalogue Printing*

BIENNIAL WORKSHOPS

Mary Virginia Swanson

Robert Morton

FILM PROGRAM

Marian Luntz, *Director, Museum of Fine Arts, Houston Film Department*

Flo Stone, *Artistic Director and Founder, Environmental Film Festival in the Nation's Capital*

Andy Hernandez, *Program Officer, Environmental Film Festival in the Nation's Capital*

DANCE PROGRAM

Michele Brangwen, *Michele Brangwen Dance Ensemble*

SPECIAL SUPPORT

Hall Puckett, Workshops and Photography, American Society of Media Photographers, Houston, *Workshops and Photography*

Beryl Striewski, Photography, American Society of Media Photographers, Houston, *Photography*

Bob Abbinanti, Que Imaging

Sara Balinska, Sara Balinska Framing

Rhonda Wilson, Rhubarb Rhubarb, UK

Andreas Müller Pohle, Berlin PhotoFestival, Germany

Karla Osorio, FotoArte, Brazil

Razvan Ion, ArtPhoto, Romania

Mary Virginia Swanson, Photo Santa Fe, USA

LITERACY THROUGH PHOTOGRAPHY – BIENNIAL PROGRAM

Sean Parker, *Writer, 2006 Earth Curriculum for Schools*

Mary Stark Love, *Researcher and Contributor, 2006 Earth Curriculum; Co-coordinator Biennial School Tours*

Ping Lau, Ping's, *Designer, 2006 Earth Curriculum*

INTERNS

Bernard Agard

Laura Bennett

Gabriel Cruz Mendoza

Melinda Dan-Hanh Pham

Brandi Desselle

April Duckworth Maduzia

Kara Duval

Ewa Konopka-Tittel

Jennifer Lawrence

Sharon Lott

Teresa Munisteri

Michael Sanders

Brandy Stoesz

Chloe Walker

FOTOFEST ART BOARD

Frederick Baldwin, *Chairman, FotoFest, Inc.*

Michelle Barnes, *Director, Community Artists Collective*

Suzanne Bloom, *Artist/Professor, University of Houston*

Peter Brown, *Artist*

Jean Caslin, *Independent Curator*

Fernando Castro, *Artist/Curator*

Lynn Herbert, *Curator, Contemporary Arts Museum*

Ed Hill, *Artist/Professor, University of Houston*

Dr. David Jacobs, *Professor, University of Houston*

George Krause, *Artist*

James Maloney, *Private Collector, Attorney, Baker & Botts*

Delilah Montoya, *Artist/Professor, University of Houston*

Bill Thomas, *Artist*

Anne Wilkes Tucker, *Curator, Museum of Fine Arts, Houston*

Wendy Watriss, *Artistic Director, FotoFest, Inc.*

Clint Willour, *Galveston Arts Center*

Casey Williams, *Artist*

Anderson Wrangle, *Artist*

COMMUNITY ADVISORY BOARD

Bennie Flores Ansell, *Artist*

Mark Cervenka, *O'Kane Gallery, University of Houston-Downtown*

John Cleary, *John Cleary Gallery*

Kimberly Davenport, *Rice University Art Gallery*

Leamon Greene, *Texas Southern University Art Department*

Kimberly Gremillion, *Gremillion & Co. Fine Art, Inc.*

Dan Havel, *Artist*

Joe Havel, *Glassell School of Art*

Earlie Hudnall, *Artist*

Darra Keeton, *Artist*

Sara Kellner, *DiverseWorks Artspace*

Chelby King, *Lawndale Art Center*

Rick Lowe, *Project Row Houses*

Roni McMurtrey, *McMurtrey Gallery*

Debbie Riddle, *Artist*

María Inés Sicardi, *Sicardi Gallery*

Jose Solis III, *Artist*

Terrie Sultan, *Blaffer Galler, University of Houston*

Sally Sprout, *Sally Sprout Gallery*

Suzanne Theis, *The Orange Show*

Dr. Alvia Wardlaw, *Texas Southern University Museum*

THE EARTH · ARTISTS RESPONDING TO VIOLENCE

FOTOFEST2006 addresses issues that have been strong personal concerns of FotoFest's founders for many years. The 2006 themes represent ideas that are at the core of FotoFest's goals and purposes since the first Biennial in 1986. Having been photographers ourselves, we started FotoFest to assist talented artists from all over the world and to enable them to have access to the same opportunities available to artists from well-established art communities in the U.S. and Western Europe. Our idea was also to help mid career and emerging artists break through the spatial separation between working artists and those who head institutions determining who is invited to exhibit or publish. We began FotoFest as a platform for discovery and opportunity.

Two programs intersect to create these opportunities—the exhibitions program and the Meeting Place portfolio reviews. FotoFest curates and commissions it own exhibitions. At the same time, we have created an open (unjuried) platform—the Meeting Place—where artists can meet and show work to important national and international curators,

publishers, gallery owners, photo agents, and editors. Working from the perspectives of working artists, we have been selective about whom we invite to be reviewers. It is important that they are open to new work and able to do something for artists whose work they like. The Meeting Place is also designed to be an opportunity for reviewers to have a chance to network with their peers from across the U.S. and the world.

We are socially concerned individuals. Before FotoFest, we did our own photography from that vantage point, in many parts of the world. We are deeply interested in the intersection of art and ideas, art and social issues. We see art as central to the intellectual and political well-being of society. In fact, most art is deeply involved, figuratively or metaphorically, with the issues that shape societal existence and individual life.

For most of its Biennials, FotoFest has put forward these ideas through themes and exhibits that interconnect art, aesthetics, ideas and social issues. FOTOFEST 1986-2006

In 1990, CENTRAL EUROPE—creative photography before and after the political changes of the late 1980s and early1990s. Photography and political changes in the Czechoslovak Republic.

In 1992—EUROPE AND LATIN AMERICAN—the mid-nineteenth century to the late twentieth century.

In 1994—AMERICAN VOICES, LATINO PHOTOGRAPHERS IN THE U.S.; THE GLOBAL ENVIRONMENT; FASHION, EVOLUTION/REVOLUTION; THE NEW GENERATION, CONTEMPORARY PHOTOGRAPHY IN CUBA

In 1996, 1998, 2000—RE-DISCOVERING HOUSTON—thirty-three art exhibitions and events re-establishing public use of the city's older downtown areas and warehouse districts. Exhibitions and installations concerned Kurdish history (Susan Meiseles' *Kurdistan in The Shadow of History*), early landscape photography in Mexico, documentary work by Chinese photographer Wu Jialin, *Altered Worlds*—Slovak staged photography,*Contemporary Photographers from Korea: The New Generation*; Malian portraitist Seydou Keita; *Looking at the 90s, Contemporary Mexican Photography*; *Five South African Artists*, with William Kentridge.

In 2002—THE CLASSICAL EYE AND BEYOND—a focus on new technology, mixed media and web-based work with five classical black and white, international exhibitions, including *Russian Pictorialism*.

In 2004—WATER—CELEBRATING WATER. LOOKING AT THE GLOBAL CRISIS—thirty-two exhibitions and films, with a Global Forum, on the nature of water, its use, abuse, and the future of water in the world.

FOTOFEST2006—ARTISTS RESPONDING TO VIOLENCE AND THE EARTH—The themes chosen for FotoFest's twentieth Biennial anniversary are our response to what is happening in the world today. The institutionalization of torture. Routinized violence and violence as entertainment. Weapons of war increasing in scale, accessibility and destructiveness. Growing consumption of the world's resources. The increasing gap between rich and poor. The efficiency with which nature can be destroyed.

There is need for a space and time when we are compelled to confront these truths. Artists can create that space.

Frederick Baldwin and Wendy Watriss
Co-founders, FotoFest

CONTENTS

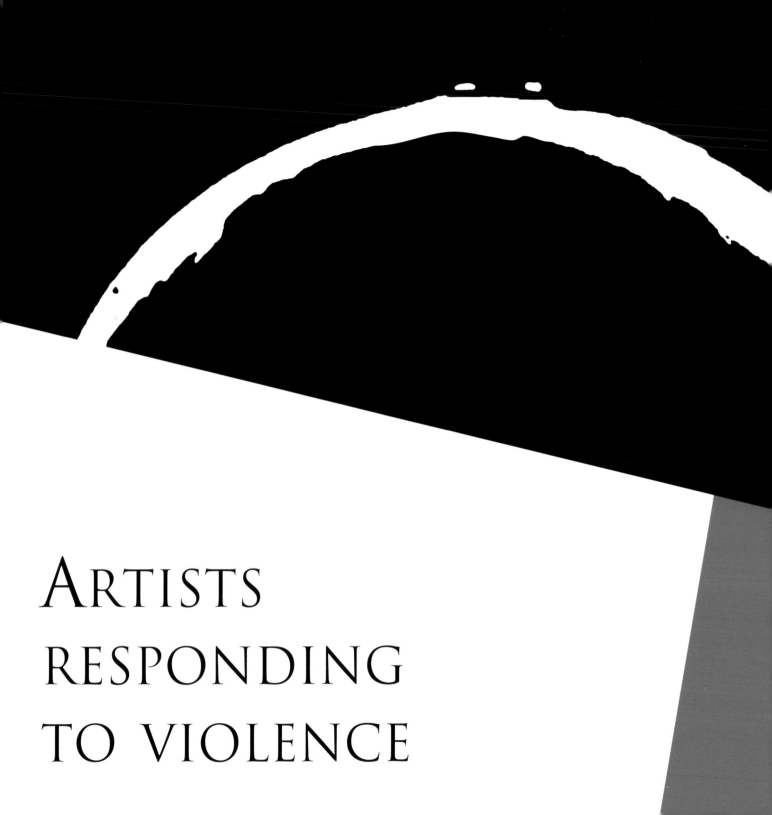

ARTISTS
RESPONDING
TO VIOLENCE

ARTISTS RESPONDING TO VIOLENCE

THE SOUND OF SILENCE

ARTIST: ALFREDO JAAR

The Shutters Come Down:
On Alfredo Jaar's *The Sound of Silence*

When it comes to political violence, we want witnesses and demand sacrifice, and sometimes the two come together. Every day, professional witnesses get into position to show us what is happening far away and out of sight. We want to see the broken bodies and sorrowful faces of those who do not have our privileges or protections. We want to be connected to these unfortunates through images. Why? Because we feel responsible to them, and we like feeling responsible *for* them. Their suffering gives a context for our comforts and a distant focus for our empathy.

The rules for this exchange are remarkably inflexible. We want those who take on the work of witnessing to show us things in the right order and in a certain light, within strict rules of propriety. It is permissible to tease the edges of these proprieties—in fact, we reward such flirtations with prizes—but not to be too insistent about it. An excess of truth can be a dangerous thing. Or, as T.S. Eliot had it in a poem about redemption, "Human kind cannot bear very much reality."[1]

Alfredo Jaar's *The Sound of Silence* is a threnody for South African photographer Kevin Carter, a committed witness who became a tragic sacrifice and a scapegoat for our guilty desire to see images of others' suffering.

Carter was born in 1960, the year Nelson Mandela's African National Congress (ANC) was banned, and came of age as a professional witness in the years leading up to the new South Africa. When political violence of the most brutal kind erupted in the black townships after the release of Mandela in 1990 (and the lifting of the ban on the ANC), Carter and his comrades in what came to be called the "Bang-Bang Club" (Greg Marinovich, Joao Silva, and Ken Oosterbroek) photographed the daily carnage as the dying apartheid government used sectarian tensions between the ANC and the Zulu-backed Inkatha Freedom Party as cover for political murder and destabilizing mayhem.

These photographers witnessed unspeakable things, day in and day out, during this time. They photographed black South Africans being beaten, tortured, hacked to death, and burned alive in Soweto and Tokoza. The worldwide market for such images was booming, and the members of the Bang-Bang Club became famous. Witnessing these things through the camera lens (being a witness to history) was a rush, but it took a toll. The photographers bonded together, but felt themselves drawing away from the rest of society and suffering various psychological maladies. Carter was especially tortured by what he saw and by the moral ambiguities of his witness role. In an article on covering conflict, he wrote, "I suffer depression from what I see and experience nightmares. I feel alienated from 'normal' people, including my family. . . . The shutters come down and I recede into a dark place with dark images of blood and death in godforsaken dusty places." One recurrent nightmare had him near

they witnessed too many murders

ALFREDO JAAR · FROM THE *SOUND OF SILENCE*, 2006 · VIDEO ANIMATION STILL

ALFREDO JAAR · FROM THE *SOUND OF SILENCE*, 2006 · VIDEO ANIMATION STILL

death, crucified to a wooden beam, while a television camera with a monstrously large lens zoomed in on his face, closer and closer till he awoke screaming.

Because of their newfound notoriety, the members of the Bang-Bang Club began to garner assignments to cover conflicts and suffering elsewhere. In 1993, Carter went to Sudan, where thousands of people were starving to death while a civil war raged on.

In South Africa, Carter had photographed the perpetrators and victims of violence. There were certainly perpetrators and victims in the Sudan, but Carter could not get into position to photograph them. What he did find was another kind of image: the image of a vulture appearing to stalk a starving child. The vulture appeared to be waiting for the child to expire and become carrion, to become food. This is a very different kind of violence than the killings Carter had photographed in South Africa. This is the inexorable violence of the food chain. The problem with this image was that it was difficult for its viewers to find, within the image, someone to blame.

The people who reacted so strongly against this image did so not because they objected to the depiction of natural violence more than that of political violence, but because of its symbolism. Though they struck out at the photographer, accusing him of being no better than a vulture, waiting to make this image while a child died, I believe the real reason for their outrage lies elsewhere. I believe they read this image, unconsciously, as a commentary on their own position in relation to the starving child. They thought that they were being called vultures in their hunger for images like this—carrion-eaters feeding off of the misfortunes of others to find satisfaction as consumers of images of violence and pestilence. And, even further, that perhaps this Sudanese child was dying there in the dirt so that we might consume her *image*.

This was too much reality for some viewers to bear. So they reacted in the normal human way: they blamed someone else. We want witnesses, but we demand sacrifice. Someone had to pay for this impropriety. Carter paid. He killed himself, at age thirty-three, on July 27, 1994, only two months after Mandela was sworn in as president of the new South Africa that Carter had spent his whole life imagining.

Blaming the photographer who makes these images is like blaming a soldier for what's going on in Iraq. The photographer and the soldier are our representatives, our surrogates. We put them in position to do our bidding. The troops didn't start the war and they don't decide how it is prosecuted. Photojournalists take the kind of pictures that they know they can sell to the news organizations, who sell them to us. Kevin Carter wouldn't have gone to Sudan on his own. We put him there. We put him in front of that starving child, and then accused him of *moral detachment* for making the image we wanted him to make. Where is our moral engagement in this? Where is our complicity? And where is our forgiveness?

David Levi Strauss

[1]T. S. Eliot, "Burnt Norton (I)," in *T. S. Eliot: The Complete Poems and Plays* (New York: Harcourt Brace & World, 1971), p. 118.

they were arrested many times

ALFREDO JAAR · FROM THE *SOUND OF SILENCE*, 2006 · VIDEO ANIMATION STILL

they were called the Bang-Bang Club

ALFREDO JAAR · FROM THE *SOUND OF SILENCE*, 2006 · VIDEO ANIMATION STILL

FotoFest at Vine
Street Studios

Artists Responding to Violence

Chechnya,

Vietnam,

Iraq,

Argentina,

Institutional torture and internal conflict,

International intervention and civil war,

Battle sites,

Video war games

As international warfare and domestic conflicts increase in scale and accessibility, it is essential to give visibility to deeper and alternative forms of analysis and expression. Through the information of personal experience and political history, these works confront both individual and societal violence.

LIST OF ARTISTS

AES + F

Sergey Bratkov

Juan Manuel Echavarría

Joakim Eneroth

Yves Gellie

Claudio Hils

Nathalie Latham

Lisdebertus aka Luis Delgado Qualtrough

Paula Luttringer

Elizabeth Mellott-Carreón

Liza Nguyen

EL LAMENTO DE LOS MUROS [THE WAILING OF THE WALLS]

ARTIST: PAULA LUTTRINGER

Paula Luttringer was "disappeared" for more than five months, at a time when she was little more than a teenager. For many years afterward, she remained silent about this period of her life when she suffered as one of the many political militants kidnapped under the state terrorism of the cruelest dictatorship ever to have seized power in the history of Argentina.

As she says, "A long time passed before I spoke to anyone about those five months I spent in a clandestine detention center. I thought that someone who hadn't lived through it would be unable to understand what I had to tell. 'How lucky you are to have survived,' was what I often heard them say to me, and so my bitter rage was never more than a mumble. I was caught up in the idea that nobody from outside would be able to understand that a noise, a smell alone, was enough to hurl us back in a matter of seconds toward the past."

The Wailing of the Walls is a project that was born of Luttringer's eventual desire to explore in depth her own experience and to extend it, through the power of testimony, to that of the almost one hundred women she came to meet while producing the work. These women are but a few of the thousands who lived through similar experiences of kidnapping, torture, and "disappearance." Indeed, the word *disappeared* came to be used on a daily basis and took on a new

and sinister meaning. It became a way of referring to those who had been kidnapped by the state security forces to be either detained in clandestine centers or murdered—those who had disappeared from daily life and were lost without a trace. During the period 1976–1983, there were over five hundred clandestine detention centers in Argentina.

In this series, a work still in progress, the word *disappeared* is added to the image as another component of the discourse, for the work here includes testimonies gathered by the artist from women who are today employed in a variety of occupations and who live in different parts of Argentina and abroad. What they share is that all of them were shut away behind those walls that Luttringer would photograph years later—walls that proved to be much more forthcoming witnesses than ever imagined by those who, upon retreating, destroyed anything that might reveal the terrible nature of what had been committed therein. Luttringer has the following to say about her work: "I don't regard the main aim of the work as being an act of denunciation, but I hope that it will encourage people to reflect on what happened, as this is essential. When violence is meted out against women, whether in times of war or in the context of civil conflict, it leaves a profound mark, one which is not erased by the passing of time and which affects their emotional world and the lives of their children and families."

I went down about twenty or thirty steps and I heard big iron doors being shut. I imagined that the place was underground, that it was big, because you could hear people's voices echoing and the airplanes taxing overhead or nearby. The noise drove you mad. One of the men said to me: so you're a psychologist? Well bitch, like all the psychologist, here you're really going to find out what's good. And he began to punch me in the stomach. MARTA CANDELORO WAS ABDUCTED ON JUNE 7, 1977 IN NEUQUEN. SHE WAS THEN TAKEN TO THE SECRET DETENTION CENTER, "LA CUEVA."

They said we were going to a place where we'd meet lots of people who had disappeared and about whom nothing more would ever be known, that we too had disappeared and no longer existed in the eyes of the world, that not even our names existed and that we should answer with the name they gave us. They left me handcuffed and blindfolded in a sort of courtyard, where they searched me and asked me about any metal objects I might be carrying, even if I had an IUD fitted. Later I found out that this routine was what they did before giving you electric shocks, to check that there was no other conductor on you. HEBE CÁCERES WAS ABDUCTED ON JUNE, 1978 IN LA PLATA. SHE WAS THEN TAKEN TO THE SECRET DETENTION CENTER, "EL BANCO."

Ants used to come in and out, and I would watch these ants because they were coming in and then going out into the world. They were walking across the earth, the outside world, and then coming back in again, and watching them I didn't feel so alone.   LEDDA BARREIRO WAS ABDUCTED ON JANUARY 12. 1978 IN MAR DEL PLATE. SHE WAS THEN TAKEN TO THE SECRET DETENTION CENTER, "LA CUEVA."

Gladis Cuervo, a nurse, says: "I was always looking. In the street, on the train, the bus, the subway, I would look at people's shoes. The image of shoes was fixed in my mind. I used to look at the shoes worn by every man who approached me." Abused and humiliated, isolated behind the blindfold or beneath the hood, she recorded the individuality of each one of her torturers through the image of those shoes, which, like a recurring obsession, is still capable of overwhelming her, as if it were an uncontrollable nightmare. Furthermore, as Luttringer says, it is terrifyingly capable of transporting her—through a process in which the mind no longer distinguishes the real from the unreal—back to that cold, damp world of nauseating smells, a world into which we as spectators enter by looking at these photographed interiors.

Concrete benches, filthy latrines, abandoned rooms, illegible graffiti, and walls torn down by time. Walls that served to stifle the desperate screams, the cries of those tortured and raped, and the indescribable, agonized moans of those who, although they were freed, remain aware of their open wounds —who feel that they will never get out of that hole.

Juan Travnik
Photographer, Curator, and Teacher, Buenos Aires

PAULA LUTTRINGER CAPTIONS:
EL LAMENTO DE LOS MUROS, 2000-2005
DIGITAL PRINTS ON FINE ART PAPER
PAGE 25: #*23* · PAGE 26: #*18* · PAGE 27: #*13* · PAGE 29: #*8*

And this marks you, it's a wounded feeling that stays with you the rest of your life. You're left with this dual task; you have to be constantly working out what comes from the trauma and what from normal life. I have this dual task in life. I have to decide which feelings are the result of the trauma and what there is beneath of less intensity, more diluted, which is what comes from normal life. So I talk to someone who was never in a clandestine prison and then I play the role of a normal person and I realize what that involves, and I step into normality. These things that happen to all of us who were victims of repression.   LILIANA GARDELLA WAS ABDUCTED ON NOVEMBER 25, 1977 IN MAR DEL PLATA. SHE WAS THEN TAKEN TO THE SECRET DETENTION CENTER, "ESMA"

REACTIVE

ARTIST: JOAKIM ENEROTH

REACTIVE

Before violence there are the accelerating thoughts, the threat, the fear, the anger. In my personal world physical violence hardly ever appears, but the conditions for it are still very much there. Sometimes slumbering, sometimes clearly shining through, reflecting the reactive mind.

Joakim Eneroth

JOAKIM ENEROTH · *ANARCHISTS ERIC AND KRISTIAN ON A DEMONSTRATION IN STOCKHOLM,* FROM THE SERIES *REACTIVE,* 1999 · INK JET DIGITAL PHOTOGRAPH

Joakim Eneroth · *A Buddhist monk in Nepal who is playing Game Boy*, from the series *Reactive*, 1999 · Ink Jet Digital Photograph

Joakim Eneroth · *Anarchist party in the suburb of Stockholm*, from the series *Reactive*, 1999 · Ink Jet Digital Photograph

Joakim Eneroth · *A cat and a Buddhist monk at the reception desk on the monastery, Wal Suanmok in Thailand,* from the series *Reactive,* 1999
· Ink jet Digital Photograph

BOCAS DE CENIZA [MOUTHS OF ASH]

ARTIST: JUAN MANUEL ECHAVARRÍA

The Art of Juan Manuel Echavarría

I was drowning in words." With that, Juan Manuel Echavarría walked away from thirty years as a writer of serious fiction. Shortly after, Echavarría's vision of his own world radically shifted. This often told story is worth repeating for, in a moment of remarkable clarity, the fledgling artist found his way.

One day while driving through Bogotá, Echavarría noticed that sidewalk sellers were displaying their wares on old battered mannequins. Busy rifling through the clothing, shoppers paid no heed. For a brief moment, the mannequins took on a different life for Echavarría. They became the raped and pillaged citizens of Colombia, the rural peasants suffering massacre after massacre, kidnapped for ransom, displaced, turned into refugees by the tens of thousands, or killed, their mutilated bodies tossed into a river or a mass grave. The damaged lives of ordinary people wrought helpless, homeless, and violent by fifty years of civil war normally went unnoticed by privileged citizens of Bogotá, buffered by wealth and security systems. The shoppers, themselves among the dispossessed, found the mannequins quite normal. But Echavarría noticed them. Cast-aside stand-ins for the human body opened his eyes.

Out of that brief moment came *Retratos/Portraits*. As the artist says, "Somehow in taking these pictures of broken mannequins, which became my first series, I understood the direction my art should take. I would explore violence through metaphor." From literature came his entanglement with metaphor; from his determination to see his country across social classes came his subject.

Whereas *Retratos* is based upon the formal portrait, trashed mannequins from the street, *Corte de florero/Flower Vase Cut* takes its form from botanical prints from the late eighteenth century Spanish expeditions into the New World. In the gallery setting, the black and white photographs appear as a row of elegant, botanical prints, one flower to a page. Gradually it dawns upon the viewer that the exquisite illustrations of flowers are made from human bones. Each print alludes to a different formalized body mutilation used to serve notice of the power of the killer even after death. Each page is titled at the bottom in old-fashioned script. The artist gives every flower its scientific name plus a second name that describes his personal response to the violence represented by the bone flowers. For example, *Maxillaria Vorx*, carries the scientific name in Latin for an orchid, Maxillaria, followed by vorix, Latin for voracious. Violence is voracious.

Then the artist turned from still photography to video— *Bolívar's Platter*, a small allegory only several minutes long based upon ten photographs. The action is simple. An object of historical importance, a platter from Simon Bolívar's banquet setting, is smashed. Simon Bolívar is the George Washington of Colombia. The subject is the total destruction of the Republic of Colombia by cocaine. The one who smashes

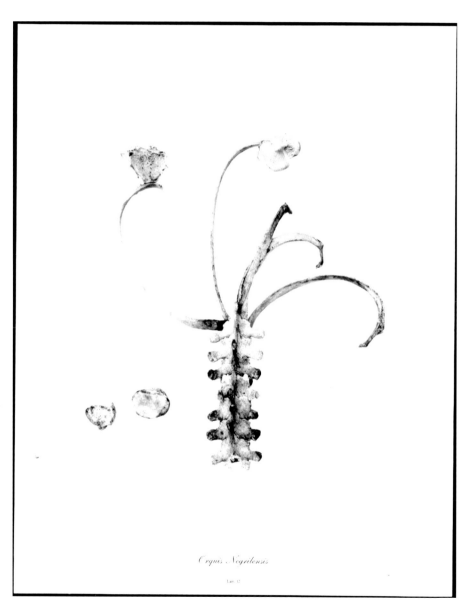

Orquis Negrilensis

JUAN MANUEL ECHAVARRIA · *ORQUIS NEGRILENSIS, FROM THE SERIES CORTE DE FLORERO / FLOWER VASE CUT.*
1997 · SILVER GELATIN PRINT · COURTESY OF NORTH DAKOTA MUSEUM OF ART

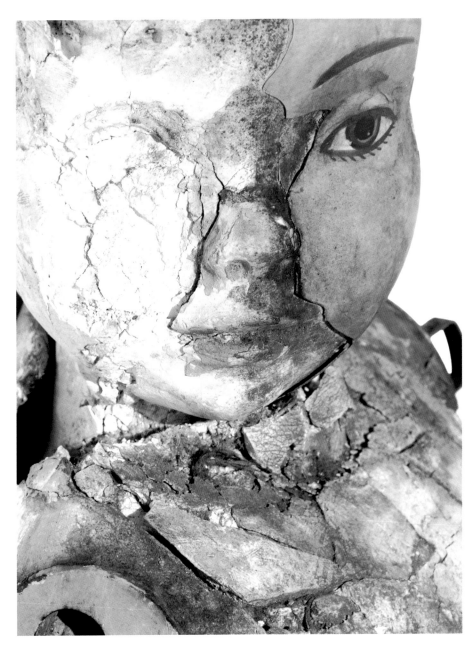

JUAN MANUEL ECHAVARRIA · FROM THE SERIES *N N (NO NAME)*, 2005 · VIBRACHROME DIGITAL PRINT ·
COURTESY OF NORTH DAKOTA MUSEUM OF ART

Juan Manuel Echavarria · *La Maria: Coleccion de insectos / Insect collection*, 2000 · Vibrachrome Digital Print · Courtesy of North Dakota Museum of Art

has no name, no singular identity. First, the viewer is startled by and then left with the reverberating sound of shattering porcelain. Against a black void, the plate is reduced to star dust. But instead of drifting off into the Milky Way as one might expect, the ceramic dust coalesces into a gleaming, glistening mound of cocaine, the last image on the screen. This is a work of art distilled to its very essence. At the end, the audience is inevitably silent. *Bolívar's Platter* seems to be the artist's personal cry for his beloved country.

Guerra y paz/War and Peace is a video version of a modern-day morality play in which two parrots personify opposing moral positions. One screams war; the other screams peace. The surreal white background suggests no place—or all places. The warring male wins, dominating from the top of his cross-like perch, suggesting that Christianity set the stage. In this work, Echavarría first introduces the question: What is the role of the Christian Church in Colombia's ongoing violence?

La María is based upon a 1999 mass kidnapping from a Catholic church in Cali during Sunday service. The artist formed his rambling narrative by photographing the seemingly inconsequential objects seven women brought back from their long months in captivity: a collection of insects and another of popular collecting or trading cards from Colombian chocolate bars that portray specimens from nature including plants, animals, and insects. Other photographs included the women's communal washing bowl with its illusion to the ecclesiastical chalice, the red rag that served as their only towel but suggests the blood-soaked cloth of Christ, and a delicate rosary. Most importantly, Echavarría also collected their stories.

La María tells the story of kidnapping for ransom. Only here does Echavarría introduce hope in the form of educated, middle-class women. The kidnapped art teacher and the botanist hold onto the promise of life through activities of the mind and the spirit. They study nature and form collections of it. They make art, and they bring their companions into their activities. They teach the young guerrilla guards about the natural world, about mathematics. Importantly, in *La María* Echavarría draws attention to the humanity of the enemy, of those who kidnap. They are children, twelve-, thirteen-, eighteen-years-old. How can they make moral choices when their language doesn't contain simple vocabulary essential to ethical thinking?

In *Two Brothers* and *Mouths of Ash*, the artist again collects stories. This time they appear in the form of songs composed by individuals who have survived massacres, which, like bards of old, they sing in public. Here they sing directly into the artist's camera. Echavarría often speaks of his desire to give voice to the voiceless. In these two works he is present but only as the sympathetic listener behind the camera lens. Like the artist himself in *Bolívar's Platter*, these Afro-Colombians at the bottom of society compose songs of mourning. With great eloquence, each sings his or her own dirge of fear and despair.

Importantly, as in *La María*, the artist finds hope for the future of Colombia with the singers. The process of turning their horrible experiences into art, and then offering that art to the public, brings a validation to their act of survival. They bear witness of their own experience which strengthens them, their families, and their community. "If I live, I will tell. If I don't live, my art will tell." And in the telling good overcomes evil.

Laurel Reuter
Director, North Dakota Museum of Art

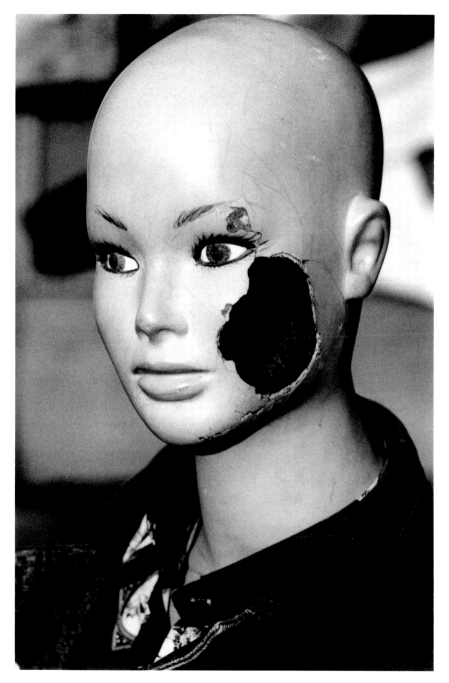

Juan Manuel Echavarría · *Retrato / Portrait #2*, 1996 · Silver Gelatin Print · Courtesy of North Dakota Museum of Art

ACTION HALF LIFE

ARTIST: AES+F

The title *Action Half Life* is borrowed from an existing computer game. Its heroes are teenagers from modeling agencies, selected in a casting call consisting of more than 500 candidates. Its landscapes are from the Sinai desert, which could have served as the location for yet another episode of *Star Wars*. Its firearms, specifically created in 3D Max and other well-known applications, are known to have performed outstandingly well in previous virtual wars.

Violence is spectacular. Scenes of combat, warriors, victories, and forced capture are constant elements in the artistic background of reality, from cave paintings and canvases of Old Masters to Hollywood 3D battles, i.e., *Lord of the Rings*, computer games, and media breakthroughs.

Violence includes visual temptation. Artists of the Renaissance were ambiguous when portraying the suffering of young martyrs with unmasked pleasure, observing the expression of the body or the stains on paintings from streams of blood. Visual violence extends from the fantasy of the hero to the reverie of the foe, the expression of a battle, and the glory of victory until it reaches an almost erotic intensity between the killer and the victim. From our childhood, we know that murder and war are "bad deeds" even though, from childhood, we reach out for a toy firearm or a button on the keyboard assigned the command "FIRE" in a computer game.

Hollywood productions show successive heroes and foes, victims and violators, drowning in blood, even though, always, like a laxative for the blood-satiated viewer, they end with a vignette of moralization about the superiority of justified onslaught, condemnations of cruelty, and so on. Viewers feel a vulgar sense of pleasure from a foe's blood or simply the cruelty of a war's horror and filth, which stains both the victor and victim, indulging in a politically correct mutation to create the idea of a "clean war" and the function "GORE MODE: OFF" in a computer game.

Susan Sontag wrote about the abundance of images of suffering and onslaught in mass media and about the paradoxical effect of creating soullessness and the absence of compassion among the public, ultimately devaluing the abundance of these images. This stunning effect of achieving just the opposite effect is joined with the very noble intention of capturing attention, provoking compassion, and encouraging the viewer/reader to actions ending the suffering of other people.

All these thoughts are present in our project *Action Half Life*. We discuss violence through methods of excluding it. We completely discourage onslaught by showing armed angels (in the commonplace angelic nature of a child) and putting them in an unidentifiable (in the sense of real and virtual) place and time (game or future). But we kept the feeling of a world "charged with violence,"—violence that hasn't yet happened or may not happen at all.

AES+F · *Episode 3, No. 2*, from the series *Action Half Life*, 2003 · Digital Color Photograph Collage stretched on canvas · Courtesy of Multimedia Complex for Actual Arts, Moscow and Ruzicska Gallery, Salzburg

Our heroes, kids at the age of innocence, belong to a heroic period of their lives, when a young shepherd defeats a giant or a bastard child extracts a magic sword from a stone and becomes king. All our young heroes are victors in a virtual world. Their enemy is absent; pain and agony are forbidden, according to the rules of the game. They are so secluded that nothing, not even a conjoined battle, can prevent them from achieving their personal exploits. They overcome their non-existent opponent. The pure manifestation of heroism in the world of a glimmering reality is the real subject of our work.

AES+F
Tatiana Arzamasova
Lev Evzovitch
Evgeny Svyatsky
Vladimir Fridkes

Translated from Russian by Anthony Svyatsky

This exhibition is presented by Multimedia Complex for Actual Arts, Moscow with assistance from the Ruzicska Gallery in Salzburg. Special assistance has come from the Trust for Mutual Understanding.

AES+F · *Episode 2, No. 12*, from the series *Action Half Life*, 2003 · Digital Color Photograph Collage stretched on canvas · Courtesy of Multimedia Complex for Actual Arts, Moscow and Ruzicska Gallery, Salzburg

SOLDIERS AND ARMY GIRLS

ARTIST: SERGEY BRATKOV

**Estrangement from Society,
Sergey Bratkov's Projects**

Sergey Bratkov first appeared in Moscow in 1994. He brought with him new Ukrainian art which, for the Russian viewer, emerged unexpectedly in the hitherto stirringly familiar and readily understood artistic space. Within the few years that had separated Russian and Ukraine into unconnected cultural spaces, Ukraine produced some artists who were the first, in the Slavonic, post-Socialist land, to ironically interpret the twentieth-century history, including its latest, and still raw, episodes in the "estranged"[1] manner stripped of the Soviet stereotypes.

Bratkov moved to Moscow in 2001. At the time Moscow art was painfully devoid of the analytical principle, those reflections on the moments in time that had marked Russian art throughout the past three centuries of its development. At the outset of the twenty-first century, Russia's contemporary art seemed to have lost both its messianic fervor and its holy fool's clowning, which had been left behind in the 1990s as represented by the few unruly artists who disturbed the general public (not just Bohemians alone) with their seemingly senseless artistic gestures that, with time, came to be reinterpreted as the paradoxical images of the times, conveying the distorted and subjective transformations of the latest changes. By 2000, this penchant for gestures, mostly manifested in performances and happenings, had generally faded. The coming of Bratkov was like a bolt of thunder from cloudless, decorative, neo-Academic and narcissistic sky under which metropolitan Bohemians live.

It was natural that Bratkov settled in Moscow rather than in St. Petersburg. This old city is the center of the circulatory system in the organism that is Russia. It is not Russia's brain, as distinct from the cold rationality of the artificially constructed and bizarre creation called St. Petersburg. Moscow is the flesh, raw meat, sensuality and emotions that can storm the whole country. The first year Bratkov spent in the capital resulted in his *My Moscow* exhibition where the surface which showed the unbridled barbarism of the old capital didn't hide the anguish of the end of history. The city-dwellers as recorded by Bratkov in the festive atmosphere of the capital are turned into archetypal figures. The paratroopers splashing in the fountain on their celebrity day seem to merge with water like water deities, while the long-legged girls up the hill are shot in such a way that their skinny modern-looking figures have something in common with goddesses of fertility.

The *Army Girls* of 2000 is notable among Bratkov's projects of the period. The project was shot on the premises of a military school for woman in Kharkov and is a travesty of a fashion magazine photo session. The artist managed it only by introducing himself as a fashion photographer for heads of military school. But that posing as fashion turned the very act of shooting into a play within the contexts of the current art process. The overall effect is a parody of PlayBoy's and

Sergey Bratkov · *Untitled*, 2000 · Digital Print · Courtesy of Regina Gallery, Moscow

Sergey Bratkov · *Untitled*, 2000 · Digital Print · Courtesy of Regina Gallery, Moscow

Helmut Newton's fashion shots which, themselves have been turned into mass consumption products in the country that had lost one set of stereotypes and had not yet embraced another set.

Practically at the same time Sergey Bratkov produced the series characteristic of his attitude to the war in Chechnya. At the turn of the 1990s and 2000s, this subject divided Russian society not only in terms of the political preferences of people, but also over their being tired of war, over their illusions, natural peacefulness, or their readiness to be swayed by the massive brainwashing from mass media to accept war. Bratkov presented two stories. One story was that of a woman-sniper, formerly a sportswoman who was hired by the Islamist resistance and later recognized as a terrorist. The second story is that of soldiers who ordered their portraits done before being sent to fight in Chechnya. Here we have iconography representing a bizarre mix of memorial portraiture rooted in the Fayuim funereal images of Roman colonists and soldiers with fiery backgrounds that offer associations both with fire worshippers and with the famous posters that carried portraits of the World War II heroes and the postwar Soviet cult of the heroes who had fallen during the war.

At the time, there was hardly anybody else on the art scene who could create his own work without manifesting some political ambition or without seeking some political support be it from those who were pro or those who were contra. The artist's stand is in line with Leo Tolstoy's "philosophy of the common sense" which enables one to understand a story in the absence of a moral or comment. Outwardly straightforward, Bratkov is an artist of nuance, capable of accentuating the present-day reality in his own way. As to the genre of the artist's expression, Bratkov can be defined as a brilliant narrator with a good nose for paradoxical stories. At the same time, his stories are so artfully simple that they could be interpreted as the expression of the vox populi.

All Bratkov's projects are subtly interrelated and interspersed with self-quotations. His photos are simply arranged, occasionally frontal, and ironically smack of cheap popular prints, echoing the principles of city folklore. The soldiers in the pictures look into the camera with a naïve and unself-conscious trust in the photographer and in the history of which, as they believe, they may become part. The same naiveté can be seen in Bratkov's portraits of children in his series *The Pilots, The Stewardesses* and *The Kids*. Brought together, the photos of soldiers and children become blatant. Today, various analysts and philosophers who observe the current state of Russian society are disturbed by the failure of the intelligentsia to perform its function. Having lost its ethos when flirting with the ruling power, and having accepted the rules of their game, even intellectuals have come to treat the people as children, thus implying a possibility of mass manipulation in the style of the 1930s. Unlike those who work with words and orchestrate the new relationships between the powers-that-are, the intelligentsia and the people, here and now, Bratkov managed, as early as five years ago, to watch adults slipping back into childhood, the immersion of the whole people in slumber.

Dr. Irina Tchmyreva
Moscow Museum of Modern Art
Translated from Russian by Marina Polevaya

[1]The term offered by Viktor Schklovsky, Russian theorist of literature, in the 1920s to denote the stand of an artist who is outside the text of his narration and is thus capable of self-reflection and self-observation.

[2]An interview between the film director Aleksey Germann, the younger, and the film critic, sociologist, and editor-in-chief of the magazine Art of Cinema Daniil Dondurey—two issues of the monthly magazine *Afisha*, No. 2, 2006, Moscow.

This exhibition has been done with the help of Evgeny Berezner, Deputy Director, Moscow Museum of Modern Art, and Vladimir Ovcharenko, Regina Gallery, Moscow. Special support has come from the Trust for Mutual Understanding.

Sergey Bratkov · *Untitled*, 2000 · Digital Print · Courtesy of Regina Gallery, Moscow

UNFATHOMABLE HUMANITY

ARTIST: LISDEBERTUS AKA LUIS DELGADO QUALTROUGH

A World of Hurt

At first glance, *Unfathomable Humanity* may seem like an irresponsible work of art. The series of photo collages appropriates images from a variety of sources without regard for context or attribution. It freely mixes images of torture, murder, and mutilation with portraits of some of the most powerful and influential men in world history. But Lisdebertus intends not to obscure the lines of responsibility, but to call for greater accountability. He employs a blunt visual language to postulate the links between unspeakable acts of violence and the high-ranking perpetrators who often get away with them.

Through their distinctive visual alchemy, the collages tell buried stories, outline hidden connections, and make scandalous accusations. Although the juxtapositions may feel jarring and random, they generate new meanings, pushing viewers to make their own associations. Lisdebertus's cut-and-paste approach may seem brash and heavy-handed, but its boldness is entirely strategic. The works decisively level all historic and academic hierarchies, and cut through the official accounts, circumlocutions, and justifications that lull us into accepting brutality as a necessary part of everyday life. They remind us, forcefully, that violence is inexcusable, and that someone is always responsible.

Sharon Mizota

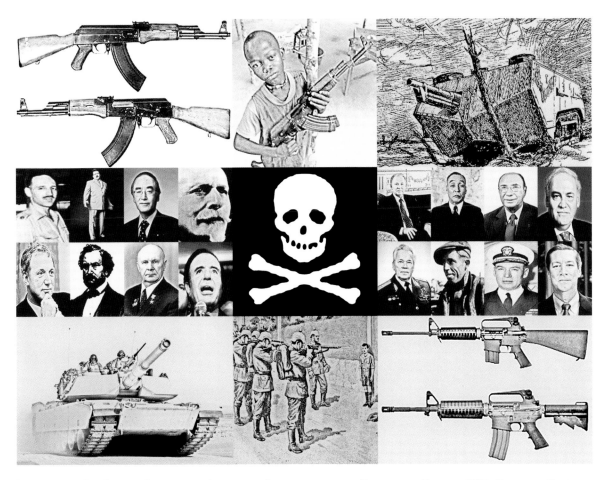

Lisdebertus aka Luis Delgado Qualtrough · *Arms for the Poor*, from the series *Unfathomable Humanity*, 2005 · Pigment on Paper.
Courtesy of De Santos Gallery

Lisdebertus aka Luis Delgado Qualtrough · *Falcon Negro*, from the series *Unfathomable Humanity*, 2005 · Pigment on Paper, Courtesy of De Santos Gallery

LISDEBERTUS AKA LUIS DELGADO QUALTROUGH · *INQUISITION*, FROM THE SERIES *UNFATHOMABLE HUMANITY*, 2005 · PIGMENT ON PAPER · COURTESY OF DE SANTOS GALLERY

DISTINCT PERCEPTIONS

ARTIST: YVES GELLIE

In 1996, Yves Gellie began a series of trips to Iraq. Working on assignment for several magazines, he photographed people who had lived under an embargo since the first Gulf War and a country plunged into a disastrous economic and social situation. Throughout the different trips, he traveled to almost every part of Iraq, and in 1999 he pushed further to Syria and Iran, two countries that have played a direct role in the recent history of Iraq.

He slowly began to have doubts about the accumulation of visual documents reproducing the same stereotypes of a region hit by war— the same images of distress, poverty, and suffering shot to arouse empathy and indignation. Gradually, Gellie moved away from this concept of shooting a concise image that is immediately visible, loaded with the symbols of an event and an easily perceptible emotion.

This evolution is visible in his more iconographic works, which treat the event while also giving due to daily life in all its triviality. In a region ravaged by war, Gellie no longer photographs the urgency of the present, but instead concentrates on the aesthetics of the mark. In his images, he doesn't show acts of violence, but rather the signs of human violence, the marks it leaves on objects, the landscape, or architecture.

For example, he isolates a detail of a worker's dress in a shipyard in southern Iraq or the shoes of a surgeon at the entrance to an operating theatre in a hospital in Bassora, foregoing a more violent vision of the state of decay of the shipyard and the operating theatre. His approach is no more to prove or to denounce, but to show. He maintains a sort of silence, a stance of neutral reportage and detachment. He widens his frames and adopts a frontal vision that intensifies the image's apparent objectivity, following the theory that "it is the motive which makes the photo, the model which imposes the image."[1] Gellie works at bringing out the implicit reality below what he is showing and at revealing the intimate moment in a public or collective scene. In truth, he occupies this fringe where the invisible arises from the visible; he explores the ambiguous relation between a photograph and reality, and experiments with the fictional power of the image.

Isabelle Bernard

[1] Olivier Lugon, *Le style documentaire d'August Sander à Walker Evans: 1920–1945* (Paris: Macula, 2001).

Yves Gellie · *Basra, Iraq; Embargo, Surgical Shoes*, 1998 · Ink Jet Print

Yves Gellie · *Raqqa, Syria, The War of Water*, 2001 · Ink Jet Print

Yves Gellie · *Abadan, Iran, The Wall of Martyrs*, 2003 · Ink Jet Print

Elizabeth Mellott-Carreón · *June 2003*, from the series *Diaries of Enlistment, 2003-2004* · Clay, Rose Petals and Polaroid Transfers, 2005

DIARIES OF ENLISTMENT, 2003–2004 AND ONE DAY

ARTIST: ELIZABETH MELLOTT-CARREÓN

In *Diaries of an Enlistment, 2003–2004*, Elizabeth Mellot-Carreón has personalized the effects of war by presenting communications exchanged between a newlywed couple during long periods of separation. Thirteen calendar months are made tangible in a series of small, dark clay boxes, where the couple's time apart is memorialized and inscribed. During this time, the husband, a combat soldier, is trained in seclusion and then deployed to Afghanistan and Iraq, while his artist wife, Mellot-Carreón, waits and continues with her daily life.

Akin to jewelry boxes, the clay containers hold beloved keepsakes commemorating extended moments in time, fetish objects that were made or collected separately by each lover. United in a tiny shared physical and psychological space, they mark time, serving to honor and remember the other, to kindle desire, and to nurture a precious spiritual connection. The power of this memento mori resides in the hand, for every item has been empowered by touch, either made or selected by hand. Indeed some objects bear fingerprint witness to a particular time and place. There are the beautiful, perhaps to be expected romantic objects: rose petals, a small jar of water from melted snow collected on Valentine's Day, small Polaroid transfers of intimate nude studies, and miniaturized copies of love letters and billet-doux ephemera sealed with lipstick kisses. Other objects appear more abstract and esoteric: a small piece of knotted twine, tiny jars of earth and pine needles, a small book of photograms, wax-encrusted ladybugs, spiky clay thorns, and downy feathers. Each item harbors a code that only the lovers can unlock, while viewers must imagine their significance.

The repetitive arrangement of the boxes and their still-life secrets exhale a funerary air. Presented on spotless antimacassars, reminiscent of lacy coffin linens, the small clay tombs hold and protect the cherished items within; their dark serenity suggests rows of caskets holding the bodies of returning soldiers. Yet Mellott-Carreón admits that she made a conscious attempt to avoid political rhetoric in her creative response to war. She is not interested in patriotic sound bites or visual clichés. Her concern is not with statistical data or language about casualties, supplies, the financial costs of nation-building, or votes. Indeed she eschews yellow-ribbon hope and the public face of a military wife in favor of sharing her private devotion and attempts to personalize her soldier husband. Her interpretation of the violence of war is an intimate meditation on the emotional effects of prolonged separation for a husband and wife. Violence here is psychological. It comes in the form of the love, loneliness, longing, and fear felt by two people, a timeless violence conveyed as a visual elegy with the nostalgic stillness of a Civil War daguerreotype.

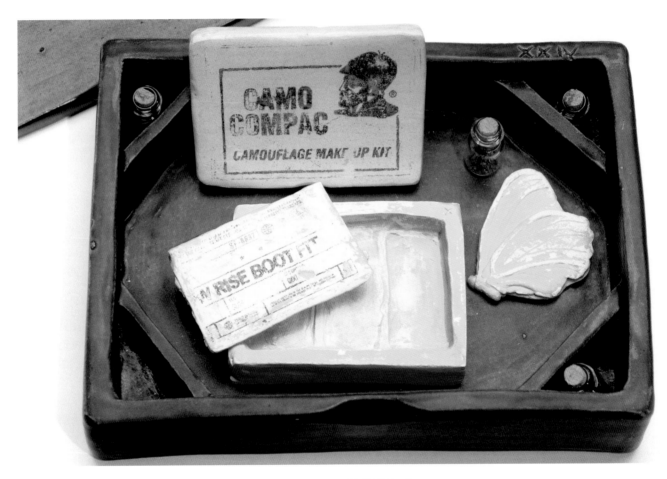

Elizabeth Mellott-Carreón · *October*, from the series *Diaries of Enlistment, 2003-2004* · Clay,
Glass Jars and Handmade Camo Box, 2005

One Day

The installation *One Day* addresses the statistic that 720 women are reportedly raped every day in the United States. Containing 720 paper cast figures that have been embedded with a wide range of objects, making each one unique, the installation invites the viewer into the space to be engulfed by the many paper casts. Maneuvering through the installation, the viewer is forced to acknowledge this type of violence, but it is through the viewer's scrutiny of the figures that the whole truth is revealed. Alone, the viewer notices the crowded "emptiness" of the installation amidst the unforgiving, disfigured female forms. Tackling this social taboo of violence directed towards women, *One Day* forces us to face the appalling number of rapes in our society.

Sara-Jayne Parsons
Curator, University of North Texas Art Gallery, Denton

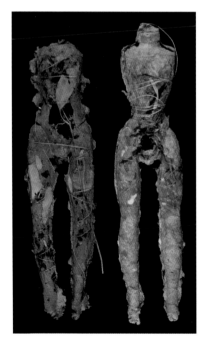

ELIZABETH MELLOTT-CARREON · FROM THE SERIES *ONE DAY, DETAIL FROM INSTALLATION,* 2005 · CAST PAPER FIGURES AND FOUND OBJECTS

#65

ARTIST: NATHALIE LATHAM

I knew very little about City No. 65 because little information existed about the place. During the Soviet era, it was one of the secret cities where military activities took place. Such cities were designated with numbers instead of names and didn't appear on maps. No. 65 was particularly special because it was where the first Soviet atomic bomb was made. It was also the site of history's greatest nuclear accident, in 1957, decades before Chernobyl.

I traveled to No. 65 with three scientists from Columbia University who were studying, with Russian colleagues, the effects of radiation on the chromosomes of people who had worked at the Mayak plutonium plant, the city's main employer. I was interested in the scientists' work because they were directly addressing the issue of what it really means for human beings to be exposed to, and live with, radiation. The scientists were keen to involve me as an artist/photographer in order to disseminate ideas about their work outside the scientific realm. This visit meant I was the first photographer from the West to enter this "closed" city.

When the Soviet Union collapsed, the city lost its numerical designation and was given the name Ozyorsk—"City of Lakes." I was told that the city was still closed today because its 80,000 inhabitants had voted to keep it closed. They could leave, but no one could come in. What did it mean to live in a closed city all one's life? Why on earth would people vote to keep it closed?

I was told not worry about radiation but to prepare for the cold, around minus 20 degrees Centigrade (-4 Fahrenheit). I found some articles on the environmental consequences of radiation in the area and tried to decipher Dr. David J. Brenner's papers on chromosomal damage. Ozyorsk was important for his research because it is a place where several generations exposed to low-dosage radiation still live together.

Once we had entered the city and work got under way, I photographed the Russian and American scientists carrying out their procedures to make sure that the blood samples met the standards their research required.

I asked the Russians what it was like to live here. I wanted to understand why one would want to keep a city like this closed. The answers were strangely familiar. It was a good place to raise children. It was safe to walk around. There were no hooligans. There was no mafia. There were good schools and good apartments. Everyone knew one another.

Most of all, there were jobs. Unemployment in Russia is high, and the closed city grants work to all its residents. Elena, who prepared the blood samples, was eager to marry her boyfriend so he could get a permit to come live with her. Nadia, a doctor who grew up in Kazakhstan, met her Ozyorsk-born husband while studying medicine and followed him back. Igor, our driver, came back after his military service in Moscow.

Nathalie Latham · *Room 246-248.* 2003 · C-Print

Nathalie Latham · *Nina, retired Mayak Plutonium Plant worker, 2003* · C-Print

I was able to meet and photograph some of the hospital's patients. They were Mayak plutonium workers and retired general workers. Some were there for their annual checkup, which lasted four days. Others were being treated for advanced cancer.

Each meeting was moving. Each person told me about his or her life. They said what good workers they had been. One man cried when he spoke about how his life was now coming to an end. A woman spoke softly of her children and grand-children, and how her husband and all her friends had died. She told me how she loved to pick mushrooms; she felt it was being among the trees and nature that had saved her from the radiation's effects. Another told me how her sister starved in the Leningrad blockade, and how she had moved to Ozyorsk with her niece and nephew to raise them single-handedly while working at the Mayak plutonium plant.

Each life story was full of strength, fragility, beauty, and sadness. And after I met each person, what struck me the most was their desire to live a normal life, and to be able to raise their children or grandchildren in a good enough environment, a place where they could grow their own flowers and vegetables.

During the Cold War, these workers were heroes: City No. 65 had symbolically protected Mother Russia from the Americans. Now history had shifted and the city's legends had expired. There was no longer any cause, just life.

When I was growing up in Brisbane, Australia, my father, a doctor, campaigned for nuclear disarmament. He would tell us about nuclear fallout and what a bomb would do to our city. His stories turned me off my dinner and gave me night-mares. They made me question why human beings would create such awful technology.

NATHALIE LATHAM · *DISTILLED WATER,* 2003 · C-PRINT

I didn't find the answers in Ozyorsk, just dignified men and women whom history had already forgotten, and who, like me, were searching for peace in their own way.

Nathalie Latham

SURFACE AND POSTCARDS OF VIETNAM

ARTIST: LIZA NGUYEN

The Vietnam War and The Ethics of Memory: A Photographer's View

What meaning should we give to the 30th anniversary of the fall of Saigon and the end of the Vietnam War, which was commemorated on April 30th, 2005? With the passing of time, long-forgotten memories come alive and gradually transform a country's identity into a tourist destination. What memories of Vietnam will we take home?

Liza Nguyen exhibits the "Souvenirs" she brought back from the Vietnamese trip she made during the summer of 2004. In this retrospection, what you see is what you get: what you won't forget. These series of photographs show that part of history that hasn't passed away. Paradoxically, the memories of the successive war destructions are impossible to erase, having led some people to leave their country (more than two million boat-people have left Vietnam since 1978) and others to rebuild it. The remains of the artist's journey—*Surface* and *Postcards of Vietnam*—bring us back to the present and the impossibility of forgetting what happened. How can we build a collective memory of a war, which, in the United States as well as in Vietnam, still hasn't been granted the right to a fair historical trial? The brutality and inhumanity of these wars are echoed by the inhumanity of these figures: Between 1962 and 1975, some 13 to 15 million tons of bombs were dropped on Vietnam (including napalm bombs, phosphorus bombs and fragmentation bombs), 4 million Vietnamese civilians were killed or wounded, 663,000 Vietnamese soldiers were killed, 58,183 Americans died, 313,613 were wounded, and before that, the French had suffered 92,000 casualties and 11,400 injuries.

Liza Nguyen decided to travel to a familiar country (her father is Vietnamese) where she didn't grow up, a country she doesn't belong to. How can she mourn a history and a country she doesn't know? This question becomes our question. It is the issue of memory itself: how can we commemorate a historical event that still has consequences on the present?

The artist's photographs offer a cartography of memory which reproduces the cartography of the Vietnam war; from the northeast (Hanoi, Haiphong, Cat Ba, Phu To), the northwest (Dien Bien Phu), the center north (Vinh), to the center (Da Nang, Hue, DMZ, Quang Tri, Khe Shan, Doc Mieu, Cua Tung), to the south (My Lai—one of the villages designated as a "free-killing zone" where an entire population was massacred—Kontum, Dak To, Saigon, Cu-Chi, Tay Ninh). From these places, Liza Nguyen's photographs only show pictures of earth. Each photograph represents a missing image. According to the photographer, "*Surface* represents a handful of earth taken as a souvenir from places full of memories. It shows the history-laden ground on which French and American soldiers fought [the Vietnamese]. Pieces of land which are index-linked to history, to bodies turned into dust". This earth is devoid of roots, symbolizing its own exile, torn away from life. Various pieces of land of different colours put together as the expression of an absence directed towards us. The photographer's itinerary follows the bombings and the spots were herbicides were dropped on the Vietnamese territory. These chemicals, initially designed to defoliate the forests of Vietnam in order to uncover the bases of the Vietnamese guerilla soldiers and burn down their crops, became a weapon of mass destruction. Between 1961 and 1971, almost 5 million Vietnamese were exposed to herbicides. The carcinogenic effects of these chemicals, as well as their damages on the immune system, the nervous system and the reproductive system (with congenital malformations) are still visible today. In Vietnam, it is the earth as well as the people which was assassinated. Is Vietnam's soil completely dead? It has enough life left in it to testify about what happened.

Its testimony mirrors the places used to house the official memories of the war: museums, old tanks, helicopters, military trucks or ships converted into tombstones or memorials, funeral monuments or statues of war heroes and so on. How shall we react to these rearranged memories of a history of horror? The artist's photographs become *Postcards from Vietnam*, a series of 7 leaflets, each of them composed of 12 images. We are invited to look at history under its most common form: tourism. Is it the horror of these images or the horror of our distant point of view which makes us feel uncomfortable? These postcards denounce the fact that history's violence has become something ordinary, something common. How can we represent the inacceptable? The point made by Liza Nguyen is most powerfully expressed in the leaflet dedicated to children suffering from malformations and various diseases cause by dioxins and to the series of misshapen foetuses kept in jars. These victims, which are kept hidden away in their families or in hospitals and rehabilitation centers, are here photographed like the pieces of a living museum of pain and suffering. The last photograph in the series shows six children. Anyone who looks at this postcard can see for themselves; horror has a face, all these children have left is a smile.

By bringing her "souvenirs" back home, where she lives, between France and Germany, Liza Nguyen has brought us the memory of the Vietnam War. As a part of the past, the history of others is unreachable. However, it can be reached through its photographic negativity, as a memory revisited in the present. The image of others can thus become the object of a common history.

Octave Debary
Anthropologist, and Senior Lecturer at Université de Paris V. Researcher focusing on history and memory
Excerpt from the original French text translated by Andrew Gallix

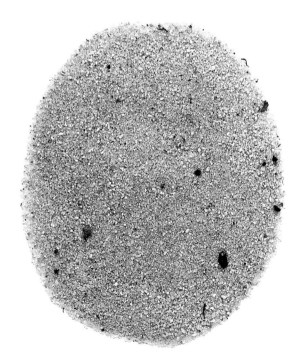

LIZA NGUYEN · *DMZ*, FROM THE SERIES *SURFACE*, 2004 · C-PRINT

LIZA NGUYEN · *DIEN BIEN PHU*, FROM THE SERIES *SURFACE*, 2004 · C-PRINT

Liza Nguyen · *My Lai*, from the series *Surface*, 2004 · C-Print

RED LAND, BLUE LAND

ARTIST: CLAUDIO HILS

The works here comprise the closing statement to my project *Red Land Blue Land*, which was published as a book of photography at the turn of the millennium (Ostfildern, Germany: Hatje Cantz, 2000). In military terminology, this succinct pair of words indicates whether one is moving across enemy or friendly territory. It superbly reflects the polar thinking and references I encountered while scouting out the military training area in the Senne region of western Germany.

This no-go zone, which extends over a total of 11,000 hectares (27,180 acres), served as a terrain for preparing for war and battle as early as the nineteenth century. Since the end of World War II, the site, where traces of its military use have been deposited like layers over many decades, has served the British allies and various NATO partners as a place for military exercises.

I carried out my inspection of the military training ground according to cartographic protocols. I began by tracking down the elements of the landscape and revealing their military maneuver-related origins. Polarities emerged even at this point because, alongside the ravished portions of the landscape, a natural protected space had been unintentionally created in which flora and fauna thrived undisturbed.

Tin City, a mock village for close combat exercises, where fights and battles are staged, is located south of the isolated area. It was obvious that the backdrop was intended to represent an archetypal rural town's infrastructure: church, post office, snack bar, betting office, bar, bank, brothel. Somewhere amidst all this was a wooden shed, painted orange, with a sign reading "Murphy's Garage." So I was not surprised at all that the rural scenario was actually signaling a turn to the worse in Northern Ireland. In his review of the book project, Stewart O'Nan also noted how the images were both unsettling and familiar, suggesting not only the possibility that atrocity lurks beneath our civilized rituals, but also that it is inevitable.

The ambivalent horror of the inevitable manifests itself in the numerous mannequins that serve as crash test dummies in the close combat zone. Each one of these life-sized dolls conveys a strong presence and collectively constitute a strange distopia. All of them are civilians (people, as I call them), who are wearing used clothing from the 1970s and 1980s, and appear to be arduously sustaining everyday rituals even as they stand in frozen motion. While one might ponder at length why they have been staged as communicative beings, what etches itself into our memory from this surreal tableau are the bullet holes, the scars, the amputated limbs. What makes us aware of the *danse macabre* as defined by James Ensor inevitably remains closely bound to the projection. A photograph—a reminder, plain and supposedly indifferent—can assist in locating it in the concrete world.

Claudio Hils

CLAUDIO HILS · *CLOSE QUARTERS BATTLE RANGE, VILLAGE CENTRE WITH CAR,* FROM THE SERIES *RED LAND, BLUE LAND,* 1999 · C-PRINT

CLAUDIO HILS · *CLOSE QUARTERS BATTLE RANGE, MAN WITH ATTACKING DOG*, FROM THE SERIES *RED LAND, BLUE LAND*, 1999 · C-PRINT

Claudio Hils · *Close Quarters Battle Range, young woman in a doorway*, from the series *Red Land, Blue Land*, 1999 · C-Print

FotoFest

Collaborations

LIST OF ARTISTS

David Farrell—Art League Houston

Wolfgang Müller—Rice University Media Center

María Martínez-Cañas—De Santos Gallery

Kim Brown—De Santos Gallery

INNOCENT LANDSCAPES

ARTIST: DAVID FARRELL

In the thirty years of conflict and atrocity in Northern Ireland, a small group of people stood apart: they were the "missing," the "Disappeared"—absent and yet somehow still present. Even their exact number was uncertain, though there were at least fifteen people whose whereabouts had remained shrouded in misinformation and doubt since the 1970s and early 1980s. Despite considerable obfuscation, their fate and whereabouts were directly linked to what was colloquially known as "The Troubles." Apart from Capt. Robert Nairac, an undercover British soldier, they were all Catholics and widely assumed to have been "disappeared" by the IRA through its internal policing of the movement and the wider Catholic community. What separated this group from other "policings" was the silence, the denial, and the absence of a body for relatives, relieved of their uncertainty, to bury. This denial continued for over twenty-five years.

On March 29, 1999, as a result of the ongoing peace process, the IRA issued a statement in which they apologized, recognized the "injustice of prolonging the suffering of victims' families," and admitted to "the killing and secret burial" of ten people. Despite internal enquiries, they only managed to locate the burial places of nine of those victims: Brian McKinney, John McClory, Danny McIlhone, Brendan Megraw, Jean McConville, Kevin McKee, Seamus Wright, Columba McVeigh, and Eamonn Molloy.

The burial locations—Colgagh, Ballynultagh, Oristown, Templetown, Wilkinstown, Bragan, and Faughart—contained a final bitter twist: they were all in the south of Ireland. This small group of people had been exiled in death, creating a poignant and, as time progressed, haunting Diaspora of the Disappeared. This became evident when on May 20, 2000, the digs, now in their second phase, were suspended: three remains had been located, three reburials permitted, leaving the remaining families with a site rather than a resting place, a closing rather than a closure.[1]

My initial response upon visiting the first burial site at Colgagh was visceral. It was some weeks after the discovery of the remains of Bryan McKinney and John McClory, and there was "nothing" to photograph—well, certainly nothing in a conventional documentary mode—but the violated landscape jarred me. It seemed to be a powerful metaphor for the violence that had taken place there over twenty years ago, which only now had become visible by the scarification of the land during the search process. I left Colgagh thinking, "They must be made to see." Somehow this small group of people epitomized the complexities of political violence, where a society becomes so brutalized that it starts to murder its own in the pursuit of the "rights" of its people.

A thread connected most of the sites, both topographically and somewhat conceptually, to the nature of photography itself. This link was in many ways an essence of the Irish

David Farrell · *Oristown*, 1999 · C-Print

David Farrell · *Ballynultagh*, 1999 · C-Print

Caption, following page:
David Farrell · *List of Individuals Kidnapped by IRA*, from the series *Innocent Landscapes*

BRIAN MCKINNEY

JOHN MCCLORY

DANNY MCILHONE

BRENDAN MEGRAW

JEAN MCCONVILLE

KEVIN MCKEE

SEAMUS WRIGHT

COLUMBA MCVEIGH

EAMONN MOLLOY

landscape—the bog, that memory bank, that witness of history and trauma. The writer Terry Eagleton has commented on the bog as revealing "the past as still present" and that objects contained within them are "caught in a living death."[2] In a similar way, *Innocent Landscapes*—like many works that deal with violence and commemoration, in particular those that are by default utilizing what has been termed "late photography"—contains a number of dilemmas. How do you photograph something that was intended to remain unseen? How do you photograph something where the referent, which in photography is normally carried forward to any future, has been completely removed from the mise-en-scène, where the experiences undergone by the disappeared were meant to be outside of memory and denied to those who experienced them? How do you photograph "nothing" in the hope that it will trigger a response? How do you photograph "the intangible presence of absence"?

As I began to visit these sites, I was struck by their beauty—they were so typical of classical representations of the Irish landscape in painting, cinema, and even within the commercial world of tourism. They exuded a rich symbol of what in some ways it means to be Irish. At first this beauty troubled me. Would it be possible to essentially aestheticize violence in a meaningful way? Could I usurp this beauty and turn it back against itself? Early within the work, a chance meeting with Mrs. McKinney (mother of Bryan), who commented that she had felt a sense of relief when Bryan had been found with nature in such a beautiful place, made me realize that the location of a place for both an absent memory and an intense loss would be a key element in my excavation of these sites, and that an inherent, almost romantic beauty somehow acted as a comforting cloak of reflection. I was aware that I was possibly questioning not only the medium's ability to furnish evidence, but also its limits when remembering, representing, and commemorating traumatic historical events. In the end, all I felt I could do was bear witness (to make the viewer bear witness) to what was essentially a framed absence.

As time passed and nature began to reclaim these locations, making them disappear from immediate consciousness, it comforted me to some extent that my involvement with these sites and the people said to be buried there was not a completely futile artistic gesture of protest: my photographs would exist as a monument of sorts, an act of remembrance in the face of voracious nature, human forgetfulness, and the folly of memory.

David Farrell

[1]Since the publication of my book *Innocent Landscapes*, the earth itself returned Jean McConville at a location approximately 500 meters (1,640 feet) from the excavated site when the shifting sands of the beach revealed her remains to a man out walking his dog in August 2003. A search was resumed, to no avail, for Colimba McVeigh at Bragan in September 2003.

[2]Terry Eagleton, *The Truth About the Irish*, (New Island Books), 1999.

David Farrell · *Oristown (night)*, 1999 · C-Print

KARAT, SKY OVER ST. PETERSBURG

ARTIST: WOLFGANG MÜLLER

To create *Karat, Sky over St. Petersburg*, I spent a total of ten months during 2000–02 photographing various groups of children and adolescents in this Russian city of four million people. I established contact with them by bringing food and the personal photos I had made of them to our meetings. The most important factor, however, was spending enough time with them to generate trust, leading in some cases to true friendships.

Teenagers experiment with a variety of drugs. As one of them explains: "Then I am free and have no more fear. Also if I am alone in the darkness in the attic and somebody is coming. And I also don't feel the beating of the policemen any longer... the soul gets lighter and I can forget all."

The daily existence of these children and adolescents, whose lives revolve around the street, is marred by violence. Although most of them have escaped the senseless beatings and negligence of chronically drunk parents, or the regimented abuse of institutions, the course of their lives on the street is hardly any less violent. Since she was ten years old, Nadja, now eighteen, has lived on the street. She sleeps on park benches, in staircases, in basements, and in attics. She not only has to fear the beatings by police, but she also has to keep a watchful eye on the other attic dwellers. "Once," she said, "I was sexually assaulted and I barely escaped with my life."

The phenomenon of direct assault is only a part of the violence facing these children. Violence usually festers as a pervasive social condition. It has forced them, as literally the weakest members of the society, to settle at its outermost fringes and to live in vacant spaces. In my experience, these living spaces consist mainly of roofs or attics, where they not only have a place to sleep, but can take drugs or earn a living through prostitution without being disturbed. According to a study by the International Labor Organization of the United Nations on working street children, forty percent of the girls and one percent of the boys are working, at least temporarily, as prostitutes.

The consumption of drugs seems to be almost a prerequisite to endure life on the street. Most of the children have already tried many different drugs. Because they are cheap, the most popular drugs are glue and shoe polish with brand names like "Karat," which gives this exhibition its title. According to a study by Médicines du Monde, the average age of a glue-sniffer is thirteen.

Sonja and Irina are using the make up to get ready for work as prostitutes.

Nadja, too, has taken drugs since she was thirteen years old. "When I am on drugs, I feel free, and I am not afraid anymore, even when it's dark and somebody comes. I also hardly notice the beatings by the police." Last year after her boyfriend Ljoscha was locked up in jail, she started to take heroin. "It makes me feel less worried and I am able to forget everything."

These children are violated even further by the sensationalist press in Russia, which, intent on increasing the number of subscribers or viewers, exploits the drama of their misery. Being stereotyped as victims, they again become objects. The reader or the viewer at home remains interested in their situation only after the level of violence and misery is ratcheted up.

Lena, 10 years is jumping over the roofs, as if the laws of gravity don't apply to her. She is entering the attic through the skylight.

The pictures in this exhibition are meant to go against this media-driven logic. They attempt to portray these children as human subjects engaged in their daily existence. The photographs do not celebrate their misery nor do they ask for the viewer's tears. These pictures cannot be reduced to simple propagandistic messages because they are too open-ended and too multilayered. The viewer is invited to explore the various picture planes or to jump back and forth among the images. Areas of tender color and scenes of intimacy are juxtaposed with brutal reality, often suggested only in the surrounding context, in small details, or in the ambiguity of a gesture.

This nonreductive approach also forestalls stylistic continuity. Alongside documentary-like pictures are portraits, snapshots, urban landscapes, trash photos, or street life scenes out of a fashion magazine. The possible answer, if any, to the misery and violence depicted in this work must be found in the language of the images. The pictorial language does not try to reinforce the viewer's stereotypical concepts of street children, but instead gives the viewer the freedom to move inside and between the images in order to form his or her own opinion.

Wolfgang Müller
Translated from German by Volker Eisele

WOLFGANG MULLER CAPTIONS:
TYPE C-PRINTS, 2001
PAGE 80: *HEROIN* · PAGE 80: *READY FOR WORK* ·
PAGE 82: *ENTRANCE* · PAGE 83: *PREGNANT*

Marina has become pregnant by her friend Slavik and cannot imagine a future with a child.

LIES AND DUSTOGRAMS

ARTISTS: MARÍA MARTÍNEZ-CAÑAS—*LIES*
MARÍA MARTÍNEZ-CAÑAS AND KIM BROWN—*DUSTOGRAMS*

María Martínez-Cañas engages with photography to make art, and only art, with elegance, virtuosity, and enthusiasm as well as clarity and constructive imagination. Of the two very distinct and different bodies of works presented at De Santos Galleries as part of FotoFest 2006, *Lies* is the latest series and perhaps a departure from most of her previous works. *Lies* is about symbols, optics, and questioning truth. *Dustograms* is a harmonious, intriguing, and intelligent work made in collaboration with Conceptualist/sculptor Kim Brown. These are excerpts from a conversation between María Martínez-Cañas, Kim Brown, and curator Ricardo Viera.

Ricardo Viera: When and why did you start your latest series, *Lies*? What is in essence the cyclical chronology of all your series and how important is it as an integral part of your work?

María Martínez-Cañas: I physically started working on the series *Lies* at the beginning of last year [2005], but the thoughts and ideas behind the series had been "brewing" in my mind earlier than that, about a year or two earlier. I had gone through a terrible personal experience in my life that made me confront head-on how easy lies can be told and believed. How easy it is to bring devastation to people's lives by telling lies that other people believe in. Without really realizing at the time the impact this event had had in my life, I started thinking about ideas for new work. The series *Lies* came very naturally for me. It was only after I finished the work, as I was talking on the phone with Catherine Edelman, my dealer in Chicago—explaining the work to her—that I realized what brought and gave life to the series. It was quite a revelation for me.

The cyclical chronology of my work is an integral part of it. I have found through the years that I work better in series—because I feel there is always a beginning and an end. Anyone who really knows me knows that I am a very structural person—this comes through in my utilization of structures as part of the act of making the work.

RV: As an artist of ideas, you always fly solo. Why have you collaborated with Kim Brown in *Dustograms*? Was it a matter of being at the right place at the right time, or finally finding someone you want to work with?

MMC: I think it was a combination of many different things. First and foremost, I believed in the endless possibilities of "mixing" our work together. When I first met Kim in March 2004 in Munich, I was very intrigued by her materials as she explained her work to me. I had no idea what her work looked like, but was intrigued by her choice of material—dust. So I asked her to send me visual samples of the works, which she did. What I saw was extraordinary and left me with a sense that I had encountered something magical. We started writing daily emails to each other, which turned into a dialogue, exchanging thoughts and ideas about the world, about life, about art, about everything. I realized after a few months of this exchange that there was this artist in Alaska with whom I had a connection based on words, images, and objects—something I had never really experienced before. So it was natural for me to ask her to come to my studio in Miami to create work together because I felt that through all this exchanging of life-things, we were already collaborating with each other. Have I always flown solo, as you said? Yes. But when I encountered someone whose work and words fascinated me so much—well, let's say that I had nothing to lose, and neither did she, I think. *Dustograms* is testament to the potential of two artists who trust and believe in each other's work.

RV: A fascinating, exciting, and challenging thing about this exhibition is the radical differences in the two bodies of work presented: *Lies* and *Dustograms*. However, I see a common denominator or conceptual thread. Am I right, and if so, why is that commonality there?

MMC: We all know that photographic images are the product of natural laws and a scientific process. That the "signs" of a photograph, if authenticated by testimony, let's say in a trial, may give truthful representations. For this reason, photography has been a tool utilized by law enforcement and others to "record" and document criminal acts. The popular notion is that photography does not lie and that what we see in an image is "truth." Evidence is but the "signs of things." Dust is also evidence—fragile and ephemeral evidence of life's presence. My English dictionary describes dust as being "the particles into which something disintegrates." Aren't our bodies supposed to become dust after we die? When Kim spoke to me about dust for the first time, I thought of DNA, of evidence of human presence. I had already started thinking about the *Lies* series, so my mind was in tune with these thoughts. So this conceptual thread between the *Dustograms* and *Lies* series exists, absolutely. What is interesting for me to think about is the chronology of both series, because I put aside working on *Lies* to collaborate with Kim on the *Dustogram* series. Now I feel that I did the right thing because I later went into creating *Lies* with a different mindset, one that felt more ready and prepared to deal with the issues, pain, and concerns that *Lies* symbolizes for me.

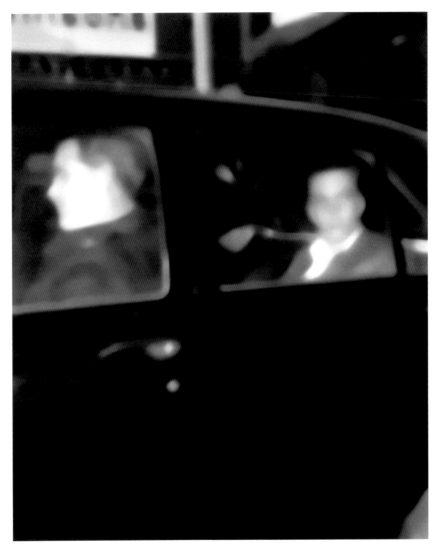

Maria Martínez-Cañas · *Back Seat*, from the series *Lies*, 2005, Pigment Print on Archival Watercolor Paper

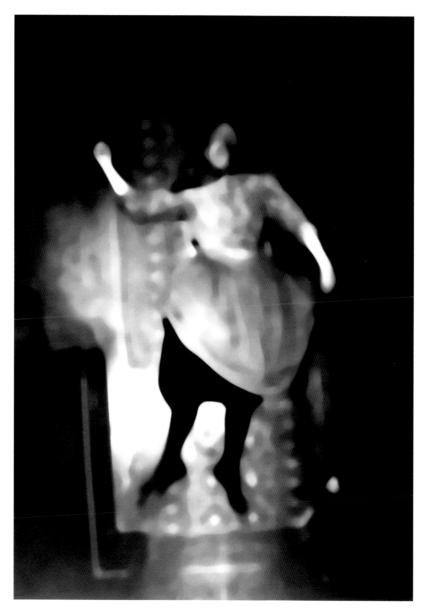

María Martínez-Cañas · *Doll*, from the series *Lies*, 2005, Pigment Print on Archival Watercolor Paper

RV: How significant and/or complex is it for a Conceptual visual artist/sculptor to work in a photo-based collaboration such as *Dustograms*?

Kim Brown: The physical collaboration was simple, because the photogram was created from the original dust sewing sewn dust sculptures .Trusting someone to create/document the way I was seeing the dust was more difficult. I did not want to lose the integrity of the dust. Seeing what Maria was doing with the dust mound sewing in the darkroom completely dispelled all my concerns.

RV: Besides the harmonious and powerful visual presence of an intelligent work of art by two individuals, what does the term *collaboration* mean to you?

KB: Collaboration means stretching out of comfort levels, trying to remain open, letting go of controlling all aspects of the work, trusting.

RV: Why do you have dust as a subject or object in an artistic composition?

KB: It is an absurd medium — it is nothing. I feel like nothing. It is everything. It is so small and so big at the same time, ceaseless like time — a reminder of the beginning and the end. It comes from everywhere and nowhere, and goes everywhere and nowhere. It is autonomous. In its silence, it speaks loudly of the never-ending. It connects us all in ways people rarely take time to understand. It holds life and death. To touch it is to destroy it. To know it is to try to know all life. This dust….

Interview with Artists by Ricardo Viera
Curator and Director, LeHigh University Art Galleries

These exhibitions were initiated by FotoFest as a collaboration with De Santos Gallery for FOTOFEST2006.

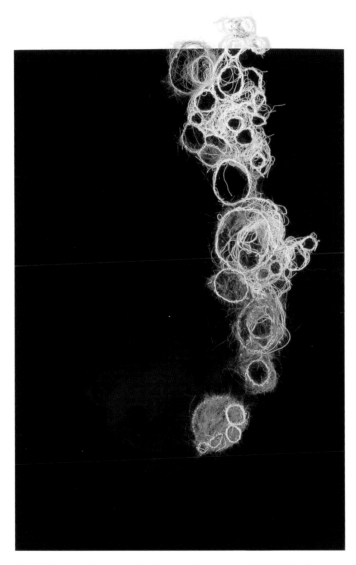

María Martínez-Canas and Kim Brown · *Dustograms XXIII*, 2004 · Silver Gelatin Print Photogram with Hand-Stitched Dust

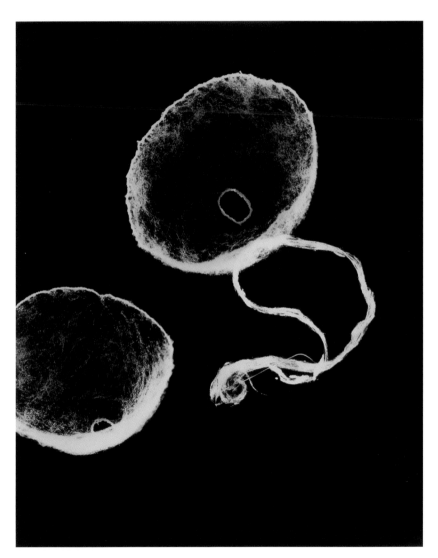

María Martínez-Cañas and Kim Brown · *Dustograms VII*, 2004 · Silver Gelatin Print Photogram with Hand-Stitched Dust

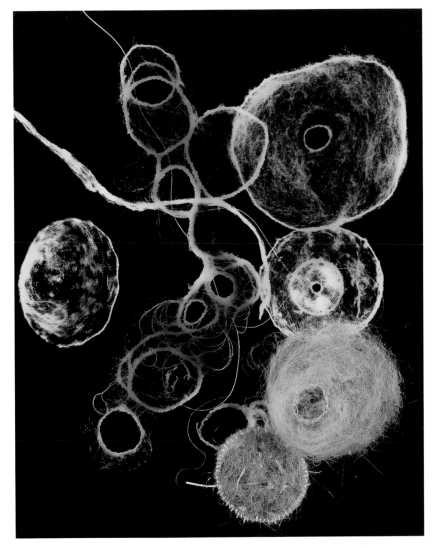

Maria Martínez-Cañas and Kim Brown · *Dustograms XXI*. 2004 · Silver Gelatin Print Photogram with Hand-Stitched Dust

THE EARTH

THE EARTH

DOUG AND MIKE STARN · *STRUCTURE OF THOUGHT #10*, 2001 · MIS AND LYSONIC INKJET PRINTS ON THAI MULBERRY, GAMPI AND TISSUE PAPERS WITH WAX

Doug and Mike Starn · *Black Pulse #15*, 2000-2005 · Lambda Digital C-Print

ABSORPTION + TRANSMISSION

ARTISTS: DOUG AND MIKE STARN

For more than two decades, Doug and Mike Starn's photographs have confounded and intrigued critics and audiences. By using unorthodox techniques, making exceptionally large and often dramatically shaped prints, and addressing subjects usually avoided by other artists, they have challenged the perception of what is accepted as "a photograph." They are not alone in such challenges. Since the mid-1980s, photography's most sacred dictums have lost their precise boundaries as the clarity of modernist principles have given way to a rich array of alternative approaches. But since their much discussed and critically praised introduction in a solo New York gallery show in 1986, followed by their inclusion in the 1987 Whitney Biennial, Doug and Mike Starn have continued to extend the definition of what we perceive as photographic and what we expect in the content of a photograph. Their work presented at FotoFest 2006 relates to FotoFest's Biennial theme *The Earth.*

A major component of their work is the creation of individual pieces that are at times both sculptural and photographic. This duality is present in some of the earth-related works they are showing at FotoFest. The very different qualities of the two media create a purposeful tension in the pieces as well as for the viewer seeking to understand them. Easy generalizations distinguishing the media include the fact that sculpture is three-dimensional and photographic surfaces are flat and smooth. Sculpture is made and photographs are taken. And, until very recently, most sculpture is produced on a grander scale than most photographs.

The surface of a Starn photograph is rarely smooth. Sometimes the photograph is torn, folded, or bent on a curved frame. In other instances, one negative is printed across many small pieces of photographic paper laid in a grid. Sheets may have uneven edges, some of which curl up and/ or overlap contiguous pieces. At times, the edges of a photograph are chipped or torn. Among other effects, this dimensional, uneven, deteriorating surface undermines the documentary nature inherent in a simple photograph. The art object becomes simultaneously a photograph that is taken of something existing in the world (a tree, a moth, a leaf) and a device conceived and constructed by the artists to be more than a factual document. It becomes a metaphor, a holder of content other than what we normally associate with the photographed object. Consequently, the picture stirs viewers to think beyond easy recognition to the work's greater implications and associations. The pieces evoke the complex systems of ideas that the Starns have been building and refining through successive bodies of work.

The pictures' subjects are also transformed by scale. A tiny moth becomes nearly eight feet high and a single leaf expands to twenty-two feet. What we can usually hold in our hands or crush under our feet now dwarfs the viewer. Subjects that are not transformed by scale are revisualized in other ways. While the Starns' photographs of trees are printed large scale, they are naturally smaller that the original subjects.

Printed by inkjet onto various translucent papers, the images of thick trunks and leafless branches are then varnished, waxed, and mounted in large freestanding frames. This flattened and highly graphic presentation emphasizes the veinlike structure of the trunks, limbs, and twigs, and thus intentionally heightens the resemblance to drawings of human circulatory systems and the branching protoplasmic organization of neurons.

Contrasting dualities abound in work by Mike and Doug Starn. They maintain balance, and yet mine the discord between photography and sculpture, fact and poetry, and reality and metaphor. Now the Starns have added the pairing of art and science to their repertoire, an ancient contrasting dichotomy that nevertheless has a fruitful history of intersection. *Absorption + Transmission* extends as well the theme of light that has been a central component of the Starns' work throughout their career. The series features the elements of nature mentioned above—trees and leaves—because there are physical and philosophical interconnections among these subjects, and between these natural elements and humans. The Starns focus the audience's attention on various aspects of those relationships, particularly the interconnections with light and its polarity, darkness.

Their images of trees compose a series titled *Structure of Thought*; the photographs of leaves belong to the series *Black Pulse*. As mentioned above, their mode of installation heightens the visual and process parallels between the flow of carbon-laden fluid in trees and leaves, and the flow of thought in neurons. Trees and leaves synthesize the carbon dioxide humans exhale. Oxygen exhaled leads to the black carbon. It is the blackness of carbon, and all the metaphorical references to blackness/darkness and light, that most inspires these artists. As they wrote in an unpublished statement, "In almost any culture in the history of the world, light is used as a metaphor for thought, knowledge, intelligence." And black historically embodies cultural negatives.

Doug and Mike Starn · *Structure of Thought #11*, 2001 · MIS and Lysonic inkjet prints on Thai
mulberry, gampi and tissue papers with wax

DOUG AND MIKE STARN · *STRUCTURE OF THOUGHT #13*, 2001-2004 · MIS AND LYSONIC INKJET PRINTS ON THAI MULBERRY, GAMPI AND TISSUE PAPERS WITH WAX

Recently, this presumption of negativity and many of the accompanying stereotypes associated with blackness have come into question. For the Starns, too, black is not a negative symbol or energy. *Black Pulse* refers to carbon pulsing through the trees' veins and absorbing the light photosynthesized by the leaves. "Carbon for us," they wrote in the same statement, "is the representation of the absorption of light (figuratively thought and information)." Or as J.D. Talasek, Exhibition Director for the National Academy of Sciences, noted, "Black is filled with light, black is a reservoir of light; in the Starns conception, black illuminates."[1]

Light and dark are also factors in the process by which these images are made. The focused light that enters the camera instigates chemical (or digital) reactions in photographic negatives (computer chips) that, transferred to paper, yields images. Light instigates and photographic black preserves the image. But as the Starns noted in an interview, the mind not only records the images that light brings to it, but interprets the information based on a lifetime of constructed memories and learning. The Starns' recurring views of trees and leaves are emblematic of the complexity of their, and our, thought processes. By layering their images, shifting the sizes and formats of their presentation, they avoid an easy lexicon of signs and remain truer to the complexity of the processes at the heart of their art.

In an earlier series, published as a book in 2003, the Starns focused on moths as their central subject. Moths, too, are intrinsically connected to light and darkness. They live in darkness but are attracted to light. If the light that attracts them is a flame, they are lured to their death; even in their frantic beating against a light bulb, they can destroy themselves. The lives of moths offer a striking reversal from the parallels established by the Starns between the process of the human mind and the photosynthesizing of trees and leaves. For instance, contrary to the growth cycles of plants, the Starns have written that science has yet to understand why moths function as they do The fragility and short life spans of moths form a dramatic contrast to those of great trees. Moths

DOUG AND MIKE STARN · VIDEO STILL FROM *BLACK PULSE VIDEO*, 2005 · VIDEO ANIMATION

are frenetic; trees are stately. If moths are contemplated, human are likely to pity them; trees are admired, even loved. In *Attracted to Light*, the series title for the photographs of moths, the Starns brought serious attention to an unexpected subject, but it proved to be a rich vein for them. Ah, the search for knowledge and understanding. For all our arrogance about what we do understand, it is equally important to be reminded of our fragility and the dangers of extreme instinctual ardor.

Beyond the sheer visual pleasure of the objects in the exhibition, *Absorption + Transmission* continues to raise questions and instigate associations that are worth a viewer's engagement, and it enhances our anticipation of where the Starn brothers will next lead.

Anne Wilkes Tucker
Gus and Lyndall Wortham Curator
Museum of Fine Arts, Houston

J.D. Talasek, introduction, Absorption + Transmission, National Academy of Sciences, 2005.

FotoFest
at Winter
Street Studios

LIST OF ARTISTS

Heidi Bradner

Dornith Doherty

John Ganis

Jules Greenberg

Vadim Gushchin

Masaki Hirano

Noel Jabbour

Vesselina Nikolaeva

Hyung Geun Park

Peter Riedlinger

Mark Ruwedel

Martin Stupich

Barbara Yoshida

The Earth

Artificial borders divide the earth and determine its use. The pathways of human migration are altered as the needs for natural resources change. Land is being cleared and consumed at a faster rate than ever before in the history of the earth. A greater number of species are disappearing. But traces of Pleistocene lakes still exist, and stone megaliths have withstood five thousand years of wind and water. There is the strange visual inter-connectedness between objects of nature and the objects of human creation. The human imprint is everywhere.

RIO GRANDE

Burnt Water/Agua Quemada 2002–2005

ARTIST: DORNITH DOHERTY

I've been invaded by a kind of lucid languor, a sense of imminence; with every moment I become increasingly aware of certain perfumes peculiar to my surroundings, certain silhouettes from a memory that formerly was revealed in brief flashes but today swells and flows with the measured vitality of a river.

Carlos Fuentes, *Agua quemada*, 1981[1]

As a place where the cultures of the U.S. and Mexico simultaneously meet and diverge, the Rio Grande exists as a watery margin of subtle and dense histories. It is a river infused with memory, charged with the presence of past lives at every bend, and yet flowing through a complex twenty-first-century passage. As the Rio Grande runs its course from Colorado to the Gulf of Mexico, it traverses landscapes ranging from managed recreational forests and agricultural land, to the densely populated urban areas around the *maquiladores* of northern Mexico. It crosses the land of the Pueblo and Navaho Nations and passes under border bridges in south Texas. As one might imagine, to navigate the river is to steer through a host of critical contemporary concerns.

Dornith Doherty's photographic series *Burnt Water/Agua Quemada* addresses the cultural landscape of the Rio Grande and reflects therein a complicated relationship between human agency and the natural environment. She began her investigations in 2002, photographing along the banks of the Rio Grande and exploring its immediate topography,

from mountain source to coastal mouth. The resulting images metaphorically reveal a natural region that is being reconfigured by a host of crucial and sometimes violent forces, including environmental politics, immigration, and economic inequities. And while they exist as re-visioned landscapes, her works are in fact straight photographs—a delicious secret that Doherty skillfully masks through a studio practice that eschews traditional documentary or expeditionary modes in favor of merging fact with aesthetics in a complicit reinvention of nature.

After photographing on the Rio Grande, Doherty returned to her studio and started to project photographic images of the river landscape onto assemblages of natural history specimens and cultural artifacts collected from her onsite work. She incorporated prickly pear plants, corn husks, soil, clothing, vinyl car seats, needles, and other found objects into the still-lifes to invoke the complexity of human experiences she had witnessed along the river, as well as refer to the immediacy of her personal experience within this landscape. Doherty then rephotographed the still-lifes, illuminated by the projected imagery, using a view camera. Presented here in mural size, reflecting the large scale of the landscapes portrayed, Doherty's photographs are exuberant, yet elegiac vignettes that trace and exhale the contemporary life of the Rio Grande, akin to the perfumed breath of memory expressed in Carlos Fuentes's poetic vision of *Burnt Water*.

Sara-Jayne Parsons, Curator

[1]Carlos Fuentes, *Agua quemada: Cuarteto narrativo* (México City: Fondo de Cultura Económica, 1981), page 17.

Dornith Doherty · *Vinyl Vista,* from the Series *Rio Grande: Burnt Water/Agua Quemada,* 2004 · Chromogenic Print · Courtesy of Holly Johnson Gallery, Dallas and McMurtrey Gallery, Houston

Dornith Doherty · *Big Bend*, from the Series *Rio Grande: Burnt Water/Agua Quemada*, 2004 · Chromogenic Print · Courtesy of Holly Johnson Gallery, Dallas and McMurtrey Gallery, Houston

Dornith Doherty · *Ground Water*, from the Series *Rio Grande: Burnt Water/Agua Quemada*, 2004 ·
Chromogenic Print · Courtesy of Holly Johnson Gallery, Dallas and McMurtrey Gallery, Houston

NO MAN'S LAND ON THE EDGE OF EUROPE

ARTIST: VESSELINA NIKOLAEVA

In my life, I have crossed countless borders— between cultures and ideologies, on countries and continents. I have always been familiar with the terms *East* and *West*, but I could never quite position either the geographical or the psychological barrier between them. I have never walked along the border between any two sovereign states, let alone two larger political unions. I thought that if I set foot on no-man's-land, I would understand the meaning of the barbed wire on either side of this thin line that is not impregnated with politics, but whose only purpose is to be a blank spot on the map of the world.

Until 1989 the Bulgarian-Turkish border marked the southeastern edge of the Soviet bloc. It was a border fiercely guarded. Nobody could freely exit or enter Bulgaria. Those leaving were either with or against the party; the latter never returned.

After World War II, making photos or filming along the border was not allowed; nobody walked on no-man's-land, so nobody has memories of it. I went there, knowing that it was now or never, with the intention of being the first one ever to walk the 259 kilometers along the thin line of barbed wire and gather photographic documentary evidence of what once was the line between "us" and "the enemy." Today the border is taking on a new face, letting time swallow the torn and sacked buildings of the frontier posts. The old symbols of repression remain only in the skeletal frames of abandoned watchtowers and wrecked airplanes.

It is difficult to define time in no-man's-land. It is timeless. It looks like the past and it also looks like the future. However, I was reminded of time whenever I entered yet another frontier post and discovered traces of history — old political maps of the world, portraits of Lenin and Georgi Dimitrov, propaganda posters of the communist regime of the Balkan wars of 1912–1913, and of World War II. I found military diaries and photographs of soldiers, glass cases displaying awards and prizes from various competitions among the soldiers living at the frontier posts, and murals embodying oaths to protect the country's borders.

This no-man's-land had been a different world, perhaps even a different country. It had its own population of soldiers, and laws and regulations understood only by them. It was a strongly male micro-society surrounded by heroic myths of victories. All of that had been left behind—abandoned, unwanted, never to be missed.

In different political environments and at different times, borders are different, too. Soon the Bulgarian-Turkish border will mark the new outer limits of Europe, a patch of land that is destined to hold the international spotlight again.

Vesselina Nikolaeva · *No Man's Land*, from the series *No Man's Land*, 2005 · Inkjet Print on Watercolor Paper

Vesselina Nikolaeva · *Border Guard with a Dog*, from the series *No Man's Land*, 2005 · Inkjet Print on Watercolor Paper

Vesselina Nikolaeva · *Falling Fence*, from the series *No Man's Land*, 2005 · Inkjet Print on Watercolor Paper

Vesselina Nikolaeva · *Threshold*, from the series *No Man's Land*, 2005 · Inkjet Print on Watercolor Paper

I felt the need to catch the last traces of these ghosts of the past. These images will allow us to look both inside the past and into the future. They make the barbed wire softer, they bring a human element into that mythical world of danger and secrecy, and they show a landscape like no other — a no-man's-land in all its desolation.

Vesselina Nikolaeva

SEGREGATION WALL

ARTIST: NOEL JABBOUR

Our era is one of weakness, and is invaded by images. Photography is repetitive and reigns supreme over an artistic milieu that stays away from politics. Artists, too busy with art festivals and biennales, are not moved by the world's commerce, and usually avoid commenting on worldly government. We care so little that the emergence of a young photographer who is troubled by her world disconcerts us.

Noel Jabbour is a Palestinian, born in Israel, and of Christian origin. Her talent does not proceed from these facts alone. We know that to be close to an object alters our analysis of it and corrupts our seeing. Noel Jabbour has chosen to study in Israel and has patiently built, by a series of "soft breaks", an alternative to the confusion of her triple roots, which must have been, for her, a source of contradictions.

Noel Jabbour must have proceeded cautiously to abstract herself from anger and violent denunciation. Armed with a press pass early on in her career, she adopted the posture of a photojournalist so she could distance herself from her own emotions. Her work opens with a series of diverted postcards, and the story of an uprooted family living among her own family. From this first work, a solid approach is in evidence as the result of its emotional distance, and a deep empathy for its subjects.

NOEL JABBOUR · *WALL STREET, JERUSALEM,* FROM THE SERIES *SEGREGATION WALL,* 2004 · PIEZO-PIGMENT PRINT, COURTESY OF LOUSHY ART & EDITIONS

Noel Jabbour · *Concrete Curtain, Jerusalem*, from the series *Segregation Wall*, 2004 · Piezo-Pigment Print, Courtesy of Loushy Art & Editions

Her departure for Europe removed her from direct relationship with the conflict, but nevertheless did not eliminate its themes from her work. Her most recent photographs bring us back to Palestine. Going back to her roots, Noel Jabbour identifies with the child who explores her native village and, while making the rounds, hits a wall. This Wall, she found, one morning, established.

Here we are in front of the concrete wall set up in the West Bank by Israel. It's an incongruity that one sees from the sky above, a Lilliputian Wall of China—a senseless object that does not know who to protect and who to lock up. This monster is called paranoia.

The wall is erect, similar to a snake which unfolds—an absolute anomaly. This monster is real. It divides and it separates. It is hatred. This illusory line of defense, a long ribbon made up of modules 1.5 meters wide and 8 meters high and loaded with electronic surveillance equipment, wants to be an instrument of power and authority. But on a land emptied of its inhabitants, it is a house of cards, a weak Lego construction that will fall in shame. And from this wall, the words of Baudelaire will spout forth: "When I will have inspired universal horror and disgust, I will have conquered loneliness."

Jabbour's images speak to us this way. The sky is heavy and the inhabitants are in hiding. It is impossible to know, in these pictures, for whom the punishment is intended. The sky, of a gray lead color, tells us that a divine anger is there, present and restrained and terribly silent.

It is perhaps this silence that Noel Jabbour cares about, and is the focus of her questions.

To deal with the power of reality, Noel Jabbour does not want to answer with the use of concept and form alone, but she organizes a staged action that resolves itself in practical work. She confronts the Wall with the controlled lighting, film grain, format and composition. The asphalt echoes the clouds and the gravel is the grain.

Noel Jabbour gives us an ageless biblical vision of this conflict. The Wall takes its place again in the fresco that is several thousand years old. When conditioned by our immediate history, and feel powerless, when we are only fed images that limit of our horizon, Noel Jabbour, takes a position and, through this position, teaches us history anew.

François Cheval
Director, Musée Nicéphore Niépce, Chalon-sur-Saône
Translation from French by Eddy Philippe

Noel Jabbour · *Before the Storm, Jerusalem*, from the series *Segregation Wall*, 2004 · Piezo-Pigment Print, Courtesy of Loushy Art & Editions

US/THEM II

ARTIST: PETER RIEDLINGER

Peter Riedlinger: Before the Wall

In 2001–2002, at the time of his second visit to Jerusalem, Peter Riedlinger started to record the dramatic changes to be seen on the outskirts of the city, known as Greater Jerusalem. These changes included an increase in the number of roadblocks, the multiplication of checkpoints, never-ending and unnecessary road construction, general closures, and settlement construction, all of which constituted the organic material out of which Greater Jerusalem was being built.

What emerges from this series of images is a study of Israel as a state and as a country in formation. With his camera, Riedlinger systematically examines the architectural concept of settlement and investigates the territory it occupies, revealing it to be divided, invaded, and thoroughly under construction. In doing so, Riedlinger manages to give the viewer an understanding of the constraints on dialogue in Israel, which started with the political and military conflict, and were compounded by decades of psychological barriers. The battle for land and for mobility within this land is inscribed in these images as a subtext that allows the viewer to see the power at play in the institutional screening and intimidation of the region's ethnic other, the Palestinian.

In their straightforward documentary manner, Riedlinger's images not only contribute to our understanding of a traumatized state, but also provide some insight into the history of the making of Israel and its "territories." His photographs are governed by the political will to bear witness while simultaneously refraining from judgmental commentary. As such, they are a prime example of the conjunction of politics and art within the history of critical documentary and—metaphorically speaking—an example as well of the role played by contested territories within cultural production. These impressive photographs, whether read as individual panoramas or as a series of images, give the viewer entry to what remains outside the norms of daily life—where a civil society intent on the formation of the state remains on high alert, and where division and hatred determine the everyday experience of many. In this way the work provides a unique view of civilization and its role in the formation of villages, towns, cities, and the countryside.

In a recent debate in Berlin, film director Michel Khleifi described Israel as "a Jewish Democratic State" and stated that putting forward the "possibility for a future modern pluralist society" means to break the "ideological wall." And film director Eyal Sivan concluded, "How do we live together with each others' trauma, sharing a positive future," while simultaneously acknowledging that the condition of "emigration to Israel was followed by ethnic cleansing of Palestinians."[1]

If artists are to play a key role in recording and writing histories, then Riedlinger's *Us/Them II* offers a bleak view of the likely outcome of any positive development ensuing from

Peter Riedlinger · *Kedar Settlement/Palestinian Farmer*, from the series *Us/Them II*, 2002 · C-Print

Peter Riedlinger · *Ma'al Adumim Settlement*, from the series *Us/Them II*, 2001 · C-Print

twenty to thirty years of settlements and the disturbance of stable ecologies and communities, including the deforestation of hills and valleys—all part of the complexity of the region that we have learned to designate as Israel/Palestine.

Israel and Palestine remain as stigmatized states — possible states "creolized" by their conjoined geography and position on the globe. Like the Silk Route, they are both nodal and yet of outstanding regional significance, occupying a place where the world has flourished, been abolished, and been reconceived. It is partly in the contemporary reality underpinning the formations of these states that Riedlinger unearths both evidence of intrigue and the surreal.

In one image, Riedlinger captures the largest settlement, Ma'ale Adumim, placed strategically on a red hill that has been completely deforested, with any potential hideouts razed to the ground. A chain of mock Mediterranean, red-tiled buildings follows the ridge of the hill, served by a network of roads that cling to the earth's undulating form. The differing elements of nature and humankind, the sky, the buildings, and the earth form a sedentary landscape reinforcing the biblical ideology of the state of Israel. It is only within the next photograph that one views the settlement's proximity to a Palestinian village further down the valley. It is within this structure of presenting and re-presenting images and power that we start to realize the interdependence of the communities, and the manifest design for control, surveillance and the defect of it all.

Before 1948 the Jewish communities were among many minorities living in Palestine. But with the advent of settlements such as Har Homa, Ma'ale Adumim, and their kin (where only their kith can live), the pluralist society that was known as Palestine has become an infertile ground.

Shaheen Merali
Curator

[1] Michel Khleifi (Palestine) and Eyal Sivan (Israel), conversation about their collaborative film *Road 181* (F/B/D/GB 2003, 270 min.), Akademie der Künste, Berlin, March 23, 2004.

Peter Riedlinger · *Mizpe Jericho Settlement,* from the series *Us/Them II,* 2002 · C-Print

THE LAND OF THE SECOND SUN

The Nenets of the Yamal Tundra

ARTIST: HEIDI BRADNER

My work documents the Nenets, an indigenous Siberian people whose nomadic journey is the longest in the world. Each year families travel more than 1,400 miles, following the reindeer herds.

This way of life, nomadism, led to humanity's spread across the globe. The first "Americans" were hunters and gatherers who followed the migrations of animals across the Bering Land Bridge into Alaska and to the Americas.

This work is also about my own background growing up in the North, and the cycle of light and life I know. Most people think of polar regions as desolate and barren—void of culture. I want viewers to question what is considered civilized or primitive, extreme or sublime, dark or light. What exactly does it mean to describe a landscape as "empty?"

To the foreign eye, the Nenets' tundra world, entirely above the Arctic Circle, seems desolate, treeless, and isolated—dark and cold. The Nenets, however, describe their world is "the land of the second sun" because the moon, clean snow, and a canopy of northern stars all create their own light in the long hours of winter darkness. In summer the Nenets know another sun, the "midnight sun" of the Arctic summer, a glorious time when days never end and the sun never sets.

Nenets families, including elderly people and children, are constantly on the move, braving storms, crossing rivers and bogs in order to follow the animal that gives them life—the reindeer. This animal provides the basis for their whole culture—clothing, shelter, food, transportation, identity and the cycle of life.

Today the Nenets who call this part of the Arctic home face their greatest threat: the development of Russia's massive gas reserves that lie underneath their tundra migration routes. In this century, Russia is emerging into a new role as energy supplier to a world hungry for gas and oil. Economists estimate that more than fifty percent of Europe's gas will come from Russia in the coming decades.

"For us the deer are everything. Without them we will not survive," one of the Nenets told me. "Our animals follow their instincts; they are wild; they migrate…If something happens to the herds, it is our end as well."

Homo sapiens are the dominant species on the plant—and the one capable of destroying it. Today, consumerism, profligate energy consumption, technology, global markets, and instant communication define modern society.

These images are about extremity and beauty, strength and fragility, life and death, movement and stillness, and our own relationship with the past. We were all nomads once.

Heidi Bradner

The artist would like to thank Blue Earth Alliance for recognizing this project.

Maxim, 18, struggles to bring his team of exhausted reindeer into camp in the evening after traveling through a difficult storm. He will go to the army this year and this is one of his last trips on the tundra before his departure.

Heidi Bradner · *Maxim struggles home*, April 2003 · Silver Gelatin Photograph

Sleds and gear lie around the frame of the family home, a tee-pee like choom made from wooden poles, at a Nenets camp during their migration north every spring on the Yamal Peninsula. Over this frame the family will drape pelts of reindeer furs sewn together.

Heidi Bradner · *Home for the Night, Serotetta Camp, March 2003* · Silver Gelatin Photograph

An elder balances standing on his shed as he rides across a stream at midnight in early June during a late snowstorm. The Nenets people migrate over 1,400 miles each year to follow the reindeer herd.

HEIDI BRADNER · *ELDER CROSSING RIVER, YAMAL TUNDRA, JUNE 2003* · SILVER GELATIN PHOTOGRAPH

John Ganis · *Mine Tailings, Bingham Canyon Mine, Copperton, Utah*, 1990 · Chromogenic Print

CONSUMING THE AMERICAN LANDSCAPE

ARTIST: JOHN GANIS

The American landscape is fertile ground for my photographic exploration of the land use issues facing our society today. I see myself as a witness to the effects of humankind's interventions and excesses, which have a tremendous environmental impact on the earth. The dialectical processes involved in modes of production and resource development infuse my photographs of the American landscape with unexpected levels of interpretation, leading the viewer to reflect on our exploitative legacy. I use straight color photographs in a way that is descriptive yet somewhat poetic. The subtly paradoxical nature of my work is intended to provoke a process of questioning in the audience and to initiate the process of rediscovering a reverence for the land, which is often beautiful in spite of its environmental distress. Much of my work is characterized by a very visceral response to the earth itself, whether it is to the red soil of the American South laid bare by development, the cross sections of strip-mined rock strata, or the disturbingly artificial color of golf course greens.

Following this approach, I spent almost two decades making photographs throughout the continental U.S., resulting in the book from which the FotoFest exhibition has been drawn. *Consuming the American Landscape* was published by Dewi Lewis Publishing, Stockport, UK, in 2003, and the work from the larger sequences of the book form an important context for understanding the works distilled from it for the

FotoFest exhibition. Some of the most aesthetically important aspects of the book were the result of my collaborations with my publisher and with the various contributors to the book. George Thompson, who wrote the afterword, provided personal guidance throughout my project. The late Stanley Diamond was a distinguished anthropologist from the New School of Social Research; for a period of a year or so, he responded to my work and the environmental concerns we shared by writing several poems for the book.

The late Robert Sobieszek made a important contribution by writing his substantive essay, "The Machine on the Verge: John Ganis and the New American Pastoral." In this introductory essay, he states: "In pictures that are broadly colorful, often lyrically seductive, and at times cooly ironic — Ganis questions the tensions that exist between photographic beauty and a not so attractive reality, while at the same time documenting those places where 'the man-made, the cultural, and the natural are entropically merged'. The subjects of Ganis's images are for the most part flagrantly clear — abandoned wrecks, desolate strip mines, clear-cut forests, industrial parks, landfill sites, and the flattening of terrains for housing developments — and just as flagrantly disturbing. His imagery is a thesaurus of the varieties of "civilized" incursions into the wildness of nature, a picturesque survey of hundreds of "minor" horrors discovered in a serene and well-lighted out-of-doors, a colorful charting of our debris-strewn topographies, and a cogent report on our abdication of any reverence towards the land."[1]

JOHN GANIS · *MAMMOTH SITKA SPRUCE IN CLEAR CUT, SAPPHO, WASHINGTON, 1997 · CHROMOGENIC PRINT*

JOHN GANIS · *ALASKA PIPELINE NORTH OF VALDEZ, ALASKA*, 2001 · CHROMOGENIC PRINT

It is my intention that this work will convey the impact that our extraction industries and overdevelopment have on the environment. My hope is that the ironic beauty found in the sites I photograph will create an opening for the viewer to discover the multiple layers of meaning inherent in the American landscape, while maintaining a critical awareness of the environmental issues revealed in these photographic explorations.

John Ganis

[1]*Consuming the American Landscape*, John Ganis, Dewi Lewis Publishing, Stockport England, 2003, page 8.

STUMPS OF SILENCE

Tasmania

ARTIST: MASAKI HIRANO

Tasmania is an island on the south coast of the Australian continent. Most of the island's magnificent temperate old growth forests are being cut down to export raw materials to Japanese paper companies. This wholesale destruction is masked by a tree-planting program: the local logging monopoly logs old growth forests and replants trees, as if that makes its actions sustainable and earth-friendly.

Surprisingly, this practice is not illegal. Even more amazingly, the Japanese citizens who use all the paper produced by the logging, mainly computer paper, are not aware of the fact that they use 90 percent of the wood chips produced in Tasmania.

Due to the continuing cross-border corporate practice of placing profit before principle, and ignorance on the part of consumers, all the old growth forests on Tasmania will be converted into plantations in just a few years. Only the Tasmanian Wilderness, on the UNESCO list of world heritage sites, and a few other primitive areas secured on May 5, 2005, by the Tasmanian people after many years of effort, will remain.

The only way to protect Tasmania's ancient ecosystem based on these iconic forests is to change the structure of consumption, quick profit, and Japanese consumer ignorance. If we do not succeed, the immense forests will disappear into the past, changing the earth forever. As the plantations replace the forests, the wild animals will change, as will the insects, microbes, and soil, until the rivers and the oceans also fall prey to the broken chain.

As the chain of life goes, so do the souls of people.

There is not much time left to protect the few remaining Tasmanian native forests from greed and ignorance. All the data available today tells us that the delicate balance of nature is being disturbed. Our Mother Earth is neither as vast nor as sturdy as we believe.

We must stare at the present moment in order to know the past.

The present moment is the embodiment of the past.

We must stare at the present moment in order to know the future.

The future will be decided by our means of living at this moment.

I am trying to stand firmly in the present moment that connects the past and the future.

Masaki Hirano

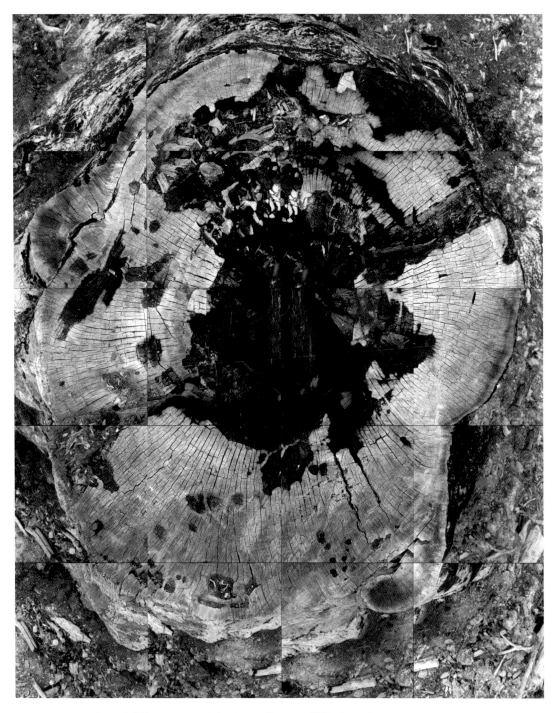

MASAKI HIRANO · *STUMP F (250 YEAR OLD TREE), SYTX VALLEY, TASMANIA,* 2001 · INKJET PRINT

Masaki Hirano · *Landscape C, Tarkene, Tasmania*, 2001 · Inkjet Print

Masaki Hirano · *Landscape A, Styx Valley, Tasmania*, 2001 · Inkjet Print

THE RED DESERT PROJECT

ARTIST: MARTIN STUPICH

The Genesis of *The Red Desert Project* and a Revelation

The Genesis

In 1996, a mountain bike crash in the central Rockies gave me a titanium femur and a sudden intimate relationship with the southern Wyoming landscape. Within a year of ditching my crutches, I moved from Boston and, using John McPhee's *Rising from the Plains* as my atlas, settled on the edge of the high windy Great Divide Basin, Wyoming's Red Desert country.

The Red Desert occupies an area the size of Yellowstone, Yosemite, and Grand Teton Parks combined. The landscape seems stark, the horizon crisp and always a day away. The desert is populated by scores of herds of rare desert elk, wild horse, and antelope. It is home to exotic species of finch, eagle, hawk, and owl. Humans live there, too, in tiny numbers in small settlements around the basin's rim.

Rumors of a coming economic boom, with its epicenter under the Red Desert, added intrigue to an already compelling landscape. By 2003 the rumors proved true. Fueled by an energy market in wild flux and a volatile world politic, the frenzy had begun.

Recently discovered directly beneath the Red Desert is one of the world's great natural gas reserves. In the last three years, the empty, remote half-million acres has flipped, transformed in one historic flash from wilderness steppe to industrial landscape. British Petroleum, Halliburton, and others have arrived. Surveyors, blasting and grading crews, rig operators and geologists now sweep the basin from edge to edge. Caravans of heavy equipment barrel across pristine playa and mesa, leaving a dense crosshatching of new roads in their wake. What had always been a blank spot on the map is now frantic with activity. When the dust clears in a decade or two —after the place has been scraped clean and pumped dry— the boom will end. The gas rigs will move on to the next sweet spot. The poisoned water table will begin to recharge. But anyone keeping time, using a clock where a second is a lifetime, will not see the desert heal.

Its transformation is under way and irreversible. I know that this vulnerable landscape cannot emerge whole. So I continue to photograph, hoping to make pictures that will serve as a collective portrait—a useful chronicle describing what was there and how we traded it away.

The Revelation

In the face of violent acts, my first impulse (like yours) is a jerk of revulsion, or horror, or disbelief. As artists and as citizens, our power is meager if our only choice, when we meet violence, is to react. We find ourselves wailing in the ruins of

Martin Stupich · *Ferris Mountains at northeast boundary of Red Desert, Carbon County, Wyoming,* 2003 · Pigment inkjet Print

a bombed village in Gaza or whispering psalms over mounds of corpses in Rwanda. Standing in the smoldering ash and mud of a newly logged hillside in the Amazon basin or in Oregon, we are swallowed by despair. And at any of these moments, if we have a camera, we photograph. We point it away from ourselves, click the shutter, and feel immediate cathartic release. Almost any picture made during that moment is going to be compelling, descriptive, eloquent. But in its virtuosity, no matter how crammed with subtle arabesque, the photograph has no practical value—no power to undo the horror, to revive the dead. But we remain voyeurs transfixed, drawn to violence like Weegee to a train wreck.

For me, making pictures of dramatically violated landscapes, or of pristine ones on the verge of being ravaged, is oddly satisfying work. The pleasure is predictable; so is the disquieting sense of righteousness. But after five years of working in the Red Desert, that landscape has finally begun to yield more than just pictures. Blunt truths surface as well, one especially clearly.

In 2005, after scores of trips crisscrossing the landscape—camping, photographing, documenting the geography of this wondrous raw place—it hit me like a skillet: They are not plundering the place. We are. I am. I look down to see that my tracks in the dust merge with theirs. They may be mining the coal and poisoning the groundwater, but they do it in our name. I am accomplice and beneficiary. Now what? Do I turn myself in—and to whom?

Martin Stupich

MARTIN STUPICH · *COOLING PONDS AT BRIDGER COAL-FIRED POWER PLANT. RED DESERT, SWEETWATER COUNTY, WYOMING,* 2003 · PIGMENT INKJET PRINT

Martin Stupich · "Boar's Tusk" Volcanic plug, Jack Morrow Hills, Red Desert, Sweetwater County, Wyoming, 2003 · Pigment inkjet Print

FALLEN

ARTIST: JULES GREENBERG

In the tradition of nineteenth-century postmortem photography (and mourning portraits painted centuries earlier), *Fallen* offers a confrontation with the dead. In this sense, the series is a sort of "corpse meditation," like that practiced by Buddhist monks who sit with dead bodies or stare at images of them for days, pondering the fleeting nature of life and the inevitability of death.

The "fallen" photographed here are bird specimens stored in natural history museums and research collections across the United States. Most of the birds were killed in the name of Enlightenment science, their deaths considered a necessary, perhaps even laudable, or at least acceptable sacrifice for the advance of human knowledge. Unlike specimens placed in dioramas and prepared for public viewing, these birds have not been made to appear alive again: they do not have artificial eyes or wings posed for flight. Their eye sockets are stuffed with cotton; their beaks and feet are bound with string. Not unlike wartime coffins or corpses that remain hidden from view by government decree, these birds and the human complicity in their deaths usually remain unseen, cloaked in the darkness of closed drawers.

Fallen is not just an elegy or a haunting and mournful lament for these beautiful birds. The series urges us not only to remember the dead and the conditions of their dying, but also to examine how the dead persist in the present and how, in the words of William Faulkner, the past is not really dead—indeed is not even past. The years identified on some of the specimen tags (1917, 1939, etc.) suggest an attention to history, particularly the history of war and violence. Indeed, *Fallen* emerged partly from my concern with how we rationalize violence and in what forms and under what circumstances we accept, celebrate, and/or hide violence. Like the wide-eyed angel in Paul Klee's painting *Angelus Novus* (1920)—which Walter Benjamin interpreted as the angel of history staring helplessly toward the past across an ever-rising pile of rubble while being propelled backwards into the future by the storm of "what we call progress"[1]—these birds raise questions about the relationship between violence, death, and destruction and "what we call progress," whether that be scientific understanding or the promise of freedom that purportedly justifies the deaths of "fallen" soldiers and others killed in war.

In this sense, the images are a call to witness, an attempt to make visible not so much the killing of these birds, or even the hundreds of thousands of other birds in collections around the world, but rather, more broadly, the increasingly disavowed entanglement of violence and "progress."

I chose to photograph birds because they embody this persistent and ironic tension. For ages, birds have been perceived as both ominous harbingers of death and envied icons of freedom. Winged creatures blessed with the capacity for

JULES GREENBERG · *FALLEN II*. 2005 · ARCHIVAL PIGMENT PRINT

flight, birds have been revered and feared as mediators between the physical and spiritual realms. They have represented liberation, transcendence, and peace, and yet mythically and materially (as scavengers and potential carriers of avian flu), they continue to be seen as messengers of mortality and devastation.

Jules Greenberg

[1]Walter Benjamin, *Illuminations*, trans. Harry Zohn (1955; reprint New York: Schocken Books, 1969), p. 258.

Jules Greenberg · *Fallen XI*. 2005 · Archival Pigment Print

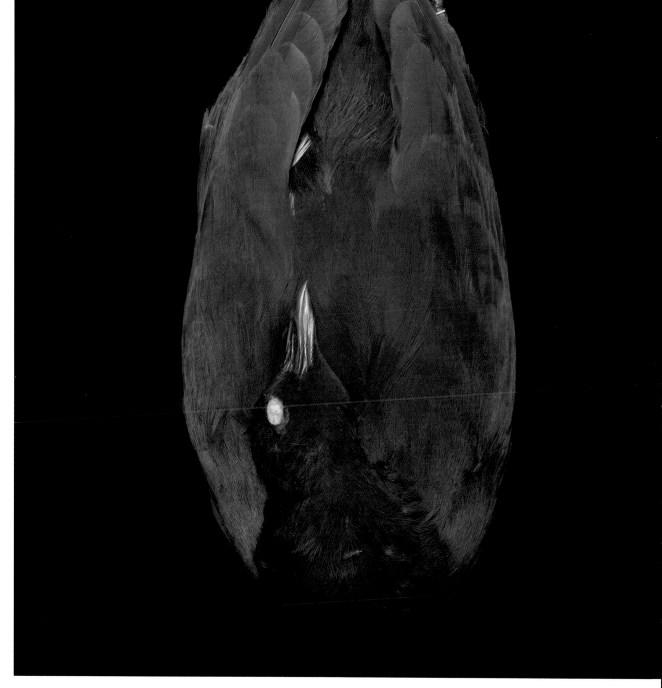

Jules Greenberg · *Fallen XIX*, 2005 · Archival Pigment Print

SELECTIONS FROM THE ICE AGE PROJECT

ARTIST: MARK RUWEDEL

Mark Ruwedel's project reminds me of the title of Thomas Bernhard's autobiography — Gathering Evidence. Ruwedel is a hunter-gatherer: of past events, of sites, of markings and the histories that they imply. What has been gathered? Individual examples of his alphabet of earth-use that he has developed into a grammar of surface history. Ruwedel explores the possibility that there is a langue, a system, and perhaps a syntax, of earth shaping, and that its overall pattern is one of disturbance evolving toward slow reclamation, with land and landscape entropically sliding along the arrow of time.

Bill Jeffries[1]

I think of the land as an enormous historical archive and am fascinated by the narrative fragments inscribed on its surface. I am most attracted to places that reveal the land as both the field of human endeavor and an agent of historical processes. Climate and geography are determining factors in the formation of cultures: mountains come first, then mountaineers. *The Ice Age* project, from which the exhibition *Gathering Evidence* comes, is a study of the physical traces of human activity on the land—the ruins of the near and distant past mapped in the context of the Pleistocene lakes that once covered large portions of the arid American West, a landscape where the bones are nearest to the skin. The lakes have largely disappeared, yet their history is clearly visible in the shorelines, deltas, and beaches inscribed on the mountains and the dry lake beds of the valleys. This land exhibits a terrific paradox: land forms created by massive bodies of fresh water are the defining features of some of the driest areas in North America.

The decline of the Pleistocene lakes roughly corresponds to the entrance of human cultures into this environment. The most conservative archaeological estimates suggest 10,500 years of human activity in the Great Basin, and as with the natural history of the lakes, evidence of succeeding human histories is written on the landscapes of the present. Histories this deep are, as Barry Lopez has suggested, "a kind of medicine," permitting "the great breadth of human expression to reverberate."[2]

Death Valley was the location of Pleistocene Lake Manly, with a maximum depth of 600 feet. The trails, campsites, and other physical traces of the hunter-gatherer cultures that lived along Lake Manly's ancient shorelines are still visible on the surface of this desert environment. In caves and rock shelters facing Lake Lahontan, now the Humboldt and Carson Sinks of the Nevada desert, archaeologists have found duck decoys and fishing nets, suggesting a way of life based on lakes and marshlands.

Evidence of more recent human endeavor overlaps these traces of ancient cultures, including the residue of exploration and settlement, and the technologized landscapes of the twentieth century. Tank tracks from World War II maneuvers cross ancient footpaths in the Yuha Basin. The ruins of Llano del Rio, a failed socialist community of the early twentieth

MARK RUWEDEL · *DEATH VALLEY: ANCIENT FOOTPATH ALONG THE SHORE OF THE DEPARTED LAKE*, 1995 · SILVER GELATIN PHOTOGRAPH

Mark Ruwedel · *Pilot Knob: Shaman's Circle,* 2001 · Silver Gelatin Photograph

century, sits on the edge of Pleistocene Lake Thompson, the setting of Space Shuttle launches. Danger Cave, cut by the waters of Lake Bonneville and inhabited over 9,000 years ago, faces the abandoned Wendover Air Force Base, where the crews of the *Enola Gay* trained in secret for the attacks on Japan. The dry lake beds of Frenchman and Yucca Flats at the Nevada Test Site became the stage upon which the U.S. government rehearsed World War III.

At Rozel Point on the north shore of the Great Salt Lake, Lake Bonneville's peripatetic descendant, Robert Smithson's *Spiral Jetty* (1970), appears and disappears with the rise and fall of the lake. Completely exposed last January, encrusted with white salt crystals, the jetty is apparently once again submerging. Landscapes are dynamic, exposing and erasing fragments of human histories embedded in it as the land continues to evolve.

Mark Ruwedel

[1] Bill Jeffries, "Symptomology in the Desert," in *Mark Ruwedel: Written on the Land* (North Vancouver, B.C.: Presentation House Gallery, 2002), pg. 8.

[2] Barry Lopez, "The Stone Horse," reprinted in *Mark Ruwedel: Written on the Land* (North Vancouver, B.C.: Presentation House Gallery, 2002), pg. 19.

MARK RUWEDEL · *CHOCOLATE MOUNTAINS: A CEREMONIAL TRAIL*, 2001 · SILVER GELATIN PHOTOGRAPH

WOOD AND BREAD

Vadim Gushchin · *Bread #7,* 2004 · Silver Gelatin Photograph

Vadim Gushchin · *Bread #1*, 2004 · Silver Gelatin Photograph

ARTIST: VADIM GUSHCHIN

Opposition and Reunification

By withdrawing an object from reality, Vadim Gushchin returns it to the viewer, and also a part of that reality, as a generalized formula or idea without creating a situational context or placing that object in the arbitrary field of "never and nowhere". Committing an act of counterpoising (opposing) image and reality, the photographer reunites reality and the idea of its being.

Philosophical deliberations of the photographic character send the viewer back to the second nature of photography that is conventionally opposed to the reality we perceive. This opposition between sensual and ideational realities takes the viewer into the realm of eighteenth-century philosophy when it was not possible to conceive that photography stems directly from the idea of empirical reason. At the time, painting alone, especially that by Chardin, could be considered as the response of an artist's intuitive perception to a philosophic idea striving to cognize universal law. Photography later came to represent the latest response to this, the latest model of the process by which the world is co-created by the idea.

From the very start, photography fully displayed its conventional opposition to sensual reality, even if it remained on the periphery of public consciousness for several decades. Yet as awareness grew closer to the fact that photography is a rational form of reflection, the less photography retained Talbot's and Hippolyte Bayard's pure experimentation that aimed to see what would happen if photography embraced reality, and the more it turned into a superficial form of technological recording which acquired the form of a philosophical and creative act only under the influence of the photographer's personality. Throughout the course of its development in the nineteenth century, photography was increasingly losing its own essential value, which was being replaced by the value of the photographer's personality, i.e. the value of personal vision. It was as late as the twentieth century, in the age of modernism, that photography, having passed through pictorial individualism, returned to an awareness of its own self-sufficient value connected, among other things, to its empirical genesis.

Conceptualism denoted the coming of age of the generalization of the new arts' experience, and that included photography. Conceptualism helped comprehend the evolution of photography's axiology in its compressed and reduced form, bringing back early photography as an empirical activity. In Russia, conceptualism, in its semiological forms especially, manifested itself in the scientific activities of the 1970s, if we discount Ilya Kabakov's studio on Sretensky Boulevard in Moscow with its hermetism group.

Vadim Gushchin's first shows came a decade later and they were already looked at in the light of the scientific knowledge of conceptualism, first as archaistic photography and, secondly, as photography that 'objectivizes' reality. Viewers were quick to recognize Gushchin's probing into the depths of photography and the rootedness of his works in philosophy, or, more precisely, in that area of cognition that constitutes the concern of philosophy. Intuitively grasped by Gushchin early in his career, this vector of interaction with an object provides the basis for his new projects.

Wood and *Bread* which continue to objectivize reality through photography. This line has been pursued by the artist over the course of the past two decades. The artist shows a tree stump or a piece of bread as a given, embodying the full scope of the semantic component of tree/bread. He endeavors to replace the whole with a fragment, implementing, together with the viewer, the transfer of meaning and a correlation of values different in scale, i.e. thinking in likelihoods and thus involving the viewer in the atmosphere of the Athenian school.

The purity of the process requires a parallel purity of form. The artist tries to obtain it by showing the object as a relief against a smooth background. This is the truly Chardinesque tradition of presenting an object, a tradition that is itself rooted in the old dispute of painters about how to approach sensual reality through painted imitation. Continuing this tradition, the artist chooses an elegant style of subtle replacement of black and white with intricately graduated tones. A philosopher, Gushchin outlines his teaching in rather refined poetry. He replaces black with noble dark-grey and he replaces white with mild, light-grey tones so that the almost terminological dryness of the philosophic utterance in his works is both sensual and sensitive, relating to sensual reality itself. With Gushchin, the fine art print relates not only to the existence of a still object but to the very nature (idea) of photography.

In *Bread*, the artist insists on creating a grid by using a table or some surface which supports his object and provides coordinates for the top-bottom and right-left position of the object as well as its three-dimensionality. Taking an object depicted and invested with humanist axiology, the artist creates the geometry of the universal, a supra-human scale. Whatever the series, Gushchin's photography belongs to the supra-national tradition. Inasmuch as a dispute on the existence of national schools of philosophy is less substantive than a dispute about schools based on some or another conception of being, so Gushchin's photography should be classed with the school that goes beyond the aesthetic and historical ideas of national photographic schools. The conception of photography embraced by this artist reaches further back than the national schools, and it is supra-national just the way the idea of being is supra-national vis-à-vis the philosophic schools of various countries.

Dr. Irina Tchmyreva
Moscow Museum of Modern Art
Translation from Russian by Marina Polevaya

Vadim Gushchin · *Wood #1,* 2004 · Silver Gelatin Photograph

Vadim Gushchin · *Wood #5*, 2004 · Silver Gelatin Photograph

NIGHT VISION

Rocks and Stones by Moonlight

ARTIST: BARBARA YOSHIDA

Some of the stones Barbara Yoshida has photographed have stood since long before humanity evolved, and others were placed by humans in their settled landscape as many as five thousand years ago. Those people's understanding of their own time and place instilled the alignments, and the stones themselves, with an ineffable sense of sanctity and wonder, a wonder now brought forth through Yoshida's photographs. While we may not know exactly how our distant ancestors approached the transporting and measuring of these stones, we can be sure of their dedication, application, and understanding. The stones speak not just of time, but of the timelessness that links the origin of the stones themselves to the role they played in the ritual and the thoughts of those who raised them.

While many have theorized as to the purpose and meaning of standing stones and circles, what cannot be doubted is that they were placed there for reasons that were of fundamental importance to the people who combined their efforts to arrange them. In the past many suggested these great monuments were meant to commemorate individuals, but the more we find out about the stones, the more it seems clear that these creations are reflective of communal enterprise rather than individual power. In communities that still live near such sites, stories still survive of fertility rituals that took place there, rituals that were focused on the dreams and aspirations of the people who raised the stones. The stones themselves tell us that the ancient peoples, living much more within the natural environment than we now do, understood how to measure and mark the turning of the seasons in order to function best within that environment. The immediacy of their involvement with nature makes it

BARBARA YOSHIDA · *TURTLE ROCK–2–MOONLIGHT, MONTAUK POINT STATE PARK,* 2002 · DIGITAL C-PRINT

Barbara Yoshida · *Aligments du Moulin−Moonlight, St. Just, France,* 2004 · Photogravure

BARBARA YOSHIDA · *RING OF BRODGAR STONE–MOONLIGHT, ORKNEY, SCOTLAND*, 2004 · PHOTOGRAVURE

sensibility underlines the continuity between us and our ancestors, and emphasizes the commonality of the human response to these ancient sites, then and now. Whether raising massive stones or picking out delicate images with the simplest of tools, our ancestors were in many ways like us. They, too, lived and died, loved and lost, laughed and cried, and tried to make sense of the universe around them. By looking at the earth and sky, they found their way to their own understanding of it, and if we cannot know precisely how they thought and prayed, we can, in these images, sense their wonder and delight at the world they inhabited.

To be able to approach these hallowed locales with an open heart and an inquiring mind is one thing; to be able to use both to capture the essence of what these stones have meant down the millennia is something else again. Yoshida has done this. Knowing some of these sites as I do, I am aware that words fail to capture their grandeur, their echoing of time passed, and their glorious relevance to the landscape that has changed and melded around them. It has been said a picture is worth a thousand words, but here these images do more than that. They bring to mind echoes of the songs that once were sung here, rhythms that surged through bodies moving in supplication and adoration of the powers of fertility and regeneration, and suggest stories we now can only grasp at like fading mist. Look and wonder.

Stuart McHardy
Storyteller and lecturer, author of *The Quest for the Nine Maidens* and *On the Trail of Scotland's Myths and Legends*

likely that for them the sacred was part of all life, the practicalities of their lives linked to the turning of the seasons celebrated at these ancient sites over incalculable periods of time.

In her spine-tingling photographs from major megalithic sites such as Calanais and the Ring of Brodgar in Scotland, Yoshida has tapped into deep levels of sensibility, showing how a talented artist can access perceptions different from those of the academics who study such places. This

Barbara Yoshida · *Pollock Mountain—Moonlight, Glacier national Park, 2002* · Digital C-Print

UNTITLED 2003-2004

ARTIST: HYUNG GEUN PARK

Most of the works I have produced recently, inspired by my imagination, show a certain way of understanding reality. Through the photographic image in particular, I attempt to see the world from more than a single dimension at any moment. For me, the actual world is not simply the object recognizable by the human eye, but something with multiple and various hidden dimensions. Thus what I am trying to do is not just record something from the real world, but rather capture the reality that I actually want to see.

For the *Untitled 2003–2004* series, I chose sites in nature marked by human beings, such as parks or Hampstead Heath in London. In these photographs, the visual image of nature is ordinary and familiar, but there is something unsettling, even chaotic, below the surface. The stillness of the image cloaks a variety of hidden narratives, histories, and events that have accumulated over a long time. I could sense something uncannily powerful and mysterious—an invisible presence—there.

However, what we often see in nature is an ostensibly beautiful or idealized version of the landscape, something we have created, desired, and possessed. Accordingly, the world we understand to be real is not the world itself, but rather something distorted by our preconceptions. The world where we live is not just a space existing at this moment, but a concept constantly being transformed. The most ambiguous of moments is that point when familiar things become uncertain, when our vision of reality grows vulnerable and indeterminate. Such a moment forces us to look at our position in this tension between real and imagined beauty.

Most of the photographs in this series were staged for the camera. I think that taking photographs as a kind of staged drama leads us to open up new possibilities of understanding and awareness.

Hyung Geun Park

Hyung Geun Park · *Untitled #1*, 2004 · Lightjet print

Hyung Geun Park · *Untitled #7*, 2004 · Lightjet print

Hyung Geun Park · *Tenseless #5.* 2004 · Lightjet print

FotoFest
at Williams
Tower Gallery

LIST OF ARTISTS

Eduardo del Valle and Mirta Gómez

Harri Kallio

Eric Klemm

Life Cycles

In the recurring cycles of life and death on earth, usually the human species has the upper hand. The story of the dodo bird is one of the first and most famous stories of species extinction in an historic encounter with human beings. On the Yucatan peninsula, there is a centuries-old tradition of recycling the resources of the earth for human dwelling places. In the ancient Canadian forests of British Columbia, however, the plants are taking over, consuming and burying the objects of human construction.

METAMORPHOSIS

ARTIST: ERIC KLEMM

The only equivalent I can think of to the lush, supersaturated greens with which these big new photographs by Eric Klemm are imbued is the lush supersaturated greens from which painter Emily Carr carved out the ancient, arboreal forests of British Columbia in paintings such as *Wood Interior* (1929–30) and *Old Tree at Dusk* (c. 1932). This makes a certain sense, since Klemm has been living and working on Salt Spring Island—Emily Carr country—for the past half-dozen years.

The fourteen chromogenic prints (each 49 x 64 inches) making up the exhibition that Klemm has titled *Metamorphosis* are a series of mysterious tableaux made in the depths of the old growth forest. Each print seems at first to be a pastoral study of the soft counterpane of the underforest, but it turns out, at second glance, to reveal the presence of a derelict automobile, quietly moldering away in the perpetual twilight of the forest floor.

Shrouded in mantles of moss and seized up in nets of vine, these decaying automobiles strangely seem less dead than their verdant embalming would lead you to believe, their headlights and bumpers and bits of brightwork gleaming dully in the green light as if they were about to stir and open their feral eyes. Sometimes the vegetation washes over the cars like a tide, clinging to their metal bones like seaweed. Sometimes only their windshields are overgrown, as if they have been blinded by the relentless greenness.

Klemm has photographed the cars—he tramps all over the island in search of them, like a hunter on safari—from all angles and in all of their fallen, post-Edenic randomness. The most haunting of his photographs, however, tend to be those in which he squares up the car so that it directly faces the viewer from within its lair of ferns and leaves. Sometimes all you can see of it is its wide smile of bumper and its unblinking headlight eyes.

It's beautifully disconcerting.

Gary Michael Dault
Art Critic, Toronto Globe and Mail

Eric Klemm · *Untitled #232*, from the series *Metamorphosis*, 2004 · Chromogenic Print

Eric Klemm · *Untitled #269*, from the series *Metamorphosis*, 2004 · Chromogenic Print

Eric Klemm · *Untitled #264*, from the series *Metamorphosis*, 2004 · Chromogenic Print

THE DODO AND MAURITIUS ISLAND, IMAGINARY ENCOUNTERS

ARTIST: HARRI KALLIO

"Why," said the Dodo, "the best way to explain it is to do it."
Lewis Carroll, *Alice in Wonderland*[1]

How can we visualize an animal we've never seen? Is it possible to breathe life back into a creature long gone from this world, to create a whole from bits and pieces of bone, long faded canvases, scraps of memories? With his project *The Dodo and Mauritius Island*, Harri Kallio aims to answer those questions and more.

Kallio's hybrid of art and science, as well as of photography and sculpture, speaks to the topic of the earth from the point of view of one of the first documented cases of animals hunted to extinction by our species—the dodo bird. The dodo, a distant cousin of the pigeon that was affected by an island-influenced gigantism, was openly mocked by early travelers to Mauritius for its ungainly appearance and lack of fear of human predators. In looking at Kallio's photographs, we see a kind and gentle creature, ironically full of the life that was snatched from it hundreds of years ago. Kallio's project examines our relationship to the earth with a humor and lightness that allows us access to the work, while at the same time opening our eyes to the loss we are complicit in. While his work allows us to see and care for this great creature, it also teaches us to mourn and, one hopes, to consider more carefully our role in species extinction, both now and in the future.

Kristiina Wilson

I'm not the first one to find the dodo compelling—more books have been written about the dodo than any other extinct species. Between 1662 and 1693, this strange giant pigeon was exterminated by humans on Mauritius Island—the only place on earth where dodos ever existed. Although the dodo became extinct hundreds of years ago, it still lives on in the collective memory of the Western world, in mythology, and in stories such as *Alice in Wonderland*.

While considering the dodo, I became fascinated with the idea of actually building models of the bird and seeing how they would look in the real world. As I worked on Mauritius, I found myself laughing all the time at the bizarre project I was doing. I knew that whatever I did with the dodos would be fun, funny, and paradoxically full of life.

Imaginary Encounters is a reconstruction and photographic study of the long extinct dodo bird. Based on extensive research, I produced life-size sculptural reconstructions of the bird, as well as a visual photo-based study of the actual dodo remains. The project culminated in a photographic series of the reconstructed dodo, made using the models in their natural habitat of Mauritius Island. While I created my photographs in the very same locations where dodos once went about their daily activities, I became acutely aware that Mauritius Island is a very different place now that it must have been in the early seventeenth century. It was a daily struggle to find land still in its natural state—not developed with crops or housing, or marred by modern human life. The resulting series is a an imaginary encounter between the viewer and the dodos on Mauritius Island.

HARRI KALLIO · *RIVIÈRE DES ANGUILLES #7, MAURITIUS,* 2002 · DIGITAL CHROMOGENIC PRINT

My idea was not so much to create a scientific reconstruction of the birds as to somehow put the *Alice in Wonderland* dodo, a character faithful to its appearances in art history, into the landscape on Mauritius Island—to create a dodo that is part myth and part real. I also wanted to recreate the kind of moments that must have occurred when the settlers arrived and the birds encountered people for the first time. Caught up in the contradiction between the historical dodo character and the real living bird, I became curious about what it would be like to combine the two—and so I decided to find out.

Harri Kallio

[1] Lewis Carroll and iIllustrated by John Tenniel, *Alice in Wonderland and Through the Looking Glass* (1865; reprint, New York, Grosset & Dunlap Publishers, 1946) p. 25

HARRI KALLIO · *BENARES #5*, MAURITIUS, 2004· DIGITAL CHROMOGENIC PRINT

Harri Kallio · *Le Gris Gris #2*, Mauritius, 2001· Digital Chromogenic Print

FROM THE GROUND UP

ARTISTS: EDUARDO DEL VALLE AND MIRTA GÓMEZ

In 1986, we visited Mexico on a two-week trip that included a three-day stop in Mérida, capital city of the state of Yucatán. On that first visit, we were struck by the diverse architecture of the region, especially the commanding presence and graceful beauty of the indigenous dwellings scattered about the city and countryside.

From the Ground Up is a three-part photographic essay that began those twenty years ago. It traces the evolution of the vernacular domestic architecture of the Yucatán peninsula, specifically the one-room dwellings of the region's Maya descendants. Customarily, these houses are constructed of earth and regional materials, such as hay, palm leaves, stones, tree trunks, and branches. These building materials, like the methods of construction, have remained the same for two thousand years. The archeological remains of the settlements that surround the ancient capitals, such as Chichén Itzá and Uxmal, indicate an unbroken continuity between past and present in both housing design and construction. This continuity is confirmed by the sculpted friezes of ancient Mayan palaces that show small dwellings clustered around the palaces in designs and arrangements similar to contemporary settlements scattered throughout the peninsula.

EDUARDO DEL VALLE AND MIRTA GÓMEZ · *SEYE, YUCATAN PENINSULA, MEXICO,* 1998 · CHROMOGENIC PRINT

In recent years, the proliferation of modern technology, industrialization, and tourism has brought with it the gradual disappearance of the natural materials that are essential for the building and maintenance of these traditional dwellings. Natural materials have been replaced by synthetic ones that compromise the structures' beauty and efficiency. In short, the indigenous dwellings of Yucatán, which are unique and emblematic of the region, are being either transformed into hybrid amalgamations of the past and present, or left to ruin and consequently to gradual extinction.

Eduardo del Valle and Mirta Gómez

Eduardo del Valle and Mirta Gómez · *Labná, Yucatán Peninsula, Mexico,* 1998 · Chromogenic Print

Eduardo del Valle and Mirta Gómez · *Sac-Chinch, Yucatán Peninsula, Mexico*, 1994 · Chromogenic Print

Eduardo del Valle and Mirta Gomez · *Topiary, Mérida, Yucatán Peninsula, Mexico,* 1998 · Chromogenic Print

FotoFest
at One City Centre

LIST OF ARTISTS

Nicholas Hughes

Elaine Ling

David Williams

Passages of Time—Light, Form and Reflection
There is that about the earth which leads us into states of contemplation about the interaction of shape, light and space.

David Williams · *Triptych 2*, from the series *one taste: (n)ever-changing*, 2003 · Giclée Print

David Williams · *Triptych 5*, from the series *one taste: (n)ever-changing*, 2003 · Giclée Print

ONE TASTE: (N)EVER-CHANGING

ARTIST: DAVID WILLIAMS

David Williams has recently traveled in Japan, where he photographed trees and garden spaces within the country's ancient Buddhist temples. The resulting series of photographs, *one taste: (n)ever-changing*, provides a meditation on nature, time, and change.

The precise location depicted in these particular triptychs is a tree-lined pathway that runs alongside the walls of the Tofuku-ji Temple in Kyoto. Established in 1236, it became one of the Five Great Temples of Kyoto and survived centuries of turmoil to be recognized as a national treasure. The many gardens within the temple complex, formal spaces of raked stone set against asymmetric plantings of moss and shrubs, are archetypes of Zen cosmography.

Something of this character is reflected in Williams's photographs. Formally, the series of eight triptychs respects a precise and elegant structure. The central image in each triptych shows the trunk of a tree from the cedar genus, *Cryptmeria Japonica*. The trunk rises in the exact centre of the photograph. Cropped at the base and again before the first branches define the tree's canopy, the trunk forms an axis for the drama of light and shade that unfolds through the series. Williams took each photograph at a different point in time, marked by how the passing sun reflects the dappled shadow of branch and leaf onto the garden wall of the temple.

This ghost image is the only evidence in the photograph of the chaos of nature that exists outside of the picture frame. Internally, there is a fusion of austere, regular patterns: the strict vertical tree trunk, the ordered horizontal striations of the garden wall, and the authoritative line of the foundation curb. This last generates a compositional centre as, combined with the vertical of the tree trunk, it creates a perfectly symmetrical cross. Each central panel is thus divided into four exact quarters. Such a formal geometry might appear to contradict the core subject in these photographs—the profoundly natural symbol of a tree shooting upwards from the earth—but in fact the rigid formalism is designed to connote the dialogue between nature and culture, permanence and change, form and emptiness, a dialogue that sits at the heart of these photographs.

These themes are present, at many levels, throughout the series of eight triptychs. Read as a linear narrative, the images unfold as a passage in time. Beginning with the cool blue light of the morning, the photographs brighten in the rising sun as subtle shades of yellow and orange color the scene. As darkness falls, a softer blue light tints the image, a light infused with the red of the sunset. Here the shadow pattern of leaves melds into a uniform darkening silhouette. This linear reading is contradicted, however, in Williams's manipulation of the triptych panels. He created the triptychs by isolating the sections of each image to the left and to the right of the tree trunk, reproducing these scenes as the flanking panels. But in each case, the section that sits to the right of the trunk is reproduced as the left-hand panel, while the section to the left of the trunk is presented as the right-hand panel. The linear progression, the sense of time unfolding, thus turns back on itself so that present, past, and future become *one '(n)ever-changing' thing*.

The conundrum of dualism transcended is echoed throughout these images—not only in the juxtaposition of horizontal and vertical framing, but also in the contrast of patterned earth and tree trunk with the uniform wall. Less explicitly, though more powerfully, the material fact of the natural and the man-made contrasts with the immaterial shadow play of sunlight and leaves. Here the thing that is not represented in the photograph is conjured as a spectre. In this sense, absence and presence coexist.

In summary, Williams presents a meditation upon the idea that a thing may be both itself and its other, that the material and the immaterial are one, and that form is emptiness and emptiness is form. These new works by Williams help to realize the essential mysticism at the core of his vision. Their formal cohesion, dark spirituality, and lyrical symbolism engage with those essential enigmas at the very heart of modern life. Simultaneously, their mood is ethereal, open, infinite, and inviting. In this way they present and re-present the puzzle of their title, *one taste: (n)ever-changing*.

Dr. Tom Normand
Senior Lecturer, History of Art, University of St. Andrews, Scotland

David Williams's project was supported by Edinburgh College of Art (eca) Research Board, The Sun Chlorella Corporation in Kyoto, and Nozomi Group (eca).

DAVID WILLIAMS · *TRIPTYCH 7, FROM THE SERIES ONE TASTE: (N)EVER-CHANGING,* 2003 · GICLÉE PRINT

EDGE

ARTIST: NICHOLAS HUGHES

…in Wildness is the preservation of the World.
Henry David Thoreau[1]

Each person's relationship to the earth may well be dependent upon location—swinging between the urban and the rural. Urban life is a barrier between people and the natural world. Often urban dwellers are unaware of this spiritual gap in their lives.

Loss of contact with nature means that for many people the earth has lost its mystique. This lack of awareness has driven a wedge between our living planet and us. For many the changing display of shop windows is the only clue to the changing seasons (often in advance of nature). Our view of the horizon is obscured, and our divorce from nature is compounded by the absence of sky. This contrived landscape further deprives our senses of the flow of the wind and the fall of the rain, while our mood is influenced and controlled by piped music. The magic of rebirth in the spring is distorted and grotesquely dressed behind glass and lit by the glow of a tungsten bulb.

The exploitative society in which we live views nature and the earth as a resource for gain. As nature disappears to meet the demands of industrialization and urban expansion, there is a constant search for the gaps left behind—for virgin territory. But what may appear as natural landscape may in fact be created by human activity over centuries. Our memories of particular landscapes or familiar terrain are emotive. The ideal remains the wilderness—a place of spiritual and mental renewal.

My work is structured by my search for the "wild" through the geometry of abstraction and finding the space to transcend the ordinary: conjuring up new visions of the pristine aided by the Minimalist mantle of undisturbed snow.

In the same manner that the tide erases the daily tracks of our presence on the shore, the fall of snow provides a newly cleared vision of wilderness. If only our exploitation of the earth could be so easily removed. The truth is the reality of irreparable damage; it is only in the space afforded by our minds that we can make room for the sanctity of our planet. This emperor's clothing is fragile as we make this reassuring metaphorical leap without the permanency required for survival.

The wilderness has long provided a frame within which one can fixe one's ideas and aspirations. To this end, I have sought to capture the essence of the human spirit and its relationship with nature. In distilling an emotional response to color, my aim is to find a form of contemporary expressionist idealism. The overburdened mind is offered the escape valve of distant vistas through utopian visions.

This fear is more keenly felt within the secure environment of our homes. We are alarmed by the news of rising tides, rather than awed by the immensity and timelessness of the ocean itself. Sometimes the sense of physical vulnerability induces a cathartic state—and creates a mental space in which to take refuge. It is in this space that I prefer to operate.

For me the visual challenge is still finding meaning in what we perceive as beauty. I am left poised on the brink of this reality as I try to grasp the value of the natural.

My intention is to focus the observer's attention on the essence of the image and avoid distracting it with negative imagery; in doing so, I draw the observer toward the spiritual. I hope that the delicate nature of my portrayal serves as a metaphor for the fragility of our relationship with the natural world. It further aims to offer a reacquaintance with what author Dawn Perlmutter has suggested is a quality that has recently fallen off the agenda but was once the nourishment of much of the world's art—the spiritual.

Nicholas Hughes

A retreat into contemplation, away from the urban noise of contemporary living, offers the opportunity to immerse oneself in compressed visualizations of the sublime. While beauty still exists, its future and ours may be on the verge of extinction. Even the ocean, subject of so much of my work and a traditional provider of this essential mental release, is contaminated by humankind.

Standing at the edge, my attempts to seek communion with Caspar David Friedrich's painting *Monk by the Sea* (1810) are tinged with the desire to raise the alarm to the danger in our midst.

[1]Henry David Thoreau, speech at Concord Lyceum, April 23, 1851; published in Henry David Thoreau, "Walking," *Atlantic Monthly 9, no. 56* (June 1862).

Nicholas Hughes · *Seascape #29, from the Series Edge,* 2003 · C-Type Photograph

Nicholas Hughes · *Seascape #14*, from the Series *Edge*, 2003 · C-Type Photograph

MONOLITHIC GUARDIANS OF THE EARTH

ARTIST: ELAINE LING

Monolith : one stone

This lyrical geological concept led me to the making of a series of portraits of stones. My fascination with these powerful lithic beings brought me into confrontation with their splendid isolation, with their numinous permanence, and with the compelling eloquence of their creaturelike, humanlike presence.

The monoliths stand in harsh and remote landscapes, each of them bearing the markings of time, shaping and reshaping their countenances. They stand—massive, silent, and immovably strong—as guardians of the earth. Their message is a promise that the natural earth, of which they are expressive inhabitants, will prevail.

Elaine Ling

In the course of writing about the works in her *Monoliths* series of photographs, Elaine Ling refers to the great stones that constitute her subject as "lithic beings" and to the resulting photographs as "portraits" of these stirring presences.

Indeed, the great stones *do* sometimes seem to possess the immediacy of beings, and as Ling points out, they often do appear capable of something she refers to as eloquence—a mute eloquence that is spatial and crystallized chronologically,

like that of venerable works of architecture. But unlike works of architecture—which Friedrich von Schelling famously described as a frozen music—the great stones are a kind of stopped-down time, a molecular rush slowed to the eon-long pace of erosion and other forms of gradual geological shift.

What makes the great stones so moving? It cannot be their anthropomorphic dynamism alone—or at all. Even though Ling's photographs of the yearning, vectoring, minaretesque stone towers of Cappadocia, Turkey, or her photographs of the dynamic, cobralike tumescences of rock made at the Giant's Playground in Namibia are persuasively animated and as dramatically lit as players on a stage, it is surely not their attainment of a kind of surrogate figuration that we find so arresting. That sort of simile-driven, stand-in status is likely to be more charming, more witty—more persuasive in an almost narcissistically mirroring way—than stirring. No, even though, as Gaston Bachelard has pointed out in his exquisite *Water and Dreams*, "everything in the Universe is an echo,"[1] it is not the imitative aspect of the stones that generates their eloquence.

What then? Well, it probably has to do with their stolidity, with their relative imperishability in contrast to the flickering, focusless moment that is the tiny trajectory of our own experience: the slow burn of erosion and other sandpaperings of time that befall the great stones of earth seem like mere sparks falling away from an ongoing fiery immutability, compared to the brief candle that is human life.

ELAINE LING · *INCREDIBLE ROCKS 6, AUSTRALIA*, 2005 · SILVER GELATIN FIBER-BASED PHOTOGRAPH

Imaginatively, if not strictly chemically, stones are monads. And it is their singularity that is so moving. Even though we know that stones are in fact hardened agglomerates of mineral, shot through with traces of water—nature's glue—they seem to be (like Søren Kierkegaard's formula for "purity of heart") essentially, imagistically, and metaphysically *one thing*. Rock is made of rock. And their Unbearable Heaviness of Being is always being thrust up at us from the mother-magma-earth as an offering of timelessness, as a shard of eternity you can walk around or stand on—or photograph.

All this is in exaggerated contrast to our own fragility. Stones are forever—or so it seems. And it is against their apparent agelessness that we posit our delicate, terrifying brevity. The stones stand, as Ling notes, "silent and immovably strong—as guardians of the earth." They move us, especially when we are assisted into our reveries by this photographer's subtle approach to their singularities, working as a lithic portraitist. Because they are axial and we are orbital. Because they are fixed, while we are endlessly ambulatory. Because they are themselves, whereas we spend most of our lives trying to figure out what that could possibly mean.

Gary Michael Dault
Writer, painter, and art critic for the *Toronto Globe and Mail*

[1]Gaston Bachelard, *Water and Dreams: An Essay on the Imagination of Matter*, trans. Edith R. Farrell (Dallas: Pegasus Foundation, 1983), p.194

ELAINE LING · *GREAT ZIMBABWE, ZIMBABWE*, 1999 · SILVER GELATIN FIBER-BASED PHOTOGRAPH

Elaine Ling · *Cappadocia Stones 3, Turkey*, 2002 · Silver Gelatin Fiber-based Photograph

FotoFest at
JPMorgan Chase,
Heritage Gallery

LIST OF ARTISTS

Barbara Grover

Muriel Hasbun

Angilee Wilkerson

Land, Place and Heritage

Migration and diaspora, forced and voluntary, have been at part of human history since the time of early settlement and the formation of communities. But ties to particular lands and places define heritage and the meaning of community, culture and self.

TRACE

ARTIST: MURIEL HASBUN

I began investigating my family's history in the early 1990s in an effort to confront the "Other" within me. Through my photo-based work, I explore notions of territory, memory, and home. I collect the voices buried deep within my diasporic self, and I confront the resulting amalgam of my identity. Through an intergenerational, transnational, and transcultural lens, I craft a language that expresses a shared humanity, while erasing the borders that maintain our "Otherness."

Trace is an embodied response to the ripple effect of violence in the world, running through four generations of my family. Faced with the outbreak of war, persecution, and/or religious intolerance, members of my family either were caught (and murdered), hid from danger, and/or fled their countries of origin. Daughter of a Palestinian-Salvadoran Christian and a Polish-French Jew, now living in the U.S., I rescue the otherwise silent voices of my family, and I try to understand the emotional repercussions of events that I myself did not live through but unquestionably carry within. The unspoken lessons of surviving the Holocaust as well as the loss of a homeland in Palestine echoed within the walls of my house as I grew up in tension-filled El Salvador.

With *Santos y sombras/Saints and Shadows*, I trace my family's various exiles and diasporas. The Palestinian desert and Eastern European ash sift and blend into the volcanic sands of El Salvador to form the texture of the path on which I define and express my experience.

With *Protegida/Watched Over*, I discover links between peoples and places that at first appear disconnected. As I examine the strangely familiar outlines of the Auvergnac volcanoes on my contact proofs, I realize that nothing is so easily separated, nothing so easily forgotten, nothing so neatly kept within its borders.

Muriel Hasbun

Muriel Hasbun · *Todos Los Santos (Volcan de Izalco, Amen)*, 1995-1996 · Silver Gelatin Print

MURIEL HASBUN · *¿SOLO UNA SOMBRA? (LEJZOR)*, 1994 · SILVER GELATIN PRINT

Muriel Hasbun · *Todos Los Santos II (Recuerdo de mi Primera Comunion)*, 1993· Toned Silver Gelatin Print

HISTORY SERIES I

ARTIST: ANGILEE WILKERSON

In this body of work, I reference the memory shared with my Oklahoma ancestors. This memory was created through handed down narratives about passing through what was once "Indian Territory," and from the multiple accounts of prophetic dreams and visions told to me by my mother, grandmother, and grandfather. In my appropriation of this inherited narrative, I re-collect and express it through a complex structure of memory, which diffuses the boundaries between what I have experienced firsthand and what I have gathered from my kin. The essence of this historical narrative remains the same, while its presence differs. In *History Series I*, my family's story makes itself present through the layering of natural elements native to the north Texas and southern Oklahoma landscape with old family photographs.

My inherited memories are constituted of Dust Bowl experiences; droughts and tornados; the red, fruitful, over-turned earth; mineral-rich well water; and the vibration of grasshoppers harmonizing with the hymn of a summertime baptism in the big warm pond west of the old house. In the complex structure of memory expressed in *History Series I*, these recollections are inseparable from my own firsthand sensory knowledge of the earth as well as from observations on the sublime coexistence of farmer and nature, tempered by a bucolic Pentecostal fervor and rural traditions quilted into deep-rooted habits of work, glorified by pride and made bearable by family-made music.

In integrating family and nature, I am articulating a new presence for the historically determined blueprint grounding the possibility of the person I am to become. In doing so, I am tending to that blueprint and thereby caring for the historical narrative of my family.

Angilee Wilkerson

ANGILEE WILKERSON · *HISTORY SERIES I, #17*, 2005 · ARCHIVAL GICLEE PRINT

Angilee Wilkerson · *History Series I, #2,* 2004 · Archival Giclée Print

Angilee Wilkerson · *History Series I, #15*, 2005 · Archival Giclée Print

Angilee Wilkerson · *History Series I, #4*, 2004 · Archival Giclée Print

THIS LAND TO ME—SOME CALL IT PALESTINE, OTHERS ISRAEL

ARTIST: BARBARA GROVER

Few other issues fuel global tension and violence as does the Israeli-Palestinian conflict, yet what do we really understand about the people who live it beyond the bloody images on the nightly news? Why is 1948 a catastrophe to some, independence to others? Why are some children willing to be suicide bombers and others willing to go to war over a "Middle Ages icon"? How can we stop this violence unless we better understand the "other" as well as ourselves?

Because what happens today in Gaza and Tel Aviv has repercussions in communities from Paris to Los Angeles, I wanted to explore these questions—not by photographing the acts of violence or the physical scars left by it, but by unveiling the rage and despair that has led people to see violence as an acceptable form of empowerment.

In the summer of 2002, I began traveling from the Gaza Strip to the Lebanese border to interview and photograph Israelis and Palestinians from all walks of life. I asked my subjects to address the main issue that is fueling the violence in this particular conflict: people's connection to the land. I had them answer the question: "What does the land that some call Israel, and others call Palestine, mean to you?" In photographing my subjects, I asked them to look into the lens of my camera—as if speaking directly to the viewer. I intentionally photographed each person in an environment that seems remarkably removed from the day-to-day violence we are used to seeing, so that the subjects' faces and words would be what resonated with—or haunted—viewers. The series of photographs and first person narratives titled *THIS LAND TO ME—Some Call It Palestine, Others Israel* came out of that journey.

The concept for this body of work came from my own life-changing experiences. More than anything I have read or seen, the candid, intimate, face-to-face encounters I have had over the years with Palestinians and Israelis helped me understand the complexities, realities, and diversity of perspectives that make this conflict so painfully difficult to resolve. They forced me to question my own fears, prejudices, and assumptions. I have tried to recreate this experience for others through an artistic approach that gives photos and text equal prominence, and thus creates for viewers a virtual encounter with people they would otherwise never meet. To make this body of work accessible to various audiences, I exhibited the same material in two different ways: In one, a series of life-size digital photographic canvases hang in a free-form arrangement alongside equally large canvases containing the first person narratives; in the other, an installation gives viewers the feeling they are walking through a larger-than-life magazine spread.

THIS LAND TO ME—Some Call It Palestine, Others Israel begins the process of unraveling the myths and misconceptions that stand in the way of peace. Since 2002, I have returned twice to the region to expand the initial body of work for future installations and potentially a book.

Barbara Grover

"I would live and die over the existence of Israel—But to die over the right to pray over the Western Wall, which is just an icon from the Middle Ages, makes no sense." Rabbi David Lazar

Barbara Grover · Rabbi David Lazar at the Western Wall, from the Series THIS LAND TO ME–some call it Palestine, Others Isreal, 2002. Carbon Ink Digital Print

"We have both lost time to live like normal people, we have both lost our children and we have both lost our lands....Peace is more important than land." Tariq Muhamed

BARBARA GROVER · *TARIQ ON THE FRONT STEPS OF HIS HOME. ISSAWIYAH, FROM THE SERIES THIS LAND TO ME— SOME CALL IT PALESTINE, OTHERS ISREAL, 2002, CARBON INK DIGITAL PRINT*

"–who knows what I would do if I wasn't pregnant. Thank god there is still something I can do for my land. I can be a good mother and teacher" Hanadi Al Mograbe

BARBARA GROVER · *HANADI WITH A PHOTO OF HER IMPRISONED HUSBAND. DEHEISHE REFUGEE CAMP. WEST BANK.* *FROM THE SERIES* THIS LAND TO ME–SOME CALL IT PALESTINE. OTHERS ISREAL. 2002. CARBON INK DIGITAL PRINT

FOTOFEST
AT ALLEN CENTER

LIST OF ARTISTS

Herman van den Boom

Keith Johnson

Abby Robinson

Keith Sharp

Re-constructing Nature

It is not enough to 'live' with nature, people need to reshape and re-make it—post-modern suburban gardens with imported vegetation, as golf courses and nature-resistant lawns. From the nineteenth century to the present, idealized landscapes have been created as hand-painted backdrops for people coming to have their portraits done by professional photo studios. And some people try to transform themselves by becoming part of nature itself.

MAN(UFACTURED) SPACE

ARTIST: KEITH JOHNSON

My work is about the planet we live on, the place we call home, and how we deal with it. As a photographer, I am interested in recording the curiosities presented to me as I travel, sometimes to interesting places, sometimes to not so interesting places. I respond to the way we have dealt with the land — the unfinished or intermediate changes that people have made. I am taken with colors and the irony of the space, the incongruity as a result of juxtaposition, and the downright weirdness that is out there.

Over the past year or so, I have been photographing reclaimed landscapes: landscapes that for whatever reason have been manufactured, carved, covered, and planted so as to seem natural, organic, and tidy. I am fascinated with the materials, colors, and look of these sites. They bear only a remote resemblance to the land that nature would have wrought.

I am an observer with a camera. I record those things and situations that make me turn my head. I am not interested in photographing to simply take an inventory, though. Instead I am drawn to a scene because it seems that photographs are hovering there, that the place offers possibilities. Then as I walk through, I work to "find my place," as Carlos Castaneda's Don Juan would suggest, or where I will plant my feet, as Garry Winogrand would say.

I am attracted to building sites and land reclamation sites in much the way a kid in a sandbox is when building roads and towns. In the real sandbox, the earth gets reclaimed after all the construction is done, remanufactured in a way. It is this stage that calls out to me the loudest. The attempt is to beautify the landscape. This of course is after we have stripped it, graded it, planted it, and covered it. There is a state when the effort is still evident, but the beauty has not yet taken hold.

My pictures are observations about the landscape and about the way the landscape is put together. I, try to make sense of that space between the organic and manmade, sometimes finding both at the same time. The stuff I make pictures of is not important stuff (it is in most cases trivial), but when abstracted by the camera, simple marks can become grand gestures. It is in this space between the abstract and the pictorial that I find resonance. I am intrigued with the intersections that take place within the frame and with my being in a place.

Information is important, as is color, and these may be the primary reasons that I stop to look. I am entertained by what is out there for me to run into and by my interaction with what is in front of me. Sometimes I shake my head with disbelief; sometimes I am just thankful I was able to be there. I couldn't make up the things I photograph, so I am glad to have intersected with them.

Keith Johnson

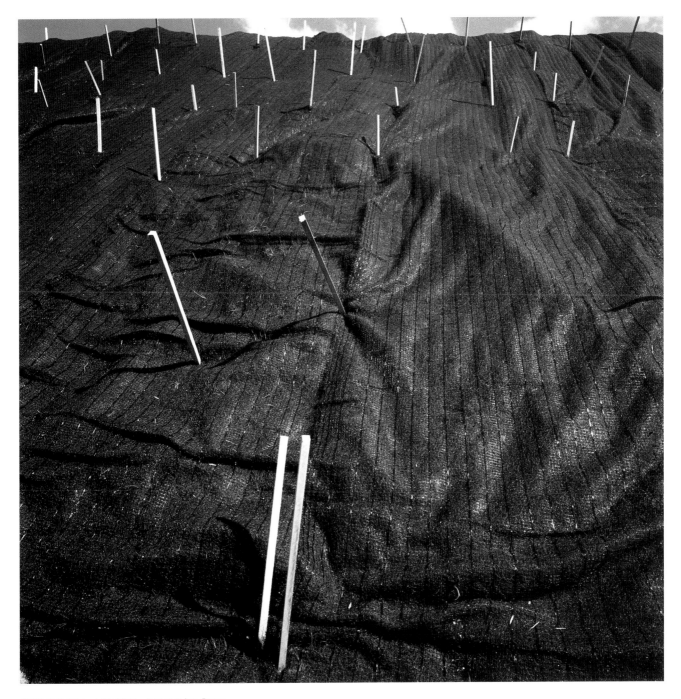

Keith Johnson · *I 95. 2004* · Pigment Ink Print

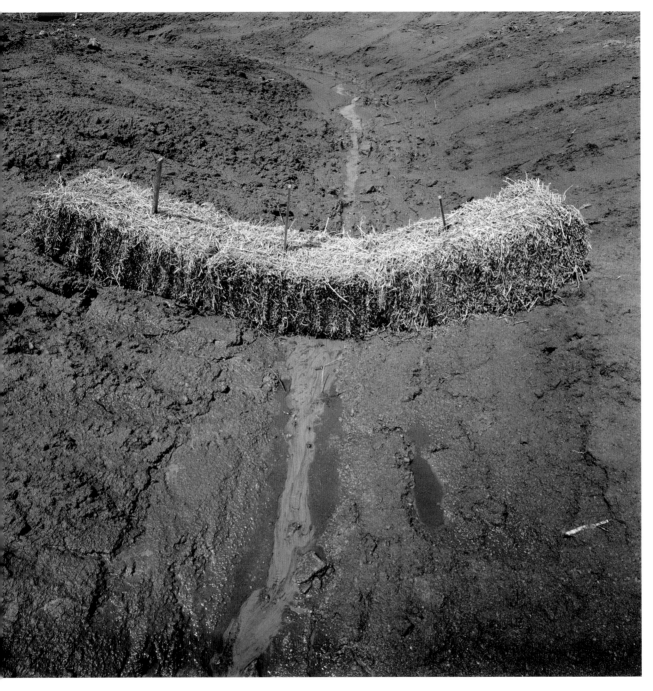

KEITH JOHNSON · *WEBSTER*, 2004 · PIGMENT INK PRINT

Keith Johnson · *Plug*. 2004 · Pigment Ink Print

IMAGINATIVE LANDSCAPES

Landscapes of the Imagination

ARTIST: HERMAN VAN DEN BOOM

...in Wildness is the preservation of the World.
Henry David Thoreau (1817–1862)[1]

The landscape changes dramatically, not only through industrialization, urbanization, globalization, and pollution, but also by "recreational gardeners" who create their own fictional Arcadia.

While looking at these front yards and gardens, it occurred to me that the fragments I was photographing could be felt and experienced as a modern-day Arcadia.

The owners themselves undoubtedly derive great pleasure from their creations, but if you put all these pieces of "Arcadia" together in your imagination on a global scale, you encounter an enormously cultivated and surreal landscape, where everthing is out of context.

What people create here as an idyllic site is not only visually absurd, but also represents a cultural and ecological implosion.

How can this "Idea of Arcadia" in reality be so different from what people feel and intend?

Herman van den Boom

1 Henry David Thoreau, speech at Concord Lyceum, April 23, 1851; published in Henry David Thoreau, "Walking," *Atlantic Monthly 9, no. 56* (June 1862).

Herman van den Boom · *Veldwezelt, from the Series Arcadia Redesigned,* 2004-2005 · Digital Print

HERMAN VAN DEN BOOM · *LO VEN JOEL,* FROM THE SERIES *ARCADIA REDESIGNED,* 2004-2005 · DIGITAL PRINT

Herman van den Boom · *Leuven*, from the Series *Arcadia Redesigned*, 2004-2005 · Digital Print

IN CAMERA

ARTIST: ABBY ROBINSON

*Stare. It is the way to educate your eye, and more. Stare, pry, listen,
eavesdrop. Die knowing something. You are not here long.*
Walker Evans[1]

ABBY ROBINSON · *ROAD / SRI LANKA*. 2002 · CIBACHROME PRINT

ABBY ROBINSON · *PALMS / SRI LANKA*, 2002 · CIBACHROME PRINT

My interest in interior spaces and the way they convey values, aspirations, class, and taste dates to my undergraduate studies in architectural history. During my M.F.A. years, I turned my attention in a more pragmatic direction by studying interior design—learning about materials and design problems as well as the matching of spatial requirements with specific programs. Even then I was involved with questions of how interiors reveal their owner's or user's personalities and the connection of function with form. Initially photography was merely a tool for taking architectural notes. But I switched to the photography department when I realized that the photographic frame functioned like a room and that the photographer served as builder, decorator, and host. Besides, photography was a lot more fun.

Walker Evans was a major influence. In his photographs of interiors he let the facts of a room's materials, furnishings, and decorations inexorably guide the viewer to imagine the room's absent occupants. Evans always showed that there was something to be valued in these places, no matter what their economic station, and that there was an eloquence and poignancy to the people who created, inhabited, or abandoned them. I learned from Evans to find poetry in plain, prosaic fact.

When I got out of school, I worked for a private investigator. I learned not only to be sneaky but also to pay even closer attention to detail, to look for clues in the way objects were positioned in a room. I also developed a writing career from these adventures when my novel, *The Dick and Jane*, was published. Around that same time, I got itchy feet and started to travel. Exposure to different cultures and aesthetics made my head spin. Morocco taught me how decoration energized and filled space. Egypt, with its vast desert landscapes, taught me about scale. Asia introduced a glorious new color palette.

In all these travels, I thought a great deal about time, ruminations that led to the first of my interior investigations (*interior* can be used here in a double sense). Time is a critical factor in photography, and Western photography is propelled by what Henri Cartier-Bresson called the "decisive moment." But this rapid-fire, split-second approach has little relevance in Asia, where art has at its center a profound sense of stillness and where time is perceived as cyclical rather than linear.

On my first trip to Vietnam in 1994, I found a country undergoing profound change under the political policy of Doi Moi ("Change Anew"). What riveted me—especially during 1996–97, when I lived there on a grant from the Asian Cultural Council—was the solid core of Vietnamese tradition in the midst of great transformation. So I photographed rooms where the old cohabited with the new, where curious juxtapositions of the secular and the spiritual were commonplace. I made my first pictures of photo studios in Vietnam, then more during my Fulbright Fellowship to India and Sri Lanka in 2000, and still more when I went back to those countries—and Pakistan—on my own. The series builds on notions of traditional documentary photography, but adds in painterly and cinematic elements. And the panorama camera I use is perfect for this work.

Abby Robinson

[1]Belinda Rathbone, *Walker Evans: A Biography*, First Mariner Books/paperback, 2000, pg. 28.

ABBY ROBINSON · *BRIDGE / SRI LANKA*, 2002 · CIBACHROME PRINT

ABBY ROBINSON · *SEASCAPE / SRI LANKA*, 2002 · CIBACHROME PRINT

NATURE BOY

ARTIST: KEITH SHARP

Dr. Moreau's Secret Garden

In Duane Michals's sequence *Paradise Regained* (1968), a young couple poses stiffly in their furnished den. In five succeeding images, they slowly shed their formal clothes, and plants begin to appear as the furniture vanishes bit by bit. In the last frame, they have been returned to a state of grace, posing naked amidst their own private jungle, an Adam and Eve for modern times.

Keith Sharp takes this devolution a step further. Positing a kind of parallel evolutionary track, he assumes the guise of two alternate, yet related characters. One's clothing is literally a living entity—a tunic of forsythia flowers, and pants of ivy or tree bark—that seems to have possessed and become part of him, transformed into a kind of living skin. The other character seems to be going in the opposite evolutionary direction: a plant assuming human form. Sharp provides a number of variants. A vine-covered man, arms akimbo, seems like the kind of creature Dorothy would have encountered in Oz — had the book been written by R. Crumb. A man with the torso of a tree but the arms of a person may have been enchanted by a Greek goddess, or perhaps, like the first fish that walked ashore, he is exploring a new ecosystem. A potted tree has human legs, while another creature, even more human, has vines wrapping around his legs and hips. And lastly, a human figure (presumably female), seated in a chair with her back to us, sports an impossibly huge, curly head of hair, except that the hair consists of a very convincing plant with a tangle of small leaves. These characters are denizens of *Dr. Moreau's Secret Garden*.

Sharp's elaborate costumes blend elements drawn from the outrageous fancy brigades of the Philadelphia Mummers, the shape-shifting of Cindy Sherman, and the intricate setups of Sandy Skoglund. And his performances — for that is what these are after all — echo the work of Charles Ray and early William Wegman, a temporal and ephemeral phenomenon of which these photographs are the only surviving document.

Frederick Sommer once said, "Some speak of a return to nature. I wonder where they could have been."[1] This modern feeling of alienation from nature is nothing new. From the beginnings of industrialization with the mechanization of labor, where the clock rather than our natural circadian rhythms ruled day and night, we have set nature at a distance. Our food magically appears in the supermarket, shining brightly in neat stacks in vegetable bins, or divided into pieces and wrapped in clear plastic. How many people could reconstruct a chicken from the various bits set so nicely in Styrofoam containers? Today, more city children have seen an elephant than a cow.

Keith Sharp · *Tree Man*, 2004 · Toned Silver Gelatin Photograph

KEITH SHARP · *POTTED TREE*, 2005 · TONED SILVER GELATIN PHOTOGRAPH

The rise of the suburbs in the mid-twentieth century was an attempt by city folk to reconnect with the landscape. Yet what have we wrought? Suburban sprawl, miles of asphalt, malls the size of small cities, SUVs. Why does excessive consumption take precedence over the husbanding of our resources for future generations? Forget the death and destruction in Iraq. How can we tolerate a president who considers global warming and evolution a mythology foisted on us by the liberal left? No wonder Sharp feels like an outsider vainly trying to reconnect with the natural world. If empathy is the key to understanding the other, then perhaps we would all benefit from spending some time as plants.

Stephen Perloff
Editor, *The Photo Review*

¹Frederick Sommer, *Words not spent today, Buy smaller images tomorrow* (New York, N.Y., *Aperture*, 1962), Volume 10, Number 4.

KEITH SHARP · *HAIR*, 2004 · TONED SILVER GELATIN PHOTOGRAPH

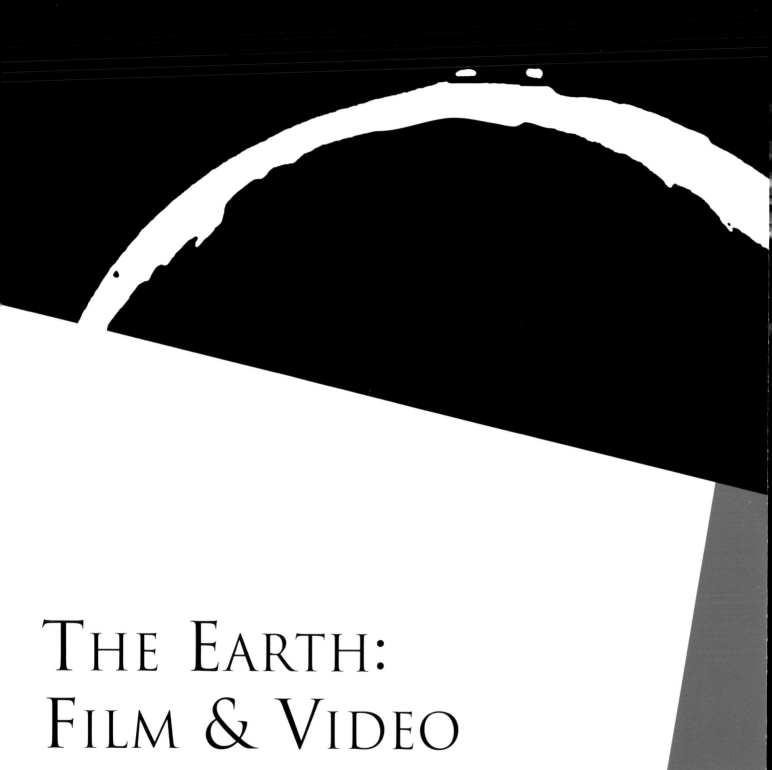

THE EARTH:
FILM & VIDEO

LIST OF FILMS

Dersu Uzala

Earth and Ashes (Terre et Cendres)

Genesis

Global Shorts Program, *Dutch Light*

Nausicaa of the Valley of the Wind (Kaze no tani no Naushika)

Rivers and Tides: Andy Goldsworthy Working with Time

All films shown at the Museum of Fine Arts, Houston, Brown Auditorium

THE EARTH: FILM & VIDEO

FOTOFEST2006   FILM   AND   VIDEO   PROGRAM
In recognition of the short distance that lies between the still and moving image, FotoFest turns again to film and video to broaden and deepen the experience of creative visual expression. Most importantly, the moving image—through feature films, documentaries, and animation— brings new ways of "seeing" to large-scale issues such as The Earth. The collaboration of the Environmental Film Festival in the Nation's Capital and the Museum of Fine Arts, Houston Film Department, with Flo Stone as the invited guest curator, is central to the programming and vision of FOTOFEST2006. — Wendy Watriss, FotoFest

Pieter-Rim DeKroon and Maarten DeKroon · *Dutch Light*, 2003 · Still from Film

NATURE PLAYS A ROLE

FOTOFEST2006 Film Program, presented in collaboration with the Environmental Film Festival in the Nation's Capital and the Museum of Fine Arts, Houston

R Buckminster Fuller, the architect and inventor, once described the environment as "everything but me." He challenged the often expressed idea that environmentalism is a narrow band of interests that fall between public dismay at the various hazards of pollution and the aspirations of some people to protect wildlife, open spaces, and wilderness.

Presenting the Environmental Film Festival in the Nation's Capital for fourteen years, we have celebrated an astonishing diversity of outstanding environmental films. The environment is not the realm solely of environmentalists. It is the polar opposite of a special interests. The environment

encompasses our surroundings and our planet. Most of it is ocean, seas, and bays, but it is also the shoreline and the land—urban, rural, or remote—that most people consider as *their* environment. We share with all living creatures our dependence on the earth for our survival.

When she accepted the 2004 Nobel Peace Prize, Wangari Maathai eloquently stated: "Today we are faced with a challenge that calls for a shift in our thinking, so that humanity stops threatening its life-support system. We are called to assist the Earth to heal her wounds and in the process heal our own—indeed, to embrace the whole creation in all its diversity, beauty and wonder…to revive our sense of belonging to a larger family of life…."[1]

THOMAS RIEDELSHEIMER. · *RIVERS AND TIDES: ANDY GOLDSWORTHY WORKING WITH TIME,* 2001 · STILL FROM FILM

The Earth as a focus of FOTOFEST2006 clearly reflects this broad viewpoint, presenting a range of creative artists who perceive the earth in new and astonishing ways. Through very different emotional journeys, their work in photography and video reaches out to a whole spectrum of viewers: families, scientists, teachers, politicians, laborers, architects, children, and both urban and rural citizens of this country and from around the world. The same is true of the filmmakers whose work will also be presented at FOTOFEST2006. Through live action and animation, in documentary and feature films, they tell stories that let us feel and hear the pulse of the earth as it continually shifts and changes.

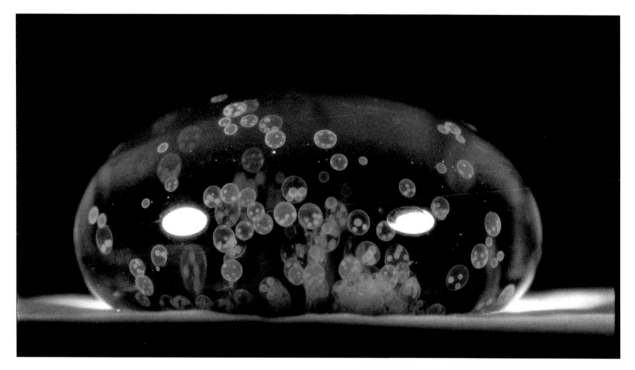

Claude Nuridsany and Marie Pérennou · *Genesis*, 2004 · Still from Film

At the Museum of Fine Arts, Houston, the film series entitled *Nature Plays a Role* gives audiences a remarkable glimpse of the incredible diversity of works broadly defined as environmental films. Included are the extraordinary anime settings and characters of Miyazaki's *Nausicaa*, the endless changes of a 360-degree Dutch landscape in *Dutch Light*, Bill Plympton's wry animation of grass growing against all odds in a parking lot, the remarkable micro-photography of life in *Genesis*, Andy Goldsworthy magical transformations of nature to sculpture in *Rivers and Tides*, Afghanistan's war-torn setting in *Earth and Ashes*, and Siberia's formidable white wilderness in Kurosawa's *Dersu Uzala*.

Also presented in March 2006 in Washington, D.C., the 2006 Environmental Film Festival illustrates the beauty, complexity, and importance of all that surrounds us, a bond to the earth on which our health and future depend. By presenting feature, documentary, animated, archival, and children's films, we wish to give audiences of all ages the chance to experience the best films from around the world. They explore the joys, the horrors, the amazing diversity, and the wonder of the natural world as well as the built environment, from our most crowded cities to distant shores. With a striking range of concerns and approaches, the 2006 Environmental Film Festival hopes to engage audiences with a hundred films screened at nearly fifty museums, libraries, universities, embassies, and theaters as well as at the spaces of international, environmental, and grassroots organizations. Film, as we see it, mirrors all of life.

At FOTOFEST2006 in Houston, the quality of the cooperative photographic arts exhibits and related events that are brought to the city from around the world during March and April creates a generous and spectacular program in which the Environmental Film Festival is proud to take part.

Flo Stone
Artistic Director, Environmental Film Festival in the Nation's Capital and Guest Curator for *Nature Plays a Role*.

[1] Available online at http://gbmna.org/a.php?id=34.

The FOTOFEST2006 film series at the Museum of Fine Arts, Houston showcases many audience favorites screened in recent years at the Environmental Film Festival Washington D.C. Featuring numerous genres—fiction, documentary, anime, animation, and short subjects—it spotlights global concerns and, in particular, the individual confronting his or her surroundings.

From the visions of two great and very different Japanese masters—Akira Kurosawa (*Dersu Uzala*) and Hayao Miyazaki (*Nausicaa of the Valley of the Wind*)—through the astonishingly intimate nature cinematography of Nuridsany and Perennou (*Genesis*), the selection is both entertaining and provocative.

Marian Luntz
Director, Museum of Fine Arts, Houston Film Department

CLAUDE NURIDSANY AND MARIE PÉRENNOU · *GENESIS*, 2004 · STILL FROM FILM

DISCOVERIES OF THE MEETING PLACE

DISCOVERIES OF THE MEETING PLACE

Lili Almog

Dave Anderson

Esteban Pastorino Díaz

Justin Guariglia

Fredrik Marsh

Martina Mullaney

Morten Nilsson

Luis Delgado Qualtrough

Frank Rodick

Brad Temkin

DISCOVERIES OF THE MEETING PLACE

ARTISTS:

LILI ALMOG, UNITED STATES
SELECTED BY JUAN ALBERTO GAVIRIA, DIRECTOR
OF VISUAL ARTS, CENTRO COLOMBO AMERICANO,
MEDELLIN, COLOMBIA

DAVE ANDERSON, UNITED STATES
SELECTED BY YOSSI MILO, DIRECTOR, YOSSI MILO
GALLERY, NEW YORK, NY USA

ESTEBAN PASTORINO DÍAZ, ARGENTINA
SELECTED BY BURT AND MISSY FINGER, FOUNDERS
AND CURATORS, PHOTOGRAPHS DO NO BEND
GALLERY, DALLAS, TX USA

JUSTIN GUARIGLIA, UNITED STATES
SELECTED BY ALAN E. RAPP, SENIOR EDITOR FOR
ART, DESIGN AND PHOTOGRAPHY BOOKS,
CHRONICLE BOOKS, SAN FRANCISCO, CA USA

FREDRIK MARSH, UNITED STATES
SELECTED BY JOHN BENNETTE, INDEPENDENT
COLLECTOR AND CURATOR, NEW YORK, NY USA

MARTINA MULLANEY, UNITED KINGDOM
SELECTED BY CHARLOTTE COTTON, HEAD OF
CREATIVE PROGRAMS, ART & COMMERCE, NEW
YORK, NY USA AND FORMERLY CURATOR OF
PHOTOGRAPHS AT THE VICTORIA AND ALBERT
MUSEUM, LONDON UK

MORTEN NILSSON, DENMARK
SELECTED BY XAVIER CANNONE, DIRECTOR, MUSÉE
DE LA PHOTOGRAPHIE, CHARLEROI, BELGIUM
AND MARC VAUSORT, CURATOR, MUSÉE DE LA
PHOTOGRAPHIE, CHARLEROI, BELGIUM

LUIS DELGADO QUALTROUGH, UNITED STATES
SELECTED BY FERNANDO CASTRO, INDEPENDENT
CURATOR AND CRITIC, HOUSTON, TX USA

FRANK RODICK, CANADA
SELECTED BY KATHERINE WARE, CURATOR OF
PHOTOGRAPHS, PHILADELPHIA MUSEUM OF ART,
PHILADELPHIA, PA USA

BRAD TEMKIN, UNITED STATES
SELECTED BY EVGENY BEREZNER, DIRECTOR,
DEPARTMENT FOR PHOTOGRAPHY AND MULTI-
MEDIA ARTS, MOSCOW MUSEUM OF MODERN
ART, RUSSIA AND DR. IRINA TCHMYREVA, HEAD
RESEARCHER OF DEPARTMENT FOR PHOTOGRAPHY
AND MULTI-MEDIA ART, MOSCOW MUSEUM OF
MODERN ART, RUSSIA

Esteban Pastorino Diaz · *Barrio Magdalena*, 2003 · Type C-Print

Ten years ago, FotoFest inaugurated the *Discoveries of the Meeting Place* exhibition at FOTOFEST 1996. Since that time, the exhibition has become a favorite event at each Biennial. Artists who come from all over the world form close bonds during the five to seven grueling days of showing their work at FotoFest's portfolio review program, the International Meeting Place. It is a moment of high energy and lasting consequences, with talented people competing for the attention and approbation of the influential curators, publishers, editors and gallery owners who review their work.

Formed by Frederick Baldwin and Wendy Watriss, the Meeting Place was created by photographers for photographers. Its purpose is to break down the hierarchies that distance practicing artists from the people who organize exhibits, publish books, edit magazines, and build collections. It is about creating opportunity—opportunities for artists to present work to important people in their field and opportunities for curators, publishers, and collectors to see new talent and to meet each other. At the Meeting Place, FotoFest brings people together from many parts of the world, so the context of art becomes broader and international exchange occurs more easily. In this *Discoveries of the Meeting Place* exhibition, the participating artists and curators come from eight countries in Europe, Latin America, and North America. In FotoFest's 2006 portfolio review program are participants from twenty-three countries, with thirty percent of the artist-registrants from outside the U.S.

The ten artists selected for the 2006 *Discoveries* exhibition were among the 320 artists presenting work at the 2004 portfolio review. Shortly after each Biennial, FotoFest asks ten people who reviewed artists' work at that year's Meeting Place to each select one artist whose work she/he considered to be a particularly interesting "discovery." These artists are then asked to exhibit this work at the subsequent Biennial in the *Discoveries of the Meeting Place* show.

Because FotoFest looks for a diversity of perspectives, cultural orientations, and expertise among the reviewers asked to curate the *Discoveries* shows, the exhibitions prove to be good barometers of what contemporary artists are doing in their creative work. The FOTOFEST2006 *Discoveries* show includes both staged and documentary work, intimate perspectives and large-scale deconstructions, digital processes and classical chromogenic printing. As part of the exhibition, a curatorial statement by each of the curators appears alongside the work she/he selected.

FotoFest's International Meeting Place continues to grow in size and popularity. The two-week program is fully subscribed very soon after the initial brochure is mailed nationally and internationally—nine months in advance. It remains the largest, most international program of its kind in the world. Photography events in Argentina, Germany, Great Britain, Slovakia, Colombia, Denmark, Canada, and the U.S. (Portland, Oregon) have now started their own versions of the FotoFest Meeting Place.

FotoFest has gone on to present work from the *Discoveries* shows abroad. In 2004, FotoFest took the work of five *Discoveries* artists to FotoArte in Brazil. In 2003–04, FotoFest showed the works of ten artists from four Discoveries exhibitions as part of *FotoFest—Discoveries of the Meeting Place 1996–2002* at the Moscow Museum of Modern Art and the Museum of Fine Arts in Samara, Russia.

In 2004, FotoFest opened a new section on its website to post developments in the work and careers of all Meeting Place participants—*Successes of the Meeting Place*. It's about keeping talent visible!

Wendy Watriss
Artistic Director, FotoFest

The installation of this exhibition is made possible through The Wealth Group, Eunice Fong, owner of Erie City Ironworks.

MORTEN NILSSON · *DANCERS NO. 1.* 2003. · C-PRINT

Brad Temkin · *Virginia Creeper, Chicago, IL, 2002* · Color Archival Print

Justin Guariglia · *Untitled*, 2006 · Digital C-Print

MARTINA MULLANEY · *UNTITLED*, FROM THE SERIES *TURN IN*, 2002 · TYPE C-PRINT

Lili Almog · *On her Bed #2*, 2004 · Digital C-Print

DAVE ANDERSON · *BBQ*, 2003 · SELENIUM TONED SILVER GELATIN PRINT

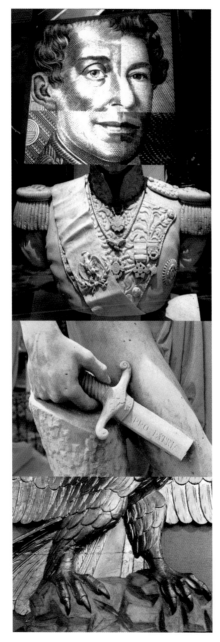

Luis Delgado Qualtrough · *Enigma 01A
Soldier*, 2003 · Pigment on Paper · Courtesy
of De Santos Gallery

Frank Rodick · *Fragments of a Celestial Abattoir*, 2004 · Silver Gelatin
Print

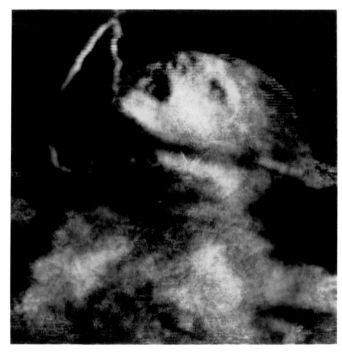

Frank Rodick · *Fragments of a Celestial Abattoir*, 2004 · Silver Gelatin
Print

FREDRIK MARSH · *SEMPER MONUMENT, DRESDEN ACADEMY OF FINE ART*, 2002 · ARCHIVAL PIGMENT ON RAG PAPER

LITERACY
THROUGH
PHOTOGRAPHY

LITERACY THROUGH PHOTOGRAPHY

SPONSORS

FotoFest's Literacy Through Photography® program is supported by foundations, government agencies, corporations, and individuals. Supporters have included:

Foundations: Vale Asche Foundation; The Favrot Fund; The William Stamps Farish Fund, The Cullen Foundation, The Bernard and Audre Rapoport Foundation, The Simmons Foundation, The Powell Foundation, The Bruni Foundation, The Clayton Fund, Houston Endowment, Inc., Susan Vaughan Foundation, The George and Mary Josephine Hamman Foundation, The Jack H. and William M. Light Charitable Trust, The Felvis Fund, Harris and Eliza Kempner Fund, Marion and Speros Martel Foundation, Education Foundation of America, The Charles Engelhard Foundation, The Kettering Family Foundation, Ettinger Foundation, Scurlock Foundation, Margaret Cullinan Wray Charitable Lead Annuity Trust, The Samuels Foundation of the Jewish Community of Houston, and the Gordon and Mary Cain Foundation.

Government: National Endowment for the Arts, Texas Commission for the Arts, The City of Houston through the Cultural Arts Council of Houston/Harris County, Texas.

Corporations: Hexagroup, TARGET, CANON USA, Fuji Photo Film USA, Inc., J.P. Morgan Chase Foundation, HEB Pantry Foods, Olympus Corporation, American General Corporation, Southwestern Bell, and Charter Bank.

Individuals: Friends of Daphne Wood Gawthrop

LITERACY THROUGH PHOTOGRAPHY

FOTOFEST2006– Literacy Through Photography and The Earth

Literacy Through Photography (LTP) is the year-round educational program of FotoFest International that uses photography to improve students' writing abilities, cognitive thinking, and classroom communication skills. LTP provides teachers with a project-based writing and photography curriculum in addition to comprehensive program training, classroom support, and teaching resources.

Currently, LTP is in 36 schools, serving more than 45 teachers and 2,000 students. With program support from school administrators, teachers, and education organizations, LTP provides quality programming that is aligned with Texas state mandated curriculum requirements for students in Grades 3-12.

2006 Biennial Curriculum — *THE EARTH*

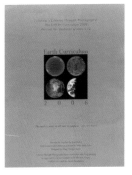

THE EARTH. LITERACY THROUGH PHOTOGRAPHY CURRICULUM, 2006

To accompany FOTOFEST2006 programming, FotoFest worked with writer and educator, Sean Parker, to create *THE EARTH*, a multi-media, multi-cultural exploration of our planet. Additional environmental resources and information were provided by Mary Stark-Love, freelance writer, photographer, and environmental activist. Working from successfully tested principles employed by the Literacy Through Photography program, *THE EARTH* is a four lesson curriculum consisting of writing and photography assignments designed to aid students in investigating the world that surrounds them. Each lesson is coordinated with TEKS objectives to ensure that this curriculum is not only fun and enriching for students, but educationally and instructionally valuable and valid.

By using *THE EARTH*, students will learn different styles and techniques of writing; stream-of-consciousness writing, point of view, and symbolism for example, and will be encouraged to think about varied topics including cause and effect, how individuals' lives vary based on their home environment, endangered species, and conservation. Through writing and photography assignments, students will gain both the verbal and visual literacy skills that they need to flourish in today's society. Throughout the curriculum, teachers will find dozens of resources selected to assist them in easily incorporating these lessons into crowded classroom schedules.

In May 2006, posters created with student writing and photography from *THE EARTH* curriculum is displayed as part of *FotoFence*, the annual exhibition of Literacy Through Photography work in a major public, Houston-area venue.

BRENT CHADDOCK · LTP STUDENTS, ST. TERESA SCHOOL, 2006

CELEBRATING 15 YEARS IN THE HOUSTON INDEPENDENT SCHOOL DISTRICT (HISD)

HISTORY

In 1987, FotoFest brought teacher and photographer Wendy Ewald and her innovative photography project to The Children's Museum in Houston. Ms. Ewald had achieved notable success using photography to stimulate children to photograph their lives and their dreams. In 1990, FotoFest expanded the project to public schools and 1,000 Houston Independent School District children. Teacher and student response was enthusiastic and led to establishing Literacy Through Photography (LTP) as a permanent school-based program. In 1991, FotoFest hired teacher and poet David Brown to expand the Ewald project into a year-round educational curriculum. The result is a twenty-seven lesson curriculum, aligned to state and national curriculum mandate. The LTP curriculum is designed to be incorporated into the classroom over eighteen weeks. It explores four themes: SELF, FAMILY, COMMUNITY, and DREAMS.

The Literacy Through Photography program has been well received by teachers and administrators in the Houston Independent School District (HISD). Executive Director of HISD's Central Region, Bonnie Collins, told FotoFest "The LTP program is helping students learn through real life experiences. [It] also provides an opportunity to heighten our students' critical thinking skills, while producing and documenting their experiences. This process has been proven to assist students in mastering their curriculum goals." LTP has also provided many unforeseen benefits to participating students and teachers. Obed Franco, former teacher at Thomas Jefferson Elementary School in Houston ISD

noted that "Students share part of [their] world with me which helps me understand them better. Talking about their families and community, I realized where they are coming from and how it is that my teaching approach needs to change to meet my students' sensible needs and their different learning styles."

It became evident early on that LTP is especially strong tool for English as a Second Language (ESL) classrooms. The program allows students' English vocabulary to grow more rapidly and reinforce new language skills through practice and peer critiques.

In the 2005-2006 school year, FotoFest released two new curricula, LTP Digital and LTP ESL. Support provided by the National Endowment for the Arts made it possible to produce and pilot each new version of LTP in HISD classrooms through an existing partnership with Project GRAD (Graduation Really Achieves Dreams) Fine Arts.

LTP DIGITAL

LTP Digital has expanded the original LTP curriculum to include lessons introducing digital technology to students and teachers. "Digital photography is a wonderful tool to help introduce young photographers to the wonder of their environment and lends itself to immediate feedback and faster acquisition of the skills that help youngsters become accomplished photographers." says Ernie Ortiz, Reading Teacher Trainer for HISD's North Region. Teachers who have piloted the LTP Digital program report that students

VISITING ARTIST EILEEN MAXSOM · DAVIS HIGH SCHOOL, 2005

are more engaged in both the photography and writing processes. Their students are able to take more risks with their photography, without fear of wasting a limited number of shots and this results in rapid improvement in their photography skills as well as increased enthusiasm which carries into their writing projects. Using digital photography equipment gives students the hands-on experience with current technology that is so critical to their ability to thrive in today's technology dependent culture.

LTP ESL

For English as a Second Language (ESL) classrooms, LTP ESL has been developed in response to requests from teachers using the basic LTP curriculum with their ESL students. The ESL curriculum not only creates a venue for students to expand their vocabulary, but also creates multiple points of contact between the students' educational environment and home life. The majority of the students who have participated in the ESL pilot program had recently come the Houston area from Mexico and Latin America and had reservations about learning English. By the end of their participation in the LTP ESL program, the majority of these students made dramatic gains in their writing skills and were no longer as reluctant to use the English language.

Each May, collages of the LTP students' best photography and writing are exhibited in a major Houston-area venue at *FotoFence*. LTP teachers, students, friends, families and community members are invited to attend a reception and participate in LTP activities. In recent years, FotoFence has been hosted by the Houston Astros' Minute Maid Ballpark and other public locations in downtown Houston.

Over the years Literacy Through Photography has been involved in special educational programs with organizations including The Artist Boat, ASPIRE (After School Programs Inspire Reading Enrichment), Brighter Futures of Planned Parenthood, De Pelchin Children's Center, Fifth Ward Enrichment Program, Galveston Housing Authority, Houston Public Library's after school program, MECA (Multicultural Education and Counseling Through the Arts), Project Bridge (Houston Housing Authority), Project GRAD's (Graduation Really Achieves Dreams) Parent University, Project Row House, Star of Hope Transitional Learning Center, Summerbridge, Teach for America, Texas Children's Hospital and most recently, Surviving Katrina and Rita in Houston.

LTP has formed lasting partnerships with education organizations including Project GRAD (Graduation Really Achieves Dreams) Fine Arts and Harris County Department of Education's programs CASE (Cooperative for After School Enrichment) and ASI (After School Initiative) to provide more students and teachers the opportunity to participate in the Literacy Through Photography program.

In fifteen school years, FotoFest has trained more than 150 teachers to use Literacy Through Photography in 112 schools with more than 20,000 students across Houston Independent School District, and Harris County School Districts including Aldine, Alief, Cypress-Fairbanks, Fort Bend, Galveston, Goose Creek Consolidated, Katy, North Forest, Pasadena, Sheldon, Spring Branch and Waller, and in Austin, Fort Worth, San Antonio and Waco, Texas, California, Colorado, New Mexico, North Carolina, and Oklahoma. To celebrate the accomplishments of students in our fifteen year history, FotoFest exhibited "Hey Listen to Me!" *Writing Pictures* in fall 2005. This retrospective of the Literacy Through Photography program featured the writing and photography of more than 100 students representing more than 30 schools.

FotoFest expands educational programming to Houston-area schools by providing classroom visits from professional photographers and writers, offering tours of all FotoFest exhibits to students and their families and by providing special curricula including *Just A Drop–Water*, written in 2004 by FotoFest and Galveston-based, The Artist Boat to teach students about water issues and water conservation. In 2006, the new *EARTH* curriculum takes its place alongside the water program.

Angela Grace
Director, Literacy Through Photography

The many professionals, interns and volunteers who have helped LTP over the past two years are recognized and thanked in the Acknowledgment section of this catalogue.

WENDY WATRISS · LTP STUDENTS, FORT BEND COUNTY, 1997

NAZAR Artist Nadia Benchallel · FotoFest Student Tours, 2005

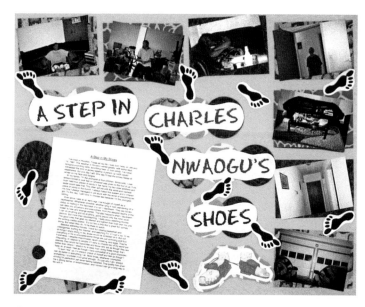

CHARLES NWAOGU · *A STEP IN CHARLES' NWAOGU'S SHOES*, 2005 · LTP BASIC

Ever since I was at an early age, I've thought of myself as a daydreamer. Whenever possible, weather lying in bed, wandering off in class, or resting in the backseat of the car, I daydream. They say books can take you anywhere an everywhere, from the depths of the ocean to new and exciting worlds. This also happens when I daydream. I can do anything and be anything, going places only my mind could venture, but more than daydreaming, I really enjoy watching movies. The good ones that grab my interest and tighten their grip over it until the credits appear. It's a long time since they made one like that. But when they do I'll be there to watch.

A Step in Charles Nwaogu's Shoes

I've lived in Houston, Texas all my life. I was born here on January 14, 1991. The weather in Houston varies greatly, with normal days bringing pounding rains, scorching heat, or cold winds. I've never withstood the kind of snowy weather a person up north would experience, but one day I will. One day I'll feel the snowy flakes of winter on my face and tongue.

In my family, I am the youngest of four children. Since birth, I was always forced to pick last on whatever was given to the four of us. If my mom held four pieces of candy in her hand, my two older brothers and sister would take first. They often left me with the worst piece of candy in the bunch. I always hated this system and it initiated how I always managed to get stuck with the worst of everything we got. To this day I will have to choose last because I'm the youngest sibling.

Besides admiring movies, I also like playing baseball and videogames, surfing the internet, and watching TV. If I had a top 10 list of things I enjoy doing in life, these would be on it. But not everything in life is enjoyable-some things are just surviving, like food. Food wise, I despise mayonnaise, ranch dressing, and eggs. They're disgusting. If I were to choose two of my biggest pet peeves they would be hypocrites and those who act as though they are better than others. I always try to tell those doing these things that I hate it so that at least I act as though I have somewhat of a good character.

To sum "me" up, I am always outside of myself and feel as though I can do better in everything I do. Most times, whenever I compose something, I consider it not good enough. It's just who I am, always striving for perfection yet never feeling satisfied. This quality has given me a strong sense of determination, and I know I can go a long way in life with it.

Charles Nwaogu
LTP Basic, 2005

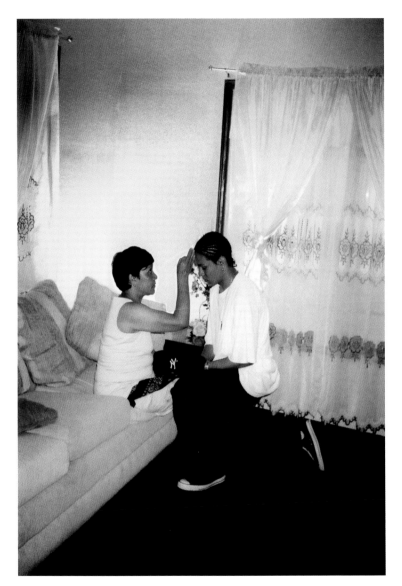

Mario Cruz · *Untitled*. LTP ESL (English as a Second Language). Wheatley High School. 2005

Untitled

In this picture you can see the love that I feel for my mom and the love that she feels for me.

This is what we do every morning before I go to school. She blesses me…all my comings and goings. She is afraid that one day I will not return from the streets of the neighborhood. This is why I always have her in my heart.

Mario Cruz
Wheatley High School, 2005
LTP ESL

ART, Davis High School, 2004 · LTP Digital

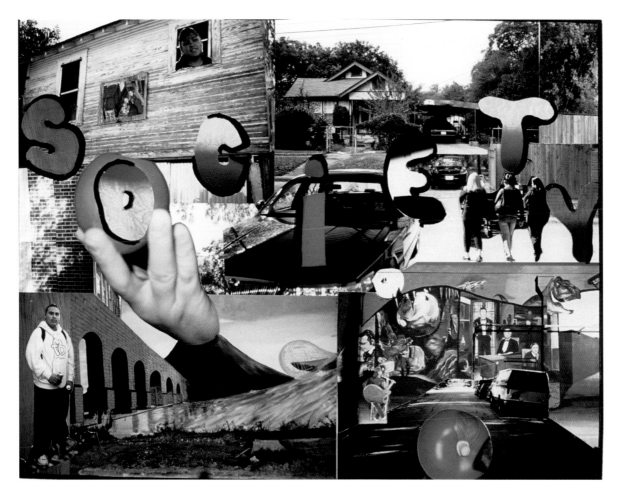

SOCIETY, Davis High School, 2004 · LTP Digital

FotoFest Exhibitions –
Artists Responding to Violence

AES+F

Three Moscow-born artists Tatiana Arzamasova, Lev Evzovich, and Evgeny Svyatsky formed the group AES in 1987. Their first exhibition abroad was in 1989 at Howard Yezersky Gallery in Boston. Since that time, works by AES have been shown in Russia and Europe at festivals, museums, and galleries. Photographer Vladimir Fridkes joined the group in 1995, and the name changed to AES+F. AES+F focuses on photo- and computer-based and video art, as well as other traditional media, such as drawing, painting, and sculpture. AES/AES+F have exhibited widely at several biennials and in a large number of important group and solo shows worldwide; their work is in the collections of major Russian national museums as well as museums in Europe, including the State Tretyakov Gallery, Moscow; State Russian Museum, St. Petersburg; Moscow House of Photography; Moderna Museet, Stockholm; La Maison Européenne de la Photographie, Paris; les Abattoirs, Toulouse, France; FNAC, Paris; and Centre national d'art et de culture Georges Pompidou, Paris.

SERGEY BRATKOV

Born in 1960 in Kharkov, Ukraine, Sergey Bratkov now lives in Moscow. In Kharkov he graduated from Repin's Art College in 1978 and from the Polytechnic Academy in 1983. In 1994 he organized Anartists' Group—Fast reaction group—with Boris Michailov and Sergei Salonsky. Bratkov has taken part in important biennials, including Manifesta 5, San Sebastián, Spain; 1st Moscow Biennial of Contemporary Art; 50th Venice Biennale; and 25th Bienal de São Paulo. His works have represented post-Soviet art in such exhibitions as *Horizons of Reality*, Museum voor Hedendaagse Kunst (MUHKA; Museum of Contemporary Art), Antwerp, Belgium; *Sans Consentement*, Centre d'Art Neuchâtelois (CAN), Switzerland; *After the Wall*, Moderna Museet, Stockholm; and *Art of Contemporary Photography: Russia, Ukraine, Byelorussia*, Central House of Artists, Moscow. His photography is in the collections of MUHKA, Antwerp, Belgium; Zimmerli Art Museum, New Brunswick, New Jersey; Stedelijk Museum voor Actuele Kunst (S.M.A.K.; Museum of Contemporary Art), Ghent, Belgium; Centro Galego de Arte Contemporanea, Santiago de Compostela, Spain; and the Collection of the Ministry of Culture of the Russian Federation. Bratkov is represented by Regina Gallery, Moscow.

MARIA MARTINEZ-CAÑAS

Maria Martinez-Cañas was born in Havana and currently lives in Miami. She received a B.F.A. from the Philadelphia College of Art and a M.F.A. from The School of The Art Institute of Chicago. An artist who works with innovative, nontraditional photographic media, she expands the boundaries traditionally associated with photography. One of her most celebrated works is *Años Continuos*, a public art commission from Miami-Dade Art In Public Places, permanently displayed at Miami International Airport's Concourse D. The forty-foot-square sandblasted photographic mural on glass was completed in January 1996. She has exhibited extensively, with thirty-three solo exhibitions and 175 group exhibitions in the U.S. and abroad. She is the recipient of a Cintas Fellowship, a National Endowment for the Arts award, and a Fulbright-Hays Grant, among others. Her works are included in the permanent collections of the Philadelphia Museum of Art; The Museum of Modern Art, New York; Whitney Museum of American Art, New York; San Francisco Museum of Modern Art; Center for Creative Photography, Tucson; Museum of Contemporary Art, Chicago; Museé national d'art moderne, Centre George Pompidou, Paris; Miami Art Museum; and National Museum of American Art, Smithsonian Institution, Washington, D.C., among others. She is represented by Fredric Snitzer Gallery, Miami; Julie Saul Gallery, New York; and Catherine Edelman Gallery, Chicago.

ELIZABETH MELLOTT-CARREÓN

Elizabeth Mellott-Carreón studied at Texas Women's University and the University of North Texas, both in Denton. She holds a M.F.A. in photography with studies in book arts. Currently, she is a professor of photography at Collin County Community College in Plano, Texas, teaching traditional and alternative photography. As an artist, Mellott-Carreón crosses boundaries constantly. The majority of her work is alternative and/or sculptural, with an emphasis on photography. The art is emotionally charged, addressing personal concerns and social issues around specific moments. The works recreate scenes with photography and other processes, capturing a personal and constructed view of the world that also engages with issues of common concern. For Mellott-Carreón, art is a means of expression and documentation, a way to communicate with others about pressing issues of contemporary life. For more information, see www.mellottcarreon.com.

JUAN MANUEL ECHAVARRÍA

Juan Manuel Echavarría was born in Medellín, Colombia, in 1947. He resides in Bogotá. A writer before becoming an artist, he published two novels, *La gran catarata* (Bogotá: Editorial Arco, 1981) and *Moros en la costa* (Bogotá: Ancora Editores, 1991). His first solo exhibition came in 1998 at B&B International Gallery in New York. A year later he was included in *Arte y violencia en Colombia desde 1948* at the Museo de Arte Moderno de Bogotá. In 2000, he showed in the Korean Kwangju Biennial. His work also appeared in *Cantos cuentos colombianos* (two-part exhibition 2004 and 2005), Daros Latin America, Zurich. His videos have been screened at many festivals and exhibitions throughout Colombia, Europe, and the U.S., including *Latinoaméamerica: Cine, video y multimedia*, Museo Nacional Centro de Arte Reina Sofía, Madrid. 2001; *Politicas de la diferencia: Arte Iberoamericano fin de siglo*, Centro de Convenciones de Pernambuco, Recife, Brazil, 2001, which traveled to Museo de Arte Latinoamericano de Buenos Aires (MALBA), among other venues; European Media Art Festival (EMAF), Ossnabrück, Germany, 2003; San Francisco International Film Festival, 2004; Toronto Latin Media Arts Festival, 2005; The 50th Flaherty Film Seminar at Vassar College; and The Museum of Modern Art, New York. He was included in the Latin American Pavilion at the 2005 Venice Biennale. The North Dakota Museum of Art organized his first solo museum exhibition in the U.S. and included him in the international touring exhibition *The Disappeared*.

JOAKIM ENEROTH

Joakim Eneroth is a Swedish artist and photographer who was born in Stockholm in 1969. His photo book *Without End* (Stockholm: Journal, 2003) was sold out one year after its release. In July 2005 Eneroth won the Prix Voies Off 2005 at the international photo festival in Arles, France, for his book *Without End*, and in October 2005 he was awarded the prize for new photography in Sweden. The exhibition *Without End* was first held at the Stockholm Culture House and has been on tour in 2005. It was presented in France at the international photo festival in Lille (*Transphotographic*) and in Arles, and at Pol Art in Paris; at the international photo festival in Tampere (*Backlight*), Finland; at the photo biennial in Santa Cruz, Spain; at Galerie Lichtblick, Cologne; at Noorderlicht, Grooningen, The Netherlands; and at Usine Gallery, Brussels. Many positive reviews of the book and exhibition have been published in international photo magazines as well as in daily newspapers. During 2005 Eneroth also received a two-year working scholarship from the Swedish Artist Department and is now working on new photo book projects.

DAVID FARRELL

Born in Dublin 1961, David Farrell studied chemistry at University College Dublin, graduating with a Ph.D. in 1987. Currently serving as a part-time lecturer in photography at Dun Laoghaire Institute of Art, Design & Technology (IADT), he has worked independently and on "communal" projects with his partner Gogo della Luna (Gudók). Farrell received the European Publishers Award for Photography in 2001 for *Innocent Landscapes*, and in 2004 he participated in the "European Eyes on Japan" project. He was included in the 2005 publication *Est-ce ainsi que les hommes vivent* (Paris: Editions du Chene) to mark the fiftieth anniversary of *The Family of Man* exhibition/publication.

YVES GELLIE

Yves Gellie was born in Bordeaux, France, in 1953. After medical studies at the Université Bordeaux, he practiced tropical medicine in Gabon for two years. In 1981, he started his practice of photography with a work on cocaine in Colombia. After receiving a World Press Award in 1986, he joined the Gamma agency for two years. Since 1996, his work has moved away from photojournalism to explore the documentary field. He started drawing up a regional portrait of the Middle East, including countries such as Syria, Lebanon, Saudi Arabia, and Turkey, which history is closely linked to the recent changes in Iraq. His work on Iraq was exhibited at the Institut du Monde Arabe, Paris; Mois de la Photo, Paris; Lianzhou International Festival, Lianzhou City, Guangdong, China; Festival de la Photographie "L'Oeil en Seyne," Seyne-sur-Mer, France; Dach Galerie Katia Rid, Munich; and Galleria Franca Speranza, Milan, Italy. He is the author of a photographic essay on Cambodia entitled "La Pluie des Mangues" (Paris: Marval Edition), and of a book on Iraq entitled *Iraq(s)* (Paris: Marval Edition).

CLAUDIO HILS

Claudio Hils was born in 1962 in Mengen, Germany. From 1985 to 1993, he studied visual communication at the Universität-GHS (Polytechnic University) in Essen, Germany. Since then he has worked for renowned national and international magazines. Besides his work as a journalist, Hils has realized his own independent, long-term photographic projects. He has both written and edited a number of books since 1997. Over a period of ten years, Hils traced East German–West German history. The book documenting this long-term project, *Neuland*, was published in 1999 (Neustadt an der Weinstraße, Germany: Umschau-Buchverlag). Following this examination of the problems of a reunited Germany, Hils analyzed urban developments in metropolises in Asia, the U.S., and South America. *Dream City* was published in 2001 (Ostfildern, Germany: Hatje Cantz). In 2003, the City Council of Northern Ireland invited Hils to Belfast to produce a work on the conflict in Northern Ireland. The focus of his research was the city's archives, which he attempted to redefine as a medium of localization and memory. The book *Archive Belfast* was published in 2004 (Ostfildern, Germany: Hatje Cantz). In addition to his freelance documentary projects, Hils has taught at various universities since 1998, and he is currently a university lecturer at the Fachhochschule Dornbirn (Dornbirn University of Applied Sciences) in Austria. From 2000–05, Hils was curator and project manager under an international photography grant from the City of Ravensburg in Germany. Hils was nominated to the Deutsche Fotografische Akademie (German Academy of Photography) in 1991 and to the Deutsche Gesellschaft für Photographie (German Photographic Society) in 2004. www.claudio-hils.com.

ALFREDO JAAR

Alfredo Jaar is an artist, architect, and filmmaker who lives and works in New York. He was born in Santiago de Chile in 1956. His work has been shown extensively around the world. He has participated in biennials in Venice (1986), São Paulo (1985, 1987), Johannesburg (1997), Sydney (1990), Istanbul (1995), and Kwangju, South Korea (1995, 2000), as well as at Documenta (1987, 2002) in Kassel, Germany. Important individual exhibitions include shows at the New Museum of Contemporary Art, New York (1992); Whitechapel, London (1992); Museum of Contemporary Art, Chicago (1992); Pergamon Museum, Berlin (1992); Moderna Museet, Stockholm (1994); and Red Cross Museum, Geneva (2000). In 2005 he had exhibitions at the Museum of Fine Arts, Houston, and the Museum of Contemporary Art, Rome. He received a Guggenheim Fellowship in 1985 and was named a MacArthur Fellow in 2000. The artist's *Rwanda Project 1994–2000* has been seen around the world. He is now dedicated to a major project on Angola that will include photography and film. More than thirty publications have been published on his work.

NATHALIE LATHAM

Nathalie Latham was born in Brisbane, Australia, and completed her post-graduate studies in Japanese at universities in Kyoto, Japan, and Sydney. She is based in Paris. She travels extensively and bases her work on the people she encounters through her journeys, using text and photography or video. Through her work, she attempts to break down preconceptions the viewer may have, and allude to the universality of the human experience and the relationship to oneself, others, and one's environment. Latham recently exhibited a video work, *Sleeping Angels*, as one of three artists taking part in *Passing Through*, a major lens-based exhibition at Ffotogallery, Cardiff, Wales. She presented Do You Vote, a photo-text work, at Trace Gallery in Weymouth, England, and participated in the Photographer's Network Exhibition in Seigen, Germany. In 2006 her work is being exhibited at Galleri Image, Aarhus, Denmark; Centrum för Fotografi, Stockholm; and the Houses of Parliament, London. Her work has been published in the *Australian Financial Review*, *Pluck* (UK), *Le Monde 2*, *Frankfurter Rundschau*, *Fotomagazin*, and Italy's *Domus*.

LISDEBERTUS AKA LUIS DELGADO QUALTROUGH

Like the blind soothsayer Tiresias, Lisdebertus reappears in our time to take up the hammer of twelfth-century sculptor Gislebertus at the bequest of the FotoFest muse and to chisel out a modern-day pantheon of hellish visions. Lisdebertus recently exhibited in Mannheim/Ludwigshafen, Germany, at the *7th Internationale Fototage*. He lives and works in Califrisco, San Fransonia, on the North American West Coast.

Luis Delgado Qualtrough became a photographer in Mexico, where he grew up. He began his work documenting folk mores and customs, as well as pre-Columbian artifacts. Today he is particularly interested in exploring different aspects of visual narrative with an emphasis on iconography and gesture. He creates photography-based prints, books, and installations with history and societal systems as the theme, specifically the concept of the hero and the anti-hero. He uses a visual language of icons and gestures assembled into compound images to create narratives that address this concept. This language consists of photographs of iconography and inanimate representations from many historical and mundane settings throughout the world, as well as imagery taken from mass media. Delgado's goal is to achieve a uniquely personal social commentary and analysis using iconography as its voice. He has recently received the Peter S. Reed Foundation Award and the Communications Arts Award of Excellence, and he was named a "Discovery" in Houston's FotoFest 2004. His work has been exhibited and published widely in Latin America, Europe, and the U.S., and is held in museums and private collections including those of the San Francisco Museum of Modern Art; Museum of Fine Arts, Houston; Stanford University, California; Lehigh University, Bethlehem, Pennsylvania; Harry Ransom Humanities Research Center, The University of Texas at Austin; Bibilothèque national, Paris; and Union of Culture, Germany.

PAULA LUTTRINGER

Paula Luttringer was born in La Plata, Argentina, in 1955. Her studies in botany were cut short in 1977, when she fled Argentina to live in exile after having been kidnapped and held for five months in a secret detention center. Upon returning to Argentina in 1995, she turned to photog-raphy as a means of expression. The subject matter of her photographic work concerns the meeting point between her country's recent history and her own personal one. In 1996 she was chosen by the Museo Nacional de Bellas Artes in Buenos Aires to exhibit her work as one of twenty photographers of the "New Generation." In 1999 she won the best portfolio prize at *PhotoEspaña* for her project *El Matadero (The Slautgherhouse)*. The following year, she was awarded an artist's grant by the Fondo Nacional de las Artes (National Arts Fund) of Argentina for her project *El Lamento de los Muros (The Wailing of the Walls)*, which also won her a fellowship in 2001 from the John Simon Guggenheim Memorial Foundation, New York. Her works have entered the collections of the Museo Nacional de Bellas Artes (MNBA), Buenos Aires; Museum of Fine Arts, Houston; and George Eastman House, Rochester, New York. She currently lives and works in Buenos Aires and Paris.

WOLFGANG MÜLLER

Before embracing photography, Wolfgang Müller was involved in many different pursuits. After years of active participation in social movements, the last one as a toolmaker, he finally looked for an introduction to the world of art. He investigated theater projects and studio courses in painting at the Frankfurt Städel-Hochschule, then decided on photography. While studying photography at the Dortmund Fachhochschule, he turned to the countries of the old Soviet Union as the focus of his work. For his graduate project, he gave up his apartment in Dortmund and spent the next ten months, up to the year 2002, photographing the work in this exhibition, *Karat: Sky over St. Petersburg*. Published as a book, the series of photographs was shown in museums and galleries in Germany, France, Great Britain, Italy, and the U.S. Supported by the BFF Prize in 2002, the Wüstenrot Prize in 2003, and assistance from the VG Bild-Kunst in 2004, he was able to finish other photography projects in Siberia and in the Russian-Chinese Amur border region. Müller is a member of the photography agency OSTKREUZ, and today he lives and works in Berlin.

LIZA NGUYEN

Liza Nguyen was born in France and splits her time between Paris and Düsseldorf, where she participates in the Thomas Ruff workshop at the Staatlichen Kunstakademie (Academy of Fine Arts). She has a M.A. from the Sorbonne, Paris, and a second M.A. in photography from the Ecole Nationale Supérieure Louis Lumière, Paris. Her work explores representation, memory, and aesthetics: how to represent the past, how memory is built in the present, and how to create the link between aesthetics and ethics. She has exhibited her work in France, Sweden, Spain, Germany, Japan, Canada, and the U.S. Her artist book *My father* received several awards in France, including La Bourse du Talent. *Souvenirs of Vietnam* recently received the Prix Fnac de la Photographie and the grand prize at the International Biennial of Art of Lulea in Sweden. For more information, see www.liza-nguyen.com.

FotoFest Exhibitions – The Earth

HERMAN VAN DEN BOOM

Herman Van den Boom has been an artist/photographer since 1971. He was born of Dutch-Belgian parents in Belgium, but was raised in The

Netherlands. As soon as possible, he started to travel worldwide. Crossing borders is part of his culture and his artistic approach. "What is seen as an important issue, fact, or belief in one culture is often seen as a hostile artifact in another." He is now working and living in both Belgium and The Netherlands "as a foreigner." He has been a guest professor at the Higher Institute for Fine Arts, Antwerp, Belgium, and at the Academy of Fine Arts, Maastricht, The Netherlands. His work was exhibited at the Photography Biennial of Moscow; Musée de la Photographie, Charleroi, Belgium; Laforet Museum, Tokyo; and Van Abbemuseum, Eindhoven, The Netherlands. His work is included in the collections of the Museum voor Fotografie, Antwerp, Belgium, and the Stedelijk Museum, Amsterdam.

HEIDI BRADNER

Alaska–born photographer Heidi Bradner has documented Eastern Europe, Central Asia, Russia, and the Caucasus since 1991, when she moved to Russia. Her most recent work concentrates on the Arctic. An ongoing project about the Nenets, reindeer herders of Siberia, titled *Land of the Second Sun*, was awarded a World Press Photo Award in 2003. She is a graduate of the University of Alaska, Anchorage, and a recipient of the Leica Medal of Excellence and the Alexia Foundation Prize for her work documenting the Chechen conflict, Europe's longest but least visible war. Her work is published and exhibited internationally. For more information, visit www.heidibradner.com.

KIM BROWN

Kim Brown's current work involves collecting and sewing dust and detritus. Brown's recent exhibitions include shows at the Museum of Contemporary Art, Miami; Anchorage Museum of History and Art, Alaska; Art Basel Miami Beach, Florida; International Gallery of Contemporary Art, Anchorage, Alaska; Decker/Morris Gallery, Anchorage, Alaska; Kimura Gallery, Anchorage, Alaska; University of California, Berkeley; and Otis/Parsons and Bolsky Gallery, Los Angeles. Her work continues to be exhibited in Washington, D.C., New York, Munich, Los Angeles, Seattle, Portland, Oregon, and Anchorage, Alaska. Selected public artworks by Brown can be seen in Alaska at the Ted Stevens Anchorage International Airport, South Anchorage High School, Anchorage Jail, and Mirror Lake Middle School, and she is currently working on a public art commission for Eastern Washington University. Brown lives and works in Seattle and Anchorage, Alaska.

DORNITH DOHERTY

Dornith Doherty is represented by Gerald Peters Gallery in Dallas and Bassetti Fine Art Photographs in New Orleans. Her photographs have been featured in more than sixty-five national and international exhibitions, and are included in the collections of the Museum of Fine Arts, Houston; Milwaukee Museum of Art; and Minneapolis Institute of Art. A recipient of grants from the Fulbright Foundation, Japan Foundation, U.S. Department of the Interior, Indiana Arts Commission, and Society for Contemporary Photography, Doherty received a B.A. cum laude in Spanish and French language and literature from Rice University, Houston, and a M.F.A. in photography from Yale University. She is currently associate professor of photography at the University of North Texas, Denton.

JOHN GANIS

John Ganis is currently a professor at the College for Creative Studies in Detroit, where he has taught since 1980. His monograph *Consuming the American Landscape* (Stockport, England: Dewi Lewis, and Heidelberg, Germany: Edition Braus, 2003) features an essay by Robert Sobieszek, poetry by the distinguished anthropologist Stanley Diamond, and an afterword by George Thompson of the Center for American Places. Ganis received a B.A. from Ohio Wesleyan University and a M.F.A. from the University of Arizona, Tucson. His color photographs of land use have been exhibited widely and published in *Camera Austria International, Photo Technik International, Blue Sky #36, Aperture's* "Beyond Wilderness" issue, and the San Francisco Museum of Modern Art exhibition catalogue *Crossing the Frontier: Photographs of the Developing West....* Photographs by Ganis are included in the collections of the San Francisco Museum of Modern Art; Brooklyn Museum of Art, New York; Center for Creative Photography, Tucson; and Detroit Institute of Arts.

JULES GREENBERG

Jules Greenberg is the recipient of the 2005 Betty & Jim Kasson Award from the Center for Photographic Art, Carmel, California. A San Francisco native, Greenberg studied at the University of California–Berkeley and Yale University, as well as at Tyler School of Art in Rome. Originally drawn to photography by the work of the Farm Security Administration photographers, she continues to address questions of social justice in her work, but often reaches beyond traditional documentary to explore diverse forms of portraiture and more conceptual projects. Her work has appeared in books published by Chronicle Books, Leica, and the University of California Press, and has been exhibited at the Blue Sky Gallery, Portland, Oregon; *Internationale Fototage*, Mannheim, Germany; Museum of Photographic Arts, San Diego; and elsewhere in the U.S. and abroad. In addition to working as a photographer, Greenberg is currently an associate producer with Farallon Films, working on a documentary about the atomic bombings of Hiroshima and Nagasaki. For more information, see www.julesgreenberg.com.

BARBARA GROVER

Barbara Grover's travels to more than forty countries, many struggling with conflict and poverty, led her to leave her career as a political consultant and take on the creation of photographic works that would affect social change. After teaching herself photography, Grover began her journey as a freelance photojournalist in 1996. Working largely for nonprofit organizations, she has published her work in *Time* magazine, *Stern*, the *LA Weekly*, and various Rizzoli publications. Over the last year, she has had solo shows at the Sherry Frumkin Gallery in Santa Monica, California; The Godwin-Ternbach Museum in Queens, New York; and the Kansas City Public Library. Currently, she is working on expanding her project *THIS LAND TO ME—Some Call It Palestine, Others Israel* into a book. Grover is based in her native Los Angeles.

VADIM GUSHCHIN

Vadim Gushchin was born in Novosibirsk, USSR, in 1963. He has worked as a free-lance photographer since 1988. Gushchin lives and works in Moscow, and he has had recent solo exhibitions at Galleria Contarte, Rome; Kultur Bahnhof Eller, Düsseldorf, Germany; and Fotosouz Gallery,

Moscow. His work is in the collections of the Museum of Modern Art, Moscow; National Centre of Contemporary Art, Moscow; Museum Moscow House of Photography; Museum of Fine Arts, Santa Fe; and Museum für Photographie, Braunschweig, Germany.

MURIEL HASBUN

Muriel Hasbun describes her work as an exploration of the intricacies and emotional reverberations of identity through art, and she uses photography and personal histories as vehicles for exchange. Through an intergenerational, transnational, and transcultural lens, she crafts a language that expresses a shared humanity, while erasing the borders that maintain our "Otherness." Hasbun received a B.A. from Georgetown University in 1983 and a M.F.A. from George Washington University in 1989. She has participated in exhibitions at the Corcoran Gallery of Art, Washington, D.C. (2004); Venice Biennale (2003); Noorderlicht Photofestival, Fries Museum, Leeuwarden, The Netherlands (2002); Bienal Internacional de Fotografía, Centro de la Imagen, Mexico City (1999); and 29th Rencontres Internationales de la Photographie, Musée de l'Arles Antiques, France (1998). She has been awarded four individual artist fellowships from the D.C. Commission on the Arts/NEA and the 2001 Janice Goldsten Community Artists Program Grant. Her work is included in the collections of the Art Museum of the Americas, Washington, D.C.; Bibliothèque Nationale de France, Paris; Lehigh University, Bethlehem, Pennsylvania; Smithsonian American Art Museum, Washington, D.C.; George Washington University, Washington, D.C.; and numerous private collections. She currently is a member of the faculty and coordinator of fine art photography at the Corcoran College of Art + Design in Washington, D.C.

MASAKI HIRANO

Masaki Hirano was born in 1952 in Yaesu, Japan. He now lives and works in Tokyo. Starting as an apprentice at Azabu Studio in 1976, Hirano established his own practice in 1986. In 1992 he participated in the joint exhibition for young photographers at Sinjuku Konica Plaza. In 1993 he presented *After the Festival*, his first solo exhibition, at Ginza Nikon Salon. His later work includes a series entitled *HOLES* that focuses on the shell-scarred walls of Bosnia Herzegovina, another series on problems created by the land reclamation project at Isahaya Bay in Kyushu, and others exploring various problems facing society in the post-cold war years. He has since exhibited in solo and group exhibitions in Croatia, Slovenia, and Japan. In 2000, he published his first monograph, *Down the Road of Life* (Umag, Croatia: Marino Cettina Gallery). He participated in the 1st Berlin Photography Festival 2005 with After the Fact, presented at Martin Gropius Bau in Berlin.

NICHOLAS HUGHES

Nicholas Hughes is a London–based photographer who works mainly on the British coast, in Switzerland, and in Germany. His work has recently been shown in Seoul, Paris, and London. He has pursued a career as a photographic artist since obtaining a first-class B.A. in 1998, followed by a M.A. from the London College of Printing in 2002. His work is currently represented by The Photographers' Gallery in London and by Gana Art

Center in Seoul. His work examines the space between the world that people inhabit and that which nature still claims as its own, and in this intermediary space he seeks to explore the essence of the human spirit and its relationship with nature. His work has appeared in numerous publications, including *The Photographer*, the *British Journal of Photography*, and *Next Level*, and is held in photographic collections worldwide.

NOEL JABBOUR

Noel Jabbour was born in Nazareth in 1970 of Palestinian descent. She currently lives and works in Berlin. For over a decade now, Jabbour has been placing the marginal at center stage, forcing her viewers to take notice of the overlooked. Her photographs consistently expose a human dimension, an angle of vision, or a profound insight that usually goes unseen or is ignored. In this, she performs one of art's important tasks: rendering visible what is otherwise invisible. Jabbour's art-making has a transformative dimension as well: it expands our range of vision and shows us things that are important to see. Her early work derived its power from a deliberate affinity with documentary photography. Some of her more recent pieces have diverged from reality and moved into a more poetic realm. Jabbour studied photography at the Hadasah College Jerusalem and in the postgraduate Young Artist's Programme at the Bezalel Academy of Art in Jerusalem. She had recent solo exhibitions at the Museum of Art Ein Harod, Tel Aviv; Tel Aviv Artist's Studios; and f.a. projects, London. Recent group shows include exhibitions at the Aperture Foundation, New York; Bruce Silverstein Photography, New York; FotoFest at Vine Street Studios, Houston; Noorderlicht Photofestival, Fries Museum, Leeuwarden, The Netherlands; Deichtorhallen Hamburg; Israel Museum, Jerusalem; The Station, Houston; and Patrimoine Photographique, Hôtel de Sully, Paris. Her work is in collections worldwide including those of the Israel Museum, Jerusalem, and Zabludowicz Art Trust, London. In 2005 she won an art residency from the Musée Nicéphore Niépce; in 2003 she was artist-in-residence at Ateliers d'Artistes de la Ville de Marseille; in 2000 she received the Young Artist of the Year Award, A.M. Qattan Foundation, Ramallah, Palestine; and in 1999 she held a scholarship from the America-Israel Cultural Foundation.

KEITH JOHNSON

Keith Johnson has been involved in photography since the early 70's. He graduated in 1975 form RISD with an MFA and studied with Harry Callahan and Aaron Siskind after spending a year at Visual Studies Workshop with Nathan Lyons. Ten years of teaching led to a move to the business side of photography completing an MBA in 1987. He supports his fine art making as a Manufacturers' Representative in the northeast. He has exhibited throughout the United States most recently in solo shows at George Eastman House in Rochester, NY, The Print Center, Philadelphia, PA and Art Institute of Boston, Boston, MA. His work is included in collections at RISD, George Eastman House, and Visual Studies Workshop, and he is a recipient of a Connecticut Commission on the arts Fellowship grant for 2002. He is on the summer faculty for Maine Photographic Workshops and Santa Fe Photography Workshops. He lives in Hamden, CT, with is wife Becky of 34 years. www.keithjohnsonphotographs.com

HARRI KALLIO

Harri Kallio was born in Finland in 1970 and holds a B.F.A. and M.F.A. from the University of Art and Design, Helsinki. He also studied at Oxford Brookes University, England. Kallio is the recipient of the European Publishers Award for Photography 2004, BFF Promotion Award 2003, 2002 and 2003 Finnish Cultural Foundation Grants, and 2000 and 2004 Finnish Art Council Grants. The exhibition *Dodo and Mauritius Island, Imaginary Encounters* has already traveled in several locations in Europe and will be shown extensively in the U.S. during 2006, including at Bonni Benrubi Gallery, New York; FotoFest, Houston; George Eastman House, Rochester, New York; and ICP Triennial, New York City. This work has also been shown in *Fotofinlandia* in Helsinki and at The Victor Barsokevitsch Photographic Centre in Kuopio, Finland. Kallio's work deals primarily with the strange relationship between humans and nature. Kallio currently lives and works in New York City. His work is represented by Bonni Benrubi Gallery, New York.

ERIC KLEMM

Born in a small German town in 1939, Eric Klemm pursued a five-year course at an art school in Trier, Germany. After working for seven years as an art director in Heidelberg, he turned seriously to photography in 1968, when an image of his was published in *Twen*, one of Germany's top magazines at the time. He was offered a job at the magazine by Willi Fleckhaus, the influential art director. That same year, Klemm was recognized by the prestigious Art Directors Club New York for one of his *Twen* photographs that jumpstarted his career. Klemm's first book, *Leute* (Mannheim, Germany, Mannheimer Verlagsanstalt, 1971), was followed closely by *Girls Girls* (Munich, Germany, Verlag Laterna Magica, 1973), which included a foreword by Willi Fleckhaus and a text by Karl Pawek, organizer of *Stern* magazine's second and third *World Exhibition of Photography* (1968 and 1973), both of which included work by Klemm. It was at this time that Klemm had his first exhibition in Heidelberg. In 1974 Klemm moved to Duesseldorf, opened a studio, and worked with numerous advertising agencies and art directors. His work was published in magazines such as *Stern*, *Zeit-Magazine*, *Freundin*, *PHOTO*, and *Lui*. From 1973 until 1980, Klemm was a major contributor to German *Playboy* under the direction of Rainer Woertmann. He became a member of Germany's Deutsche Gesellschaft fuer Photographie, and *Professional Camera* published in 1980 an eight-page portfolio about his work. Then Klemm left Germany for Cocoa Island in the Maldives, which was to become his home for the next fifteen years. In 1990 he published two books on the Maldives. Both contained a foreword by his friend, the photographer Leni Riefenstahl. Klemm spent seven years in France, then immigrated to British Columbia in 1998. In Vancouver he began to paint, which strongly influenced his photographic approach. Klemm now lives on Salt Spring Island near Vancouver.

ELAINE LING

Seeking the solitude of deserts and the abandoned architectures of ancient cultures, Elaine Ling explores the shifting equilibrium between nature and the man-made. Photographing in the deserts of Namibia, North Africa, Mongolia, India, South America, Australia, and the American Southwest, and in the citadels of Persepolis, Petra, Cappadocia, Machu Picchu, Angkor Wat, and Great Zimbabwe, she has captured that dialogue. Ling's recent solo exhibitions include *Foto Arte*, Brasilia, Brazil; *FotoRio*, Rio de Janeiro; *Britanico*, Lima, Peru; *Encuentros Abiertos*, Buenos Aires; *Bratislava Photofest*, Bratislava, Slovakia; *Fototage*, Mannheim, Germany; and exhibitions at Museo de Antioquia, Medellin, Colombia; Houston Center for Photography; Musée de la Photographie à Charleroi, Belgium; and Prague House of Photography. She has been published in *The Polaroid Book, Powerhouse Review, Aperture, Photo Technik Int*, and *View Camera*. Her photographs are in the permanent collections of the Museum of Fine Arts, Houston; Henry Buhl Foundation, New York; Brooklyn Museum of Art, New York; Musée de la Photographie à Charleroi, Belgium; Bibliothèque nationale de France, Paris; and Museet for Fotokunst, Odense, Denmark. Based in Toronto, she has work in the collections of the Royal Ontario Museum, Ryerson University, and the Canadian Museum of Contemporary Photography, Ottawa. Born in Hong Kong, Ling has lived in Canada since the age of nine.

VESSELINA NIKOLAEVA

Vesselina Nikolaeva is a Bulgarian-born documentary photographer who graduated from the Art Academy in Utrecht [Hogeschool voor de Kunsten Utrecht (Utrecht School of the Arts), the Netherlands. She lives and works in Bulgaria and the Netherlands. Her work examines the sociocultural relationships in contemporary Europe in the context of a diverse continent struggling for unification. Her ongoing projects, *Coming of Age in an Adolescent Society* and *No man's land: On the edge of Europe*, explore the metamorphosis of a historically marginalized society into a European nation-state that is partaking in the cultural transfer of globalization and modernization. Nikolaeva's work in progress is internationally renowned, bringing her the Canon Award for 2004 in the Netherlands (for best young photographer under thirty within the framework of *The Silver Camera 2004*), the Grand Prix of the 4th International Festival of Photography 2005 in Lodz, Poland, and the Descubrimientos prize for best young photographer at *Photoespaña 2005*, Madrid.

HYUNG GEUN PARK

Hyung Geun Park was born in Jeju do in Korea and has an M.F.A. in fine art photography from Gwangju University in Gwangju. He completed the MA Image & Communication Course at Goldsmiths College in London in 2005. This series was made on Hampstead Heath and in various forested parks in London. He has exhibited at Fotografie Forum International, Frankfurt; Gana Art Center, Seoul; and Martini Art internazionale, Turin, Italy, and he has forthcoming solo exhibitions at Asia House, London, and Kumho Museum of Art, Seoul.

PETER RIEDLINGER

Peter Riedlinger was born in Löffingen, Germany, in 1966; he currently lives and works in Berlin. Since the 1990s Riedlinger has been realizing comprehensive projects. Photography serves him as an expressive and powerful tool to explore social realities through the critical approach that documentary means can offer, on the one hand, and to create work inspired by the aesthetically autonomous artistic possibilities of the medium, on the other. He often generates extensive series that analyze reality and its differences in a wide sense beyond the material complexities. Riedlinger studied photography at the Hochschule für Gestaltung und Kunst Zürich (University of Art and Design Zurich) and at the Hochshule für Grafik und Buchkunst (Academy of Visual Arts), Leipzig. He has had recent solo exhibitions at Centre Culturel Franco-Allemand Karlsruhe, Germany; Städtische Galerie Schwarzes Kloster, Freiburg, Germany; Gallery Anadiel, Jerusalem; and Kunstverein Leipzig, Projektgalerie Elsterpark. His work is in museum collections in Europe, including those of Staatsgalerie Stuttgart; Galerie für Zeitgenoessische Kunst Leipzig; and Museum für Gestaltung, Zurich, and he has received numerous scholarships and grants.

ABBY ROBINSON

Abby Robinson came to New York City for school and never left. After receiving an undergraduate degree in architectural history, she went to art school to study interior design. Instead she wound up a photographer. After completing her M.F.A., she worked for a private investigator; wrote a novel, *The Dick and Jane*, based on her detective experiences; and began teaching photography at the School of Visual Arts in New York. She simultaneously got itchy feet and started to travel; exposure to different cultures and aesthetics made her head spin. Her current work started with an Asian Cultural Council grant for a trip to Vietnam and continued through a Fulbright stay in India and Sri Lanka, and additional trips to Asia on her own, most recently on a fellowship from the American Institute of Sri Lankan Studies. She received a Siskind Grant in 2005; her work is in the collection of the Whitney Museum of American Art, New York, and the Museum of Fine Arts, Houston.

MARK RUWEDEL

Mark Ruwedel is an artist who divides his time between Long Beach, California, and Vancouver. He taught at Concordia University, Montreal, for twenty years and is at present on the faculty at CalState, Long Beach. Ruwedel's work is represented in many collections, including The J. Paul Getty Museum, Los Angeles; Los Angeles County Museum of Art; National Gallery of Australia, Canberra; National Gallery of Canada, Ottawa; Metropolitan Museum of Art, New York; San Francisco Museum of Contemporary Art; Princeton University Art Museum, New Jersey; FNAC, Paris; Canadian Centre for Architecture, Montreal; and The Library of Congress, Washington, D.C. He exhibits and publishes extensively, and has had recent solo exhibitions at Gallery Luisotti, Santa Monica, California, and Stephen Bulger Gallery, Toronto. A ten-year survey, *Written on the Land*, was organized in 2002 by Presentation House Gallery, North Vancouver, and has been touring Canada since then. His photographs are featured in *Robert Smithson: Spiral Jetty"*, recently published by the Dia Art Foundation and University of California Press.

KEITH SHARP

Keith Sharp studied photography at the University of the Arts, Philadelphia, where he received a B.F.A. in photography and a M.A.T. in art education. He has exhibited in solo shows at St. Joseph's University, Philadelphia; Silver Eye Center for Photography, Pittsburgh; Arts Club of Washington, Washington, D.C.; Muse Gallery, Philadelphia, and Zone One Gallery, Philadelphia. His work has been included in various group shows across the country, including exhibitions at Perkins Center for the Arts, Moorestown, New Jersey; Westmoreland Art Nationals, Latrobe, Pennsylvania; James Madison University, Harrisonburg, Virginia;

Maryland Federation of Art, Baltimore; Toledo Friends of Photography; Delaware Art Museum, Wilmington; and the Delaware Center for the Contemporary Arts, Wilmington. Public and corporate collections holding Sharp's work include the Allentown Art Museum, Pennsylvania; Free Library of Philadelphia; Smithsonian American Art Museum, Washington, D.C.; State Museum of Pennsylvania, Harrisburg; West Collection at SEI Investments Company, and Wyeth Pharmaceuticals. In 2003–2005, he was a fellow with the Center for the Emerging Visual Artists (CEFVA), formerly Creative Artists Network (CAN).

DOUG AND MIKE STARN

Mike and Doug Starn were born in New Jersey in 1961. Working collaboratively with photography since they were thirteen, they continue to defy categorization by effectively combining traditionally separate disciplines such as sculpture, painting, video, and installation. Their conceptual approach to photography has earned them a unique position in the history of contemporary art. The 1987 Whitney Biennial brought them international prominence. Their survey solo exhibitions have been presented in museums worldwide. Their most ambitious projects were realized in 2004: *Behind Your Eye*, a multimedia installation inaugurated at the Neuberger Museum of Art, New York, coincided with the release of *Attracted to Light* (New York City, NY, PowerHouse Books, 2004), a new monograph; in the fall, the Färgfabriken Kunsthalle, Stockholm, premiered *Gravity of Light*, seven mural-size photographs illuminated by a single blindingly bright, monumental carbon arc lamp. In 2005 the National Academy of Sciences, Washington, D.C., premiered *Absorption + Transmission* in its core version; Fotofest 2006 with The New World Museum, followed by the Wood Street Galleries, Pittsburgh, are featuring a largely expanded selection of these works in 2006. Doug and Mike Starn have regular solo exhibitions at galleries in the U.S., Europe, and Asia, and they have received critical acclaim in *The New York Times, Art in America, Artforum,* and *Flashart*, among other international publications. Their photographs are in more than thirty public permanent collections, such as those of The Museum of Modern Art, New York; Metropolitan Museum of Art, New York; Whitney Museum of American Art, New York; San Francisco Museum of Modern Art; Solomon R. Guggenheim Museum, New York; Corcoran Gallery of Art, Washington, D.C.; Jewish Museum, New York; Los Angeles County Museum of Art; La Maison Européenne de la Photographie, Paris; National Gallery of Victoria, Melbourne, Australia; National Museum of Contemporary Art, Seoul; and Yokohama Museum of Art, Japan. They have received two National Endowment for the Arts grants (1987, 1995) and The International Center for Photography's Infinity Award for Fine Art Photography (1992), and were recently commissioned by the New York City Transit Authority to create a work for the South Ferry Subway Terminal, the largest permanent installation to date.

MARTIN STUPICH

Martin Stupich received an early education in painting and sculpture in Milwaukee in the 1960s. In the early 1970s, he studied photography with Emmet Gowin in Ohio, and in 1978 he earned a M.A. degree in photography from Georgia State University, Atlanta, after studying with John McWilliams. He stepped from graduate school into a career photographing industrial landscape, with early grants from the National Endowment for the Arts, jobs with the U.S. Department of the Interior, and work as a photographer documenting sites from Panama to Providence for the U.S. Army Corps of Engineers. Throughout Stupich's career, the line between commerce and art has been blurred. Pictures of Cape Canaveral launch pads hang in galleries in Tokyo, while his industrial panoramas reside happily in official state archives, folded into dense historical reports. His current work in Wyoming's Red Desert reaffirms his hunch that all landscape is cultural—and that good photographs made there can contribute to the literature of this place and time.

EDUARDO DEL VALLE AND MIRTA GÓMEZ

The Cuban-born husband and wife team of Eduardo del Valle & Mirta Gómez has worked collaboratively for more than thirty years, receiving international acclaim for their photographs of subjects in a state of flux. They have received fellowships from the John Simon Guggenheim Memorial Foundation, Oscar B. Cintas Foundation, South Florida Cultural Consortium, National Endowment for the Arts, Florida Art Council, and New York State Council for the Arts. Their photographs are widely exhibited and were included in the groundbreaking *Inaugural Exhibition 2004*, marking the reopening of The Museum of Modern Art, New York. Their work is housed in the permanent collections of The Museum of Modern Art, San Francisco Museum of Modern Art, and New Orleans Museum of Art. Del Valle and Gómez are professors of art and photography at Florida International University, Miami, where they have taught since 1983. They are the authors of several monographs, including *From the Ground Up* (Tucson: Nazraeli Press, 2003), *Four Sections of Time* (Tucson: Nazraeli Press, 2004), and *Fried Waters* (Tucson: Nazraeli Press, 2003). Their work is represented by Chelsea Galleria, Miami; Hemphill Fine Arts, Washington, D.C.; Jim Kempner Fine Art, New York; and Yancey Richardson Gallery, New York.

ANGILEE WILKERSON

Angilee Wilkerson lives and works in the Dallas-Fort Worth metroplex. She is an artist, university instructor, and professional editorial photographer. Wilkerson has participated in more than thirty national and regional exhibitions since 2002, including five solo shows. Wilkerson has been recognized and honored by the Dallas Museum of Art; New Museum of Contemporary Art, New York; Solomon R. Guggenheim Museum, New York; George Eastman House International Museum of Photography and Film, Rochester, New York; Temple University, Philadelphia; SOHO Photo Gallery, New York; Society for Photographic Education; *Aperture* magazine; and many others. Her photographs have been featured in fine art journals, editorial magazines, and newspapers, including *The Photo Review, Photographer's Forum, Harper's & Queen—London, The Wall Street Journal*, and countless others. Wilkerson is active in her community, leading workshops for institutions such as the Dallas Museum of Art and the Girl Scouts of America. She has also worked with students in various local universities, colleges, high schools, and cultural centers. In 2001, Wilkerson was voted the Best of Southwest Photographers in Higher Education by the Council for the Advancement and Support of Education (CASE). In 2005, she curated *Works on Water*, an international exhibition of multimedia artists celebrating the art, science, and philosophy of water-related issues, as part of the 2005 WaterWays

Symposium at the University of North Texas, Denton. Wilkerson's work frequently examines memory and identity, family narratives, and the nature of alterity through landscapes.

DAVID WILLIAMS

Born in Edinburgh in 1952, David Williams is head of photography at Edinburgh College of Art. He studied English literature before becoming a professional musician/composer in the mid-1970s. He took up photography in 1980, and since that time his work has been extensively published and exhibited. He is the recipient of a number of awards and prizes, including the BBC Television 150 Years of Photography Prize. Williams's abiding interest in Eastern philosophy and its relationship to contemporary art practice is evident in *one taste: (n)ever-changing*. These images were made at Tofuku-ji Zen Temple, Kyoto, during one of several recent trips Williams has made to a variety of Buddhist temple sites in Japan. He plans to return to Japan on a regular basis in order to carry on with this project, visiting new sites and adding to what is evolving into a major body of work. For further details, visit www.davidwilliamsphotographer.com.

BARBARA YOSHIDA

Barbara Yoshida lives and works in New York City, where for the past several years she has looked for opportunities to come directly in touch with her audience, through teaching, panel discussions, public talks, and residencies (Graciela Iturbide selected her for one such residency). She has recently been invited to jury the 2006 Minnesota Print Biennial. Yoshida has four one-person shows scheduled for 2006, two in New York City and two in Scotland. Recent solo exhibitions have been held in Overland Park, Kansas; Bar Harbor, Maine; and Poland. Her photogravures were shown at Atelier Lacourière Frélaut in Paris as part of *Le Mois de l'Estampe* 2005, and seven prints have been featured at the Southeast Museum of Photography in Daytona Beach, Florida. Yoshida's work is in various public collections, including those of the Museet for Fotokunst, Brandts Klaedefabrik, Odense, Denmark; Southeast Museum of Photography; Frederick R. Weisman Art Museum, Minneapolis; The Huntington Library, Art Collections, and Botanical Gardens, San Marino, California; International Polaroid Collection, New York; and Light Work, New York.

Curators – FotoFest Exhibitions

FREDERICK BALDWIN

A founder of FotoFest in 1983–84, Frederick Baldwin was a photographer for many years. He has worked around the world, and his photographs have been published in *Esquire, National Geographic, Life, The New York Times, Newsweek*, and *Geo*, as well as many other national and international publications. Baldwin taught photography at the University of Texas and the University of Houston. He was a Peace Corps director in Borneo during the 1960s. Baldwin's book, *We Ain't What We Used to Be* (Savannah, Ga.: Telfair Academy of Arts and Sciences, 1983), documents the Civil Rights movement in Georgia. He is coauthor of the book *Coming to Terms, the German Hill Country of Texas* (College Station, Texas: Texas A&M Press, 1991). He is the recipient of a Humanities Fellowship from The Rockefeller Foundation. His photographic work is represented in many public collections, including those of the Bibliothèque nationale de

Paris, the Museum of Fine Arts, Houston, and the Harry Ransom Humanities Research Center at the University of Texas in Austin. Baldwin was born in Lausanne, Switzerland, and served as a U.S. Marine in the Korean War, where he was wounded and decorated. He has been president and chairman of FotoFest since 1984

LAUREL REUTER [JUAN MANUEL ECHAVARRÍA]
Laurel Reuter was born and raised in the Spirit Lake (Dakota) Nation in North Dakota, where she attended reservation schools. She completed her B.A. in English and M.A. in American literature at the University of North Dakota, founding the North Dakota Museum of Art in 1974. She is the author of many publications, including *Whole Cloth* (New York: Monacelli Press, 1998), with Mildred Constantine; *Under the Whelming Tide: The 1997 Flood of the Red River of the North* (Grand Forks: North Dakota Museum of Art, 1998); the closing chapter of *Immortality? The Legacy of 20th Century Art*, ed. Miguel Angel Corzo (Los Angeles: The Getty Conservation Institute, 1999); *Will Maclean: Cardinal Points* (Grand Forks: North Dakota Museum of Art, 2002); *Machiko Agano, Portfolio Series* (London: Telos Art Publishing, 2003); *Juan Manuel Echavarría: Mouths of Ash* (Milan: Charta Publishing, 2005); and *The Disappeared* (Milan: Charta Publishing, 2006). She is currently writing a biography of Chinese artist Xu Bing. Since founding the North Dakota Museum of Art, Reuter has curated numerous exhibitions by regional, national, and international artists. CBS News "Sunday Morning" produced two segments about Reuter in 1997, and ARTnews profiled her in its November 1998 issue. In 1999 Reuter received the Award of Distinction from the National Council of Art Administrators, recognizing "her dedication to art and to culture in North Dakota and her struggle to create a world-class museum in a remote environment." Furthermore, she was cited for "helping a devastated community draw together and recover its spiritual existence."

JENNIFER WARD
Jennifer Ward, a photographic artist, is exhibitions coordinator for FotoFest. She joined FotoFest's staff in the summer of 2003 as assistant exhibition coordinator and took on her current position in the fall of 2003. She coordinated the FotoFest exhibitions and the Participating Spaces programs for the FotoFest 2004 Biennial on the theme of *Water*, and supervised the inter-biennial programs in 2004–2005. She co-curated FotoFest's *Home and Garden* inter-biennial exhibition of emerging Texas artists in late 2004. Ward has exhibited her photography at Cora Stafford Gallery and Union Gallery in Denton, Texas, as well as at The Griffin Museum of Photography in Winchester, Massachusetts. She received a B.F.A. in photography with a minor in advertising from the University of North Texas, Denton, in 2003. She was born in Houston.

WENDY WATRISS
A founder of FotoFest in 1983–84, Wendy Watriss worked as a freelance photographer, writer, curator, newspaper reporter, and producer of television documentaries from 1965 to 1993. Since 1991, she has been artistic director of FotoFest, curating and organizing international exhibitions on Latin American photography, U.S. Latino photography, Central European photography, the global environment, new media, and water, among other themes. She conceived and produced the award-winning

book *Image and Memory, Photography from Latin America 1865–1994* (Austin, Texas: University of Texas Press, 1998). Photo-documentary essays of her own work have been published in national and international publications such as *Stern, Life, Geo, The Smithsonian, Newsweek, The New York Times,* and many others. She is the recipient of numerous awards, including the World Press Photo Feature of the Year, the Oskar Barnack Prize, the Mid-Atlantic Arts Alliance/National Endowment for the Arts Award, and a Humanities Fellowship from The Rockefeller Foundation. She is coauthor of *Coming to Terms, the German Hill Country of Texas* (College Station, Texas: Texas A&M Press, 1991). She was born in San Francisco.

Film and Video — The Earth

ENVIRONMENTAL FILM FESTIVAL IN THE NATION'S CAPITAL
Each March, the Environmental Film Festival in the Nation's Capital presents a broad diversity of documentary, feature, animated, archival, experimental, and children's films, selected to provide fresh perspectives on environmental issues affecting our planet. Screened at a wide variety of venues throughout the Washington, D.C., area, including museums, embassies, universities, and theaters, the films are enhanced by discussions with filmmakers and scientists. Most films are free. Founded in 1993 by Flo Stone, the Environmental Film Festival has grown to become a major annual event in Washington. In its inaugural year, the Festival presented fifty films to 1,000 people over five days, while the 2005 Festival screened 108 films for a record 15,000 people during an eleven-day period. A national leader in showcasing the finest in environmental filmmaking, the Festival seeks to expand public knowledge and understanding of our world. www.dcenvironmentalfilmfest.org

MUSEUM OF FINE ARTS, HOUSTON FILM DEPARTMENT
Established in the 1930s, the Museum of Fine Arts, Houston's film department is the largest of its kind in the southwestern U.S. Under the direction of Marian Luntz, curator of film and video, the department showcases a broad range of classic and contemporary Hollywood films, foreign language films, and premieres of independent films, many by local artists. www.mfah.org/films

Discoveries of the Meeting Place

LILI ALMOG
New York–based Lili Almog began working as a photojournalist for several international news publications in the 1980s, focusing on fashion and portraiture. After graduating with honors from the School of Visual Arts, New York, in 1992, she turned exclusively to art. Over the past ten years, Almog has explored representations of the feminine body and psyche. With her spirit of adventure, she captures the spiritual and cultural identity of various women as they are influenced, reflected, or morphed by Western culture. Almog's work has been shown in museums and galleries throughout the U.S., Europe, Australia, and Israel, including the Herzliya Museum of Contemporary Art, Israel; Godwin-Ternbach Museum, Queens, New York; Prague House of Photography; Still Gallery, Sydney, Australia; Alternative Museum, New York; Center for Photography at Woodstock,

New York; and Galerie Pennings, Eindhoven, The Netherlands. Her work is included in the collections of the New York Academy of Art; Samuel Dorsky Museum, SUNY New Paltz, New York; Norton Museum of Art, West Palm Beach, Florida; Musée de la Photographie, Charleroi, Belgium; Museet for Fotokunst, Odense, Denmark; and Herzliya Museum of Contemporary Art, Israel. She has been commissioned to design and create both book and compact disk covers, and her art has appeared in *New York* magazine, *The New York Times, Photo District News, La Fotografia Actual* (Barcelona), and *Photonews* (Hamburg), among others.

DAVE ANDERSON

A former television producer in the Clinton White House and at MTV, Dave Anderson takes photographs that cast a wistful eye on the people, places, and objects occupying the landscape. His spare, otherworldly black and white images project a kind of isolated romanticism. His work has appeared in publications and exhibitions all over the world, and is in the permanent collections of the Museum of Fine Arts, Houston, the Worcester Art Museum, Massachusetts, and the University of Louisville Photographic Archive, Kentucky. Anderson's work is also in the private collection of fashion designer Todd Oldham as well as the collections of W. M. Hunt/Collection Dancing Bear and Houstonians James Edward Maloney and Ed Osowski. Anderson's first solo show was organized by curator Clint Willour and opened in October 2004 at the Galveston Arts Center, Texas. He is represented by Yossi Milo Gallery, New York; Halsted Gallery, Birmingham, Alabama; Vicki Bassetti Gallery, New Orleans; Watermark Fine Art Photography, Houston; Candace Perich Gallery, Ketonah, New York; and Susan Spiritus Gallery, Newport Beach, California. Anderson is a native of East Lansing, Michigan, and resident of New York. He is also a published writer, with a story entitled "A Failed Execution" in Paul Auster's best-selling anthology of nonfiction *I Thought My Father Was God: And Other True Tales from NPR's National Story Project* (New York: Henry Holt, 2001).

ESTEBAN PASTORINO DÍAZ

Esteban Pastorino Díaz was born in Buenos Aires, Argentina, in 1972. During his childhood and adolescence, he was fascinated by the manual work involved in making airplane models, his hobby for several years. Interested in mechanics, he decided to attend Escuela Técnica Otto Krause in Buenos Aires. In 1993 he graduated as a mechanical technician, and after three years of studying mechanical engineering, he became interested in photography. After doing a short basic course in the medium, he decided to give up his formal studies and to focus on photography. During 1995–96 he took a two-year course in advertising photography while he worked as an photographer's assistant. Through this experience he realized that the world of commercial photography was not his place. In 1997 he met Juan Travnik, a well-known Argentine photographer/curator, and attended his workshops for more than two years. He then focused on his own projects, which draw on his technical background. For instance, the series *KAP* comprises aerial pictures taken from a kite, and his panoramic series was made with a panoramic strip camera he designed and built. In 2001, he received the Photographer of the Year Prize awarded by the Argentinean Association of Art Critics. He is currently a resident at Rijksakademie van Beeldende Kunsten in Amsterdam, where he is developing new projects.

JUSTIN GUARIGLIA

Born in 1974 in Maplewood, New Jersey, Justin Guariglia resides in New York. He lived in Venice, Beijing, Hong Kong, Singapore and Tokyo for nine years (1995–2005). At the age of twenty-one, he went to learn Mandarin Chinese in Beijing, where he took up photography to get out of Chinese character memorization classes. He did an internship with Magnum Photos in New York, where he was first exposed to the documentary photography world. In 1998, he returned to Asia to begin working on freelance commissions in Hong Kong for *National Geographic, Time,* and *Newsweek.* This work helped pay for his *Personal Journeys* projects, in which he photographed landscapes and cityscapes around Asia. In 1999-2000, Guariglia's work was nominated for the International Center of Photography's "Young Photographer of the Year" Infinity Award; he was given an Eddie Adams *"Newsweek"* award and was named by *Photo District News* as one of the top "30 Young Photographers Under 30." In 2001, feeling overwhelmed by the onslaught of the Information Age, Guariglia began to examine the calming properties of the philosophy of Zen Buddhism. Legend has it that Buddhism came to China by way of the Indian monk named Bodhidharma, the 38th disciple of Buddha who came to the Shaolin Temple 1,500 years ago. Here he gave birth not only to the branch of Buddhism known as Zen, but to kung fu, a physical practice designed to focus one's mind, body, and spirit to work as one and induce a state of Zen enlightenment in the practitioner. Going to the source of Zen to explore this subject, Guariglia worked closely with the very closed society of monks at the Shaolin Temple in China. These monks practice kung fu and Buddhist teachings as vehicles to attain Zen enlightenment. As the first foreigner to get access to the Shaolin Temple in this way, Guariglia began experimenting with video, sound, and still photography of monks practicing traditional kung fu methods and the mudras (Indian hand meditations). Guariglia's video installations, in color and black and white, occasionally with sound, are often slowed to allow the viewer to examine and experience the energy and spirit of the centuries-old movements practiced by the monks. In this ongoing work, which explores the vehicles, triggers, and states of Zen enlightenment, Guariglia attempts to "instill a greater sense of balance, inner peace and oneness within people and the world around us, through contact with these otherwise elusive experiences." He began to exhibit this work for the first time in 2005.

FREDRIK MARSH

Born in Quantico, Virginia, in 1957, Fredrik Marsh received his B.F.A. and M.F.A. from Ohio State University in Columbus. His work has been included in more than a hundred solo and group exhibitions across the U.S. since 1978, with recent exhibitions in Germany. He has been the recipient of three Ohio Arts Council Grants, a Greater Columbus Arts Council Fellowship, a NEA/Arts Midwest Regional Fellowship, and an Artists Projects Grant (with Inga Paas) from the Saxonian Ministry of Science and Art, Dresden, Germany. In 2000 he was awarded a Dresden/Saxony Artist-in-Residency through the Greater Columbus Arts Council, completed during the summer of 2002. His photographs are included in numerous public and private collections, including those of the Museum of Contemporary Photography, Chicago; Toledo Museum of Art, Ohio; Hochschule für Bildende Künste Dresden (Dresden Academy of Fine Arts), Germany; and Kupferstich-Kabinett Museum, Dresden,

Germany. *Dresden Reliquary: Past into Present*, a limited edition portfolio with essays by American and German photo historians, will be published by Podhola Press in 2006. Marsh has been a freelance photographer and teacher for twenty-five years. Currently, he is a senior lecturer of art at Otterbein College, Westerville, Ohio, where he has been teaching since 1992. He lives in Columbus.

MARTINA MULLANEY

Martina Mullaney is an Irish artist currently living and working in London, where she received a M.F.A. from the Royal College of Art in 2004. Her work looks at uncomfortable social situations, mainly those of solitude. She has worked extensively with the homeless communities of Ireland and Britain, teenage mothers, and abandoned children in China. Participation and process are important elements of her practice, and she often collaborates with large groups of people to make her work. In 1999 she was invited by the British Council to attend the International Artists Camp in Sri Lanka. Her first publication, *Turn In*, was published by ffotogallery, Cardiff, Wales, in 2002. In 2003 she was artist-in-residence at the Loft Gallery in Kunming, China. In 2005 she will have her first solo show in New York at Yossi Milo Gallery. Her work has been published by *Portfolio: Contemporary Photography in Britain, Source Magazine* (Belfast), and Zoom Italy. It has been reviewed by *Afterimage* (New York) and the *Sunday Times* (Dublin). She is currently represented exclusively by Yossi Milo Gallery in New York.

MORTEN NILSSON

Morten Nilsson lives and works in Denmark. He has exhibited his work internationally, including at Ffotogallery, Cardiff, Wales; Musée de la Photographie de Charleroi, Belgium; and Jacksonville Museum of Modern Art, Florida. He is represented by Bendixen Contemporary Art in Copenhagen, ClampArt in New York, and Photographs Do Not Bend Gallery in Dallas.

LISDEBERTUS AKA LUIS DELGADO QUALTROUGH (SEE ARTISTS RESPONDING TO VIOLENCE SECTION)

FRANK RODICK

Frank Rodick grew up in Montreal, where his parents' small but eclectic bookstore was a meeting place for the city's literati. His first body of work was a set of forty images entitled *Liquid City*, completed during the years 1991 to 1999. These photographs portray the modern city more as a personal vision than as a specific location. During 1995–97, Rodick also completed a series of images—entitled *sub rosa*—based on the nude figure. In 2002, he produced the first set of works from his project *Arena*. Stephen Perloff, editor and founder of *The Photo Review*, has stated: "Pain and pleasure, sex and procreation, dissolution and death all appear in the Arena photographs—not as opposites, but as a continuum, a dialectic in which each condition is inherent in the other. As in Mr. Rodick's other series, *Liquid City* and *sub rosa*, the *Arena* images obscure reality and force viewers to confront what they think they know and to reimagine the world and their own experience. While one can find art historical precedents of his Arena series in Bosch, Velazquez, and Goya, Mr.

Rodick's spiritual forebears are equally Werner Heisenberg and Franz Kafka." Rodick received grants from the Canada Council in 1997 and 2002, the Ontario Arts Council in 1998, 1999, 2000, and 2002, and the Canadian Department of Foreign Affairs in 2002 and 2004. Institutions that have collected his work include the Museum of Fine Arts, Houston; Museo Nacional de Bellas Artes, Buenos Aires; Museet for Fotokunst, Odense, Denmark; Musée de la Photographie, Charleroi, Belgium; Lehigh University Art Galleries, Bethlehem, Pennsylvania; and Canadian Museum of Contemporary Photography, Ottawa, Ontario. Rodick currently resides in Toronto.

BRAD TEMKIN

Brad Temkin is a working artist whose photographs have been exhibited and collected internationally. He was born in Chicago in 1956 and began photographing in 1973 as part of his interest in music. His focus quickly changed and he soon began photographing other subjects, including the landscape and portraiture, finding poetry in the world around him. Temkin currently lives in Skokie, Illinois, and has taught photography at Columbia College in Chicago since 1984. He also teaches workshops in Ireland every year. He received his B.F.A. from Ohio University in Athens and his M.F.A. from the University of Illinois, Chicago. Solo exhibitions include shows at Scott Nichols Gallery, San Francisco; Museum of Contemporary Photography, Chicago; Afterimage Gallery, Dallas; Chicago Cultural Center; Midtown Y Photography Gallery, New York; and Milwaukee Center for Photography. Group exhibitions include *Innocence Exposed: The Child in Modern Photography*, Frist Center for Visual Arts, Nashville; *Bolbart, Langes Haar...das Bildnis Jesu Christi*, Fotographie Forum International, Frankfurt; *White*, Stephen Bulger Gallery, Toronto; and *David Carol and Brad Temkin*, Stephen Daiter Gallery, Chicago. His work can be found in several permanent collections, including those of The Art Institute of Chicago, Museum of Fine Arts, Houston, and the Museum of Contemporary Photography, Chicago. He is represented by Stephen Daiter Gallery in Chicago, Scott Nichols Gallery in San Francisco, Stephen Bulger Gallery in Toronto, Afterimage Gallery in Dallas, and June Bateman Gallery in New York. www.bradtemkin.com.

Curators – Discoveries of the Meeting Place

JOHN BENNETTE

John A. Bennette, who lives in New York, is a collector, curator, writer, lecturer, and former discovery editor for *21st: The Journal Of Contemporary Photography*. He first came to the public's attention in 1996 when he spoke on a panel discussing "The Joy of Collecting," hosted by William Hunt for the Association of International Photography Art Dealers (AIPAD). He has written a number of articles for journals including *21st* (nos. 1, 2, and 5) and *Black & White Magazine*, and catalogue introductions for Lynn Bianchi and Rod Cook, as well as other artists. Bennette teaches an alternative adult course on collecting at New York's New School University and heads an independent group called The 8 X 10. Since 1996 he has spoken at photography events, trade fairs, and museums around the country, from the Birmingham Museum of Art, Alabama, to The Newark Museum, New Jersey. Articles written about

Bennette and his quirky beliefs about collecting have appeared in *Art+Auctions* (October 2003) and *Photography in New York*. In January 2005 he will curate a exhibition for Sylvia Plachy at the Hunter-Fox Gallery in New York entitled *Self Portrait with Cows Going Home*, presented in conjunction with the *Aperture* publication of her new book.

EVGENY BEREZNER

Evgeny Berezner is vice-director of the Moscow Museum of Modern Art, in charge of the Department for Photography and Multi-Media Arts. An expert in the history of Russian and Soviet photography, and in contemporary Russian, Ukrainian, and Byelorussian photography, he has organized more than 180 exhibitions, including *150 Years of Photography* (Central Exhibition Hall Manezh, Moscow, 1989), *Art of Contemporary Photography: Russia, Byelorussia, Ukraine* (Central House of Artists, Moscow, 1994), *New Art of Photography in Russia* (traveled to five cities in Germany, 1994–95), *Russian Pictorial Photography: 1890–1990* (FotoFest 2002; traveled to National Gallery of Slovakia, Bratislava, 2002), *Russian Colored Photography: 1850–1950* (Z Gallery, Bratislava; James Gallery, Moscow; and State Museum of History, St. Petersburg, 1999–2002), and *Inner Space of War: Blockade of Leningrad in Photography, 1941–1944* (Museum of History of Slovakia, Bratislava; Moscow Museum of Modern Art; and Maison de l'Homme, Paris, 2003–05). Berezner has published articles in Soviet, Russian, and international journals, including *Aperture* and *European Photography* (Germany). He has lectured on the history of Russian and Soviet photography and on contemporary Russian, Ukrainian and Belorussian photography in Canada, Germany, Portugal, Slovakia, Spain, and the U.S. Since 1995, he has been Russian co-editor and coordinator of the international magazine *Imago*. In 1995–97, he was the international adviser from Russia for the International Festival of Photography in Scotland. Since 1996 he has been adviser and curator of the Russian exhibitions at the International Festival of Photography in Bratislava, Slovakia. He has served as a reviewer at the Portfolio Review in Bratislava, Slovakia, since 1999, at PhotoEspana in Madrid in 2000, at Summer Photoschool in Poprad, Slovakia, in 2000, at Meeting Place at FotoFest 2002 and 2004, Houston, and at the First International Festival of Photography in Berlin.

XAVIER CANONNE AND MARC VAUSORT

Xavier Canonne is an art historian from the Université Libre de Bruxelles. He received a Ph.D. in art history from the Sorbonne. From 1987 to 2000, he was the director of the collection of the Province de Hainaut (modern and contemporary art). He has been the director of the Musée de la Photographie de la Communauté française Wallonie-Bruxelles in Charleroi, Belgium, since March 2000. He has organized many exhibitions and has edited and written several books and studies, especially about Surrealism, Man Ray, and Eugène Atget. Marc Vausort is an art historian who works in collaboration with Xavier Canonne. He has been at the Musée de la Photographie de la Communauté française Wallonie-Bruxelles in Charleroi, Belgium, for fourteen years and has been a curator there since 2000. Vausort previously worked in the print room of the Royal Library in Brussels. He has organized many exhibitions about Belgian photographers.

FERNANDO CASTRO-RAMÍREZ

Born in Lima, Peru, in 1952, Fernando Castro-Ramírez was awarded a Fulbright Fellowship in 1979 to do graduate studies in philosophy at Rice University, Houston. His first book, *Five Rolls of Plus-X* (Austin, Texas: Studia Hispanica Editors, 1983), alternates poetry and photography. He began a career as a critic in 1988 writing for *El Comercio* (Lima); since then he has contributed to *Lima Times*, *Photometro* (San Francisco), *Art-Nexus* (Colombia), *Cámara Extra* (Caracas), *Zonezero.com* (Los Angeles), *Artlies*, *Visible*, *Literal*, and *Spot* (Houston), *Aperture* (New York), and other publications. He is a member of the advisory board of Aperture. His essay "Crossover Dreams" is featured in the award-winning book *Image and Memory: Photography from Latin America 1867–1994* (Austin, University of Texas Press, 1998). His curatorial work includes *Modernity in the Southern Andes: Peruvian Photography 1900–1930* shown at FOTOFEST 1992 in Houston and The Americas Society in 1993 in New York. Since 1996 Castro-Ramírez has been curator of photography at Sicardi Gallery, Houston, where he presented *Traces on the Glass: The Photographic Work of Geraldo de Barros 1948–1951* (1998) and *The Culture of Books and Light: The Photography of Abelardo Morell* (2001), among other exhibitions. In 2000 he was co-curator of *The Art of Risk / The Risk of Art* at the Fototeca de Nuevo Leon, Monterrey, 1999 and *Stone* at the Centro de la Imagen, Mexico City, 2004. Since 1997 his own photographic work has taken a political turn in the series *Reasons of State*. Recently, his work was included by Spanish critic Paco Barragán in the book *The Art to Come* (Actar/Subastas Siglo XXI, 2003). His most recent solo exhibition, *The Ideology of Color* (2004), was shown at the Centro Cultural Borges in Buenos Aires and is now a virtual exhibit at Lehigh University. His works are in the permanent collections of the Museum of Fine Arts, Houston; The Dancing Bear Collection, New York; Lehigh University, Bethlehem, Pennsylvania; and Museo de Arte, Lima. He currently lives in Houston.

CHARLOTTE COTTON

Charlotte Cotton is head of cultural programmes at Art & Commerce, New York. Previously, she was head of programming at The Photographers' Gallery, London, and from 1992 until 2004, she was a curator of photography at the Victoria & Albert Museum, London. In 2001/02, she was the V&A History of Art Fellow at the University of Sussex. Currently, Cotton is a visiting professor at Surrey Institute, Farnham, England, and she teaches in the history of art department at Yale University. Her books include *Photography as Contemporary Art* (London: Thames & Hudson, 2004), *Then Things Went Quiet* (London: MW Projects, 2003), and *Imperfect Beauty: The Making of Contemporary Fashion Photographs* (London: Victoria & Albert Museum, 2000). Her exhibitions include *Stories from Russia: Melanie Manchot & David King* (The Photographers' Gallery, London, January–March 2005), *History in the Making* (Circulos des Bellas Artes, Madrid, June–July 2004, PhotoEspana), *Guy Bourdin* (Victoria & Albert Museum, London; traveled to National Gallery of Victoria, Australia; Centre Nationale de la Photographie, Paris; and Foam, Amsterdam, April 2003–December 2004), and *Stepping In and Out: Contemporary Documentary Photography* (Victoria & Albert Museum, London, September 2002–February 2003).

BURT AND MISSY FINGER

Burt and Missy Finger are the founders of Photographs Do Not Bend Gallery in Dallas. This gallery has specialized in twentieth-century and contemporary photography for more than ten years. Burt Finger had a chance to work with the great photojournalist Larry Burrows during his tour of duty in Vietnam in 1968. This gave him his start in photography, and he eventually exhibited in the early seventies at various Texas galleries and at the Contemporary Arts Museum Houston. Missy Finger studied art history during and after earning her B.B.A. in marketing from The University of Texas at Austin. Several years later, while running a successful antique business, Burt and Missy began collecting photographs. After several years of collecting, they decided to make their passion for photography their full-time pursuit. The gallery opened in April 1995. Artists exhibited at the gallery have included Bill Owens, George Krause, Keith Carter, Vik Muniz, Misty Keasler, John Albok, Chris Verene, Marta Maria Perez Bravo, Chema Madoz, Jock Sturges, and Carlotta Corpron. Theme exhibitions in the past ten years have been multifacted, as seen in these titles: *Scene of the Crime, NUDE, Un Regard Oblique, ANONYMOUS,* and *I WANNA BE A COWBOY.* The gallery's mission in photography is always evolving, but exhibiting contemporary and Latin American photography has remained its focus.

JUAN ALBERTO GAVIRIA

Juan Alberto Gaviria is director of visual arts for the Centro Colombo Americano (CCA) in Medellín, Colombia. He has created and managed an important international arts exchange program in Colombia, working with numerous institutions around the country. Gaviria has a strong commitment to international arts exchange and in that area has placed a strong emphasis on photography since the mid-1980s. Most recently he participated as co-curator for the newly created photography biennial FOTOFIESTA MEDELLIN. The CCA, founded in 1947, is a private, nonprofit international cultural center devoted to academic and cultural exchange while promoting the multicultural diversity of the world we live in. The main program areas include foreign language learning, cinema, visual arts, residencies for artists, a lecture series, dance, library programs, and academic exchange. The CCA produces publications in the areas of cinema and the visual arts. Gaviria is interested in reviewing a wide range of work, including both traditional and more avant-garde work, for exhibitions and residency projects at the CCA as well as for FOTOFIESTA MEDELLIN, which is co-produced by the CCA and the Museum of Antioquia. Gaviria holds a B.A. in fine arts and a M.A. in hermeneutics of art. He has worked for the CCA in his current position since 1983. He has been an advisor to the National Ministry of Culture, a juror for multiple national and international events in Colombia, and a reviewer for FotoFest since 1992.

YOSSI MILO

Yossi Milo is the Director of Yossi Milo Gallery in New York. Founded in 1997, the gallery specializes in contemporary photography of all types by emerging and established artists. In the past year, the gallery has hosted critically acclaimed shows by Loretta Lux, Alessandra Sanguinetti, and Alec Soth, among others.

ALAN RAPP

Alan E. Rapp is senior editor of art, design, and photography books at Chronicle Books, San Francisco. He is also a writer who contributes to such publications as *San Francisco Magazine, Metropolis,* and *Photo-Eye Booklist.*

IRINA TCHMYREVA

Residing in Moscow, Irina Tchmyreva holds a Ph.D. in art history, and is a writer on photography and a curator. She is head researcher for the Department for Photography and Multi-Media Arts in the Moscow Museum of Modern Art. Curator of more than fifty exhibitions of contemporary Russian and foreign photography, she was co-curator of *Russian Pictorial Photography: 1890–1990* (FotoFest 2002; traveled to National Gallery of Slovakia, Bratislava, 2002), *Russian Colored Photography: 1850–1950* (Z Gallery, Bratislava; James Gallery, Moscow; and State Museum of History, St. Petersburg, 1999–2002), and *Inner Space of War: Blockade of Leningrad in Photography, 1941–1944* (Museum of History of Slovakia, Bratislava; Moscow Museum of Modern Art; and Maison de l'Homme, Paris, 2003–05). She has published articles in Russian and international journals, including *Aperture* (U.S.), *European Photography* (Germany), *Fotografia Kvartalnik* (Poland), *Photo* (France), and *Foto&video* (Russia). She has lectured on the history and current state of Russian photography in Slovakia and the U.S. In 1999 she became the co-founder and editor of a Russian web-resource on photography www.photographer.ru. Since 2004 she has been a member of the editorial board of the international magazine *Imago* (Slovakia) and *Fotografia Kvartalnik* (Poland). In 1999 she was one of the curators of the Russian exhibitions at the International Festival of Photography in Bratislava, Slovakia. Since 2002 she has been a lecturer on the history of photography and visual arts at Moscow State University of Printing Arts. She has served as a reviewer at the Portfolio Review in Bratislava, Slovakia, since 2000, at Summer Photoschool in Poprad, Slovakia, in 2000, at Meeting Place at FotoFest 2002 and 2004, Houston, at the First Festival of Photography in Bucharest, Romania, in 2005, at the First International Photoschool in St. Petersburg in 2005, and at the First International Festival of Photography in Berlin.

KATHERINE WARE

Katherine Ware is curator of photographs at the Philadelphia Museum of Art. Her recent exhibitions include *Elemental Landscapes: Photographs by Harry Callahan* and *The Discerning Eye of Julien Levy: Selections from a New Acquisition.* Ware previously served as assistant curator in the Department of Photographs at the J. Paul Getty Museum, where she organized the traveling exhibitions *A Practical Dreamer: The Photographs of Man Ray* and *Vision in Motion: The Photographs of László Moholy-Nagy,* both with accompanying books in the In Focus series. She is the author of the book *Elemental Landscapes: Photographs by Harry Callahan* (Philadelphia: Philadelphia Museum of Art, 2001) and a number of essays, including "Chemist of Mysteries: The Life and Work of Man Ray," in *Man Ray* (Cologne: Taschen, 2000), and "Photography at the Bauhaus," in *Bauhaus* (Hagen, Germany: Könemann, 1999).

ACKNOWLEDGEMENTS—FOTOFEST2006

FOTOFEST2006 EXHIBITIONS

Diane Barber, *DiverseWorks Artspace*, *Houston*

Evgeny Berezner and Irina Tchmyreva, *Moscow Museum of Modern Art*

Joanna Chain, *Trizec Office Properties*, *Houston*

Luis and Gemma De Santos, *De Santos Gallery*, *Houston*

Volker Eisele, *Rudolph Projects/ ArtScan Gallery*, *Houston*

Jane Ellison, *Balcones Frame Supply*

Lorranie Houthoofd, *Village Frame Shoppe*

Sara Kellner, *DiverseWorks Art Space*, *Houston*

Julie Kinzelman, *Kinzelman Art Consulting & McCord Development Inc.*, *Houston*

Yolanda Londoño, *JP Morgan Chase*, *Houston*

Debbie McNulty, *Art League Houston*

Armando Palacios and Cinda Ward, *New World Museum*

Eddy Philippe, *Houston*

Vickie Russell, *Village Frame Shoppe Houston*

Sheila Shaw, *Fulbright and Jaworski*, *Houston*

María Inés Sicardi, *Sicardi Gallery*, *Houston*

Sally Sprout, *Williams Tower Gallery*, *Houston*

Ernest Thompson, *Vine Street Studios*, *Houston*

Margaret Regan Fletcher Thorne-Thomsen, Jr., *Vine Street Studios*, *Houston*

Rhonda Wilson, *Rhubarb Rhubarb*

VOLUNTEERS

Bonnie Snipes

Justin Ward

Kathy Ward

2006 BIENNIAL SPECIAL EVENTS

Kelly Gale Amén, *Houston*

David and Allison Ayers, *Sicardi Gallery*, *Houston*

Bering & James Gallery, *Houston*

David Brown, *Spacetaker*, *Houston*

Lindsey Brown, *Greater Houston Visitors and Convention Bureau*

Mike Casey, *Houston*

Deborah Colton, *Deborah Colton Gallery*, *Houston*

Cherry Eno, *The Houston Visitors Center*

Marta Fredricks, *Dancie Perugini Ware Associates*, *Houston*

Curry Glassell, *Houston*

Michael and Ceci Goldstone, *Houston*

Kimberly Gremillion, *Gremillion & Co. Fine Art Inc.*, *Houston*

Chelby King, *Lawndale Art Center*

Marilyn Lau, *Dancie Perugini Ware Associates*, *Houston*

Mike and Mickey Marvins, *Houston*

Apama McKay, *Mackay Gallery*, *Houston*

Katherine and David Miller, *Houston*

Jeff Messina, *Messina Group*, *Houston*

Katherine and David Miller, *Houston*

Eric Skelly, *KUHF 88.7FM*, *Houston*

Staff of Copy.Com, *Houston*

Richard Stout, *Houston*

Antoine Vigne, *Blue Medium*, *New York*

Carly Walker, *Gremillion & Co. Fine Art Inc.*, *Houston*

MEETING PLACE REVIEWERS

Peggy Sue Amison, Cork, *Ireland*

Pavel Banka, *Prague*

Jayne Baum, *New York*

Linda Benedict-Jones, *Pittsburgh*

Lucia Benicka, *Poprad, Slovakia*

John Bennette, *New York*

Evgeny Berezner & Irina Tchmyreva, *Moscow*

Vladimir Birgus, *Prague*

Suzanne Bloom, *Houston*

Sian Bonnell, *Weymouth, Dorset, UK*

Chris Boot, *London*

Sue Brisk, *New York*

MaryAnn Camilleri, *Toronto*

Krzysztof Candrowicz, *Lodz, Poland*

Xavier Canonne & Marck Vausort, *Charleroi, Belgium*

Alejandro Castellanos, *Mexico City*

Fernando Castro, *Houston*

Gary Chassman, *Burlington, VT*

Brian Clamp, *New York*

John Cleary, *Houston*

Joan Davidow, *Dallas*

Eric Davis, *Houston*

Suzanne Dechert, *Amsterdam*

Kathy Aron Dowell, *Kansas City*

Diana Edkins, *New York*

Bernd Fechner, *Berlin*

Burt & Missy Finger, *Dallas*

Marco Fiorese, *Milan*

Blake Fitch, *Winchester, MA*

Roy Flukinger, *Austin*

Juan Alberto Gaviria, *Medellin, Colombia*

Christian J. Gerstheimer, *El Paso*

Gigi Giannuzzi, *London*

Tom Gitterman, *New York*

Anna Gripp, *Hamburg*

Marek Grygiel, *Warsaw*

Zheng Gu, *Shangai*

Ellen J. Handy, *Austin*

Elda Harrington, *Buenos Aires*

Melissa Harris, *New York*

Francois Hebel, Arles, *France*

Virginia Heckert, *Los Angeles*

Gary Hesse, *San Francisco*

Eva Hodek, *Prague*

Lisa Hostetler, *Milwaukee*

W. M. Hunt, *New York*

Allison Hunter, *Houston*

Razvan Ion, *Bucharest*

Michelle Jackson, *New York*

Russell Joslin, *Minneapolis*

Mindaugas Kavaliauskas, *Kaunas, Lithuania*

Thomas Kellner, Siegen, *Germany*

Julie Kinzelman, *Houston*

Hans-Michael Koetzle, *Munich*

Paul Kopeikin, *Los Angeles*

Angela Krass, *New York*

Dewi Lewis, *Stockport, Cheshire, UK*

Maren Luebbke-Tidow, *Berlin*

Celina Lunsford, *Frankfurt*

Vaclav Macek, *Bratislava, Slovakia*

James E. Maloney, *Houston*

John Mannion, *Syracuse*

Lesley Martin, *New York*

Stephen Mayes, *New York*

Joana Mazza, *Rio de Janeiro*

Kate Menconeri, *Woodstock*

Pedro Meyer, *Los Angeles*

Yossi Milo, *New York*

Charles Dee Mitchell, *Dallas*

Chuck Mobley, *San Francisco*

Joan Morgenstern, *Houston*

Sarah Morthland, *New York*

Robert Morton, *Redding Ridge*

Ute Noll, *Frankfurt*

Alison D. Nordstrom, *Rochester*

Christine Ollier, *Paris*

Ed Osowski, *Houston*

Joaquim Paiva, *Madrid*

Ann Pallesen, *Seattle*

Samantha Profitt, *Dallas*

Alan E. Rapp, *San Francisco*

Christopher Rauschenberg, *Portland*

Rixon Reed, *Santa Fe*

Arianna Rinaldo, *Milan*

John Rohrbach, *Fort Worth*

Miriam Romais, *Bronx*

Ernestine Ruben, *Princeton*

Chuck Samuels, *Montreal*

Mark Sealy, *London*

Ariel Shanberg, *Woodstock*

Barry Singer, *Petaluma*

Teresa Siza, *Porto, Portugal*

Johan Sjostrom, *Umea, Sweden*

George Slade, *Minneapolis*

Rod Slemmons, *Chicago*

Jean-Luc Soret, *Paris*

Mary Virginia Swanson, *New York*

Barbara Tannenbaum, *Akron*

Christoph Tannert, *Berlin*

Finn Thrane, Odense, *Denmark*

Katalin Timar, *Budapest*

Issa Touma, *Aleppo, Syria*

Juan Travnik, *Buenos Aires*

Anne Tucker, *Houston*

Cynthia van Roden, *Kansas City*

Addie Vassie, *Amsterdam*

Ricardo Viera, *Bethlehem, PA*

Enrica Vigano, *Milan*

Katherine Ware, *Philadelphia*

Lorna-Mary Webb, *Birmingham, UK*

Terri Whitlock, *San Francisco*

Clint Willour, *Galveston*

Rhonda Wilson, *Birmingham, UK*

Tim Wride, *Los Angeles*

Ireneusz Zjezdzalka, *Wrzesnia, Poland*

Del Zogg, *Houston*

Manfred Zollner, *Hamburg*

MEETING PLACE VOLUNTEERS

Larry Albert
Cyndy Allard
Joy Boone
Emily Brants
Beth Brinsdon
Jennifer Brinsdon
Barbara Busbey
Rene Cervantes
Carolyn Cullinan
Melanie Dando
Linda Foot
Ivy Haynes
Rose Hock
Frazier King
Michael and Tatiana Lewis
William Liu
Alex Lopez
Mike and Mickey Marvins
Dion McInnis
Jake and Betty Mooney
Laura Nolden
Leah Orenpalmer
Beverly Parker
Therese Ramirez
Rene Rodriguez
Molly Rose
Jeremy Rountree
Royce Ann Sline
Patti Stoddart
Christina Summers
Nicolas Tamayo

Susan West
Kerry Whitehead
Peter Yenne

WORKSHOPS PANELISTS

Chris Boot, *London, UK*
Gary Chassman, *Burlington*
Bernd Fechner, *Berlin*
Judy Herrmann & Michael Starke, *Ellicott*
Dewi Lewis, *Cheshire, UK*
John Mannion, *Syracuse*
Lesley A. Martin, *New York*
Scott Martin, *San Antonio*
Robert Morton, *Redding Ridge*
Alan Rapp, *San Francisco*
Rixon Reed, *Santa Fe*
Mary Virginia Swansonm, *Tuscon*
William Tolan, *Austin*

WORKSHOP VOLUNTEERS

Cyndy Allar
Barbara Busbey
Rene Cervantes
Laura Nolden
Hall Puckett

FINE PRINT AUCTION
AUCTION ORGANIZERS

Annick Dekiouk
Nancy Douthey
Marilia Fernandes

Keith Hollingsworth
Mark Larsen
Marta Sánchez Philippe
Martha Skow
Anderson Wrangle

AUCTION VOLUNTEERS

Emily Adams
Carolina Alaniz
Cyndy Allard
Jenny Antill
Joy Boone
Barbara Busbey
Carolyn Cullinan
Rose Daly
Melanie Dando
Tatiana Davidson
Susan Davis
Delia Dockal
Lisa Duncan
Donna Durbin
Linda Foot
Ora Harrison
Ivy Hayns
Rose Cullivan Hock
Mike Kades
Danielle Lemuth
Michael Lewis
Irene Liberatos
William Lin
Alex Lopez
Sharon Lynn

Melissa Martinez

Mike Marvins

Leah Orenpalmer

Beverly Parker

Ken & Nancy Parker

Leila Perrin

Heather Reynolds

Juan Rivera

Rene Rodriguez

Molly Rose

Jeremy Rountree

June Russell

Cameron Sands

BIENNIAL VOLUNTEERS

American Society of Media
Photographers, *Houston Chapter*

Kimberly Barfield

Joy Boone

Diane Dockins

Trish Fowler

Wes Fenn

Arnold Franco

Sofia Holder

Amy Jarrous

Ping Lau

Elizabeth Lopez

Anne H. Roberts

Ana Carolina Sanchez

Camilla Sayers

Randall Sims

Bonnie Snipes

Kristen Sprague

Ryan Stoddart

Richard Stout

Craig Anthony Thomas

Lisa Ross Thomas

Dave Wilson

LITERACY THROUGH PHOTOGRAPHY

GENERAL PROGRAMMING

Lisa Caruthers, *Harris County Department of Education, CASE*

Ted Estrada, *Davis High School*

Trina Finley, *Harris County Department of Education, CASE*

Steve Gonzales, *Houston Chronicle*

Marion Harper, *The Houston Astros*

Patti Hernandez, *Marshall Middle School*

Ann Parker, *Project GRAD, Fine Arts*

George Ramirez, *Museum of Fine Arts, Houston*

Kathy Taylor, *St. Teresa's School*

R. Neal Wiley, *Director of Fine Arts Strategic Initiatives and Partnerships, Houston Independent School District*

INTERNS

Gabriel Cruz

Brandi Dessel

Michael Sanders

Brany Stoesz

Chloe Walker

FOTOFUN — KIDS FOR KIDS DAY 2005

Allyson Ayers, *Chairperson*

Ping Lau, *Station Captain*

Begonia Lopez, *Invitation Design*

Elizabeth Swift, *Food*

Sicardi Gallery

Werner & Kerrigan, LLTP

DIGITAL AND ESL CURRICULM DEVELOPMENT

Tonya Andreson, *Marshall Middle School*

Chandel Bonner-Hancock, *Marshall Middle School*

Obed Franco, *T. Jefferson Elementary School*

Susan Espinoza, *Marshall Middle School*

Ted Estrada, *Davis High School*

Patti Hernandez, *C. Martinez Elementary School*

Lisa Hooten, *Project GRAD*

Valentinia Mozia, *Marshall Middle School*

Ann Parker, *Project GRAD*

Edna Preston, *Sherman Elementary School*

Sally Valle, *Davis High School*

FOTOFEST2006

PARTICIPATING SPACES — FOTOFEST2006

The participation of over a hundred Houston-area museums, galleries, artist and educational organizations, corporate and retail spaces in the FotoFest Biennial gives hundreds of Houston-based and Texas artists an unparalleled opportunity to show their work to important national and international audience of curators, publishers, collectors and critics who come to Houston for the Biennial programs. In 2006, they are coming from 24 countries and 30 states in the U.S.

The city's commercial art galleries and non-profit art spaces also bring to Houston major artists from other part of the U.S. and the world. Many galleries that don't regularly show photography take the opportunity to exhibit photo-related art during the Biennial. It is a testament to the growing importance of photography as a marketable art form that almost all Houston's galleries have photography installations during the Biennial. This participation is central to the breadth and variety of artwork found at the Biennial and it creates a community-wide happening.

Recent studies have shown that the arts in Houston, both performing and visual, have an annual audience of over five million people. The city has 500 arts organizations with annual budgets that range in size from $32 million to less than $5,000. In addition to creating and presenting art, the Houston's arts organizations have educated the city's youth, restored inner city neighborhoods and helped to beautify public areas of the city. The arts organizations are an essential part of urban life.

FOTOFEST2006

CONTENTS

CONTENTS

CONTENTS

MUSEUMS

1

MUSEUMS

TWO WOMEN LOOK WEST

Photographs of King Ranch by Helen C. Kleberg and Toni Frissell

ARTISTS: HELEN C. KLEBERG AND TONI FRISSELL

Two Women Look West: Photographs of King Ranch by Helen C. Kleberg and Toni Frissell, an exhibition of approximately eighty-five black and white and color photographs, focuses on the dialogue between two women's photographs, revealing the women's relationship to their subject matter, King Ranch, and to each other. Dating from the late 1930s through the 1960s, their photographs provide a view of King Ranch rarely witnessed. In 1931, Helen C. Kleberg (1902–1963), a self-taught photographer, began documenting life on King Ranch, including vaqueros' cutting, roping, and branding cattle, as well as the activities of guests at the Ranch and family members. As the wife of Robert J. Kleberg, Jr., general manager of King Ranch from 1925 to 1974, she had a personal relationship with the landscape and with those who lived and worked on the property. Toni Frissell (1907–1988), a photojournalist and well-known New York fashion photographer for Vogue and Harper's Bazaar, was invited by the Klebergs to photograph King Ranch during the years 1939–44. As a professional photographer, Frissell composed her photographs with a "storytelling" quality, seeing them as part of a larger narrative she was constructing about ranch life.

Both women found the landscape of south Texas a rich setting, ripe with subject matter, and they captured similar scenes in their work. Due to their independent and distinctive relationships to King Ranch, however, their works reveal two views of ranch life, photographed from two different perspectives. While Frissell approached her subjects with a romantic eye as to what it is to live and work on the ranch, Kleberg documented the people and romanticized the photography experience. Unlike Frissell, Kleberg also had the opportunity to photograph King Ranch-owned property outside of Texas in South America and Australia. A number of these works are also on view in the exhibition. *Two Women Look West* is a rare opportunity to view Kleberg's intimate photographs, which have never before been exhibited, and represents the first time that Frissell's dramatic photographs of King Ranch have been placed in the context of another photographer's work.

HELEN C. KLEBERG · *MOVING THROUGH THE ROUNDUP HERD*. LATE 1930s–EARLY 1940s · GELATIN SILVER PRINT · COURTESY OF THE COLLECTION OF HELEN GROVES

Marisa S. Sánchez
Curatorial Assistant, Photography Department

Toni Frissell · *Vaquero, Javier Medietta, Cutting Calf from the Herd and Roping Calf for Branding, King Ranch, September 1943* · Silver Gelatin Print · Photographs by Toni Frissell, Permission of King Ranch, Inc., Courtesy of the Library of Congress

FROM THE PRINTED PAGE

Photographs from the Manfred Heiting Collection

By the end of the nineteenth century, it became possible to reproduce photographs alongside text in books, magazines, and newspapers. The new technology led to the founding of a number of commercial publications, which employed photographers who went on to establish careers in this medium. The picture essay was first developed in 1928 by *Münchner Illustrierte Presse* in Germany and simultaneously by *VU* in Paris. *Life* was founded in the United States in 1936, and *Pictures Post* appeared in England in 1938. These and other picture magazines were important venues fostering the genre of photojournalism, where the "day in the life" and the photo essay proved to be effective ways to communicate a range of issues, from serious social concerns to more lighthearted subject matter.

Photographers took advantage of the technical advances credited with making magazine photography viable. One development in particular was the invention of the handheld 35 mm camera, which was miniscule in scale compared to the older camera equipment and could make exposures with less light without using a flash. Illustrated newspapers and magazines continued to thrive well into the 1950s, but the demand for photojournalistic stories declined due to television, which offered a wide and growing audience more immediate news coverage. *From the Printed Page*, an exhibition of twenty-eight photographs dating from the late 1920s to the 1960s, highlights work made specifically with the printed page in mind. Included are photographs by Rene Burri, Alfred Eisenstaedt, Gordon Parks, Margaret Bourke-White, Lisette Model, and W. Eugene Smith, to name a few. Magnum was a photo agency established in 1947 by Henri Cartier-Bresson, George Roger, Robert Capa, and David Seymour. Photographs by all but Roger are also on view.

Anne Wilkes Tucker
The Gus and Lyndall Wortham Curator of Photography
Museum of Fine Arts, Houston

GJON MILI · *TYPEWRITER*, 1940s · SILVER GELATIN PRINT · MUSEUM OF FINE ARTS, HOUSTON, GIFT OF THE MUNDY COMPANIES

MARK SELIGER: IN MY STAIRWELL

ARTIST: MARK SELIGER

Mark Seliger was the chief photographer for *Rolling Stone* for more than ten years. In this position, he had the opportunity to photograph a wide range of celebrities, including Bob Dylan, Renée Fleming, Lenny Kravitz, Susan Sarandon, Jerry Seinfeld, Richard Serra, Matthew Barney, and Laurie Anderson. *In My Stairwell*, the most recent body of work by this Texas native and well-known editorial photographer, focuses on contemporary artists, musicians, and actors posed on the stairwell of his studio in New York's West Village. He said of this series: "The *Stairwell* project was an opportunity for me to create a collection of portraits of artists, ranging from peripheral to mainstream, to make a record of our times. The stairwell environment became the common denominator that related the subjects to one another: they could either make it into a personal space for themselves or use it as a background simply to be documented."[1] The strength of Seliger's portraits lies in his ability to portray the nuances in the personality of his sitters and intuitively capture a central characteristic of each individual's public persona. The exhibition includes a selection of platinum-palladium prints drawn from the eighty-nine photographs that make up this series, begun in 1998 and completed last year. It is the first exhibition of Seliger's work at the Museum of Fine Arts, Houston.

Anne Wilkes Tucker
The Gus and Lyndall Wortham Curator of Photography
Museum of Fine Arts, Houston

[1] Mark Seliger, www.markseliger.com

MARK SELIGER · *CINDY SHERMAN*, FROM THE SERIES *IN MY STAIRWELL*, 2005 · PLATINUM-PALLADIUM PRINT

INSISTENT OBJECT: DAVID LEVINTHAL'S BLACKFACE

ARTIST: DAVID LEVINTHAL

CURATOR: KRISTINA VAN DYKE, ASSOCIATE CURATOR OF COLLECTIONS

Through a series of large-scale Polaroids, New York–based photographer David Levinthal engages with the racist portrayal of African-Americans in everyday objects dating from the nineteenth and early twentieth centuries, drawing on imagery that continues to haunt the American memory.

Levinthal's approach toward this confrontational subject matter heightens its inherent tension. Carefully lit and almost classically composed, the photographs themselves are visually striking, even beautiful—complicating our already uneasy response to the imagery portrayed. In a series that is deliberately ambiguous, the artist seeks neither to glorify the subject matter nor to antagonize viewers. Rather he hopes to promote dialogue around a subject many are reluctant to discuss.

Many of the objects photographed for *Blackface* are from the museum's own collection of black memorabilia, acquired in connection with John and Dominique de Menils' strong interest in promoting civil rights for African-Americans. With the presentation of *Blackface*, The Menil Collection honors the commitment of its founders to confront the complex issue of racism. *Insistent Objects* is accompanied by the book David Levinthal: *Blackface* (Santa Fe: Arena Editions, 1999).

Clare Elliot
Curatorial Assistant, The Menil Collection

DAVID LEVINTHAL · *UNTITLED,* FROM *BLACKFACE* SERIES, 1998 · POLAROID

GIRLS' NIGHT OUT

ARTISTS: EIJA-LIISA AHTILA, ELINA BROTHERUS, DORIT CYPIS, RENEKE DIJKSTRA, KATY GRANNAN, SARAH JONES, KELLY NIPPER, DANIELA ROSSELL, SHIRANA SHAHBAZI AND SALLA TYKKÄ

Girls' Night Out was organized by the Orange County Museum of Art, Newport Beach, California. The exhibition is presented by Neutrogena. Additional support has been provided by James B. Pick and Rosalyn M. Laudati, Joan and Don Beall, Visionaries, LEF Foundation, the Women's Consortium of the Orange County Museum of Art, Christine and Jeff Masonek, FRAME Finnish Fund for Art Exchange, Patricia and Max Ellis, Anita Kunin Fund of the Minneapolis Foundation, The Consulate General of the Netherlands in Los Angeles, and an anonymous donor. Presentation at Blaffer Gallery is made possible by the Director's Discretionary Fund.

The exhibition *Girls' Night Out* brings together the work of an international and intergenerational group of women artists whose works in photography and video reflect a new approach to issues of femininity and identity. Central to *Girls' Night Out* is the idea of the *girl*—a term that has regained currency when applied to women in an affirmative manner, especially by other women—and the exhibition's title reflects a generational shift that has brought the use of this word back into play. The use of the term *girl*, when applied to grown women, was once considered patronizing and demeaning. In recent years, however, the word *girl* has been reclaimed by a wide range of young women. The evolution of a new girl culture—and the increasingly central and empowered role that girls and women now play in politics, mass media, and other professions—finds its parallel in the art world.

Girls' Night Out reflects a new sensibility that has grown out of the influence of feminism on art and society, and attests to the corresponding progress women artists have been able to achieve, changing the content of traditional media, such as painting and sculpture, while at the same time pushing photography, performance, video, and installation art to the fore.

The Blaffer Gallery

SALLA TYKKÄ · *THE SICKEST ONE.* 1997 · C-PRINT

WHEN THEY CAME TO TAKE MY FATHER

ARTIST: MARK SELIGER

We were mostly children in our group; we had little in common, except fear.
—Alice Lok Cahana

MARK SELIGER · *ALICE LOK CAHANA*, 1996· SILVER GELATIN PRINT

When They Came to Take My Father: Photographs by Mark Seliger is an exhibition of photographic portraits made by world-renowned photographer Mark Seliger of Holocaust survivors that include Houstonians Max, Sol, and Sigmund Jucker as well as artist Alice Lok Cahana. Accompanying each photograph is a first-person account that provides an intimate look at a harrowing experience. Taken together, this powerful collection of words and images forms a moving testimony to human dignity and a record of history that cannot, and must not, ever be forgotten.

Shawna Murland

This exhibition is underwritten by Nina and Michael Zilkha, with special thanks to Continental Airlines, the Official Airlines of Holocaust Museum Houston.

HOME SWEET HOME

ARTIST: ROBERTO MORÁN

The high level of domestic violence presently suffered by contemporary society begins at home. The behavior, the values, and all that relates to the personality of the individuals, are reflections of the home and the familial environment in which these things have developed.

Home Sweet Home is the establishment of a physical space that moves us to ponder the intra-familial violence of our current society.

An inoffensive, ordinary and daily environment is created. In this case, it is inside a home. Through the game of appearances, the concept of aggressiveness is created through covering it in cotton wallpaper, walls and objects, to convey to the spectator a feeling of extreme smoothness and cleanliness. Also, playing somewhat with the origin of opposites, these are recreated in a space which has the characteristics of the room of a madhouse, where patients with severe mental ailment, such as schizophrenia, are lodged.

The objects selected for the room are commonplace, but they deal with those things that are used, physically and psychologically, to harass others around the house. They become symbols of violation: chairs, bottles, kitchen utensils, etc.

Thus, an ambivalent interaction of closeness and rejection is created, while, at the same time, violence is alluded to, and its efficacy is annulled, with a stare that changes from prophylaxis to lyricism.

Roberto Morán

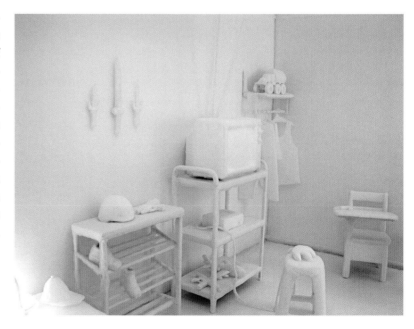

ROBERTO MORÁN · *VIEW I* FROM THE SERIES *HOME SWEET HOME*, 2006 · MIXED MEDIA

Roberto Morán · *View 2* from the series *Home Sweet Home*, 2006 · Mixed media

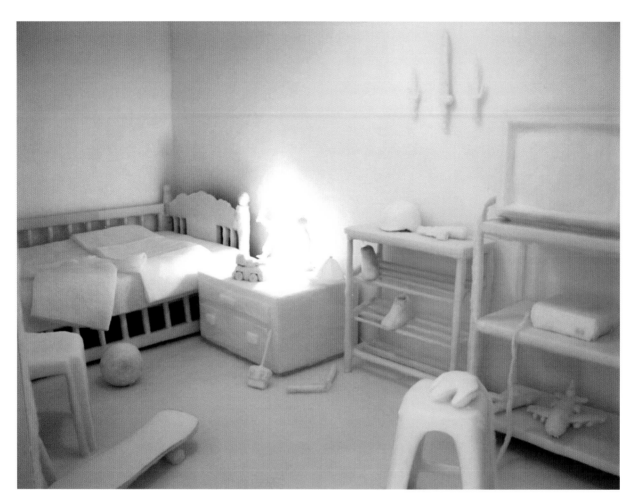

Roberto Morán · *Children's Room* from the series *Home Sweet Home*, 2006 · Mixed media

2
Non-Profit Art Organizations

NON-PROFIT ART ORGANIZATIONS

EL LLANO ESTACADO: AN ISLAND IN THE SKY

ARTISTS: PETER BROWN, RICK DINGUS, STEVE FITCH, MIGUEL GANDERT, TONY GLEATON, ANDREW JOHN LICCARDO AND DEBORAH LUSTER

E*l Llano Estacado: An Island in the Sky* presents seven interpretations of the Llano region in northwest Texas by nationally recognized photographers Peter Brown, Rick Dingus, Steve Fitch, Miguel Gandert, Tony Gleaton, Andrew John Liccardo, and Deborah Luster. These photographers, whose past work shows a deep appreciation of the Southwest's cultural and geographic landscape, were commissioned by the Southwest Collection (SWC) of Texas Tech University, Lubbock, in January 2004 to create new work for the SWC. Many works will be seen here for the first time.

The Llano region stands out as a place often underappreciated for its contradictions and for the stories etched across the land and the faces of the people who have called this place home. Today, the Llano faces a wide range of questions focusing on concerns such as the decline of cattle ranching; changes in demographics, including significant increases in minority populations and declines in traditional rural and town populations; the doubtful future of a cotton industry propped up by government subsidies; the declining availability and the increased costs of retrieving waters captured deep below the earth's surface; and the inevitable shift from the agricultural sector to an economy based on medicine and education.

RICK DINGUS · *LUBBOCK MARKED GLOBE (INTERNATIONAL CULTURAL CENTER, LUBBOCK, TEXAS)*, 2004 · EPSON INKJET PRINT

An Island in the Sky reflects upon not only the thoughts and aspirations of early settlers who broke ground in Llano during the first half of the twentieth century, but also the rich history of periodic occupation extending back 10,000 years.

Stephen D. Bogener, Ph.D.
Associate Archivist, Southwest Collection, Texas Tech University

FEAST...AGAINST THE WORD PRESENTED IN IDF

ARTIST: FEAST

FEAST is the collaborative effort of artists who look at spectacle, fashion, and art with caution and awe. We came together through good food, good drink, and great conversation, and decided to put our conversation to work. We talked about stuff, from CNN to cheerleading cowgirls, and asked of each other: Why is that interesting? Why is that doodle stuck in my head? These conversations snowballed into a conceptual lark and have now manifested as concrete images.

Beauty and terror live side by side, and we want to express that anxiety and thrill. We want to create images that can be savored like tasty roast pork. We want to create work that feels abundant, like a new boob job in a cheap sweater. We want to create art that is accessible in every way if you sit and watch the everyday.

The photographs are conversations, and each of us gives a little part of ourselves to them. The conversations talk about etiquette and loose restraint. They blend faux pas with quiet recklessness and spin on dirty secrets. They walk without care but make sure no one is looking. The images are formal things. They are rooted in the discourse of art and pruned with the shears of a quick wit. The intent is to celebrate the anomalies of the normal while we simultaneously critique the structures of function (if there is such a thing). Enjoy the images and join the conversation. We made these things to be talked about.

FEAST

FEAST · *Becca and Bridget—Long Shot*, 2005 · C-print

ERIKA HARRSCH / EROS-THANATOS

ARTISTS: INSTALLATION BY ERIKA HARRSCH WITH SOUND COLLABORATION BY EDMUND MOONEY

Eros-Thanatos, Erika Harrsch's latest project, takes the form of a multilevel installation and sound environment representing the cycle of life on earth. Positing women as objects of desire, and hence engaging with representations of the body, affection, emotion, psychic and social experiences, and the narcissistic pleasure of being possessed as a loved object, Harrsch suggests that the construction of identity and the development of personality is a condensation of sex and psyche. This installation focuses on the butterfly as a visual icon and metaphor for women. In this case, the femme fatale is caught in a constant struggle between subordination and liberation, sublimation and humiliation, life and death.

Using film and sound recordings made on visits to the monarch butterfly sanctuary in Michoacan, Mexico, Harrsch has recreated the experience of witnessing this amazing natural phenomenon firsthand. By juxtaposing a large-scale projection of butterflies in flight against the backdrop of the gallery space with a floor both littered with synthetic replicas of thousands of dead butterflies and superimposed with images suggestive of the female anatomy, Harrsch exposes both the grace and the violence of the natural realm. Such violence is a part of nature, shown here through the forces of destruction and chaos. Although we may build a world where work and reason prevail, there remains an undercurrent of violence at the root of our being. Despite this, the radiance of life seems to appear in the realm where death and eroticism merge. At brief moments in human experience—most notably involving intimacy, birth, and death—we experience the continuity of life. The passage of the monarch becomes the emblem of that understanding.

Diane Barber

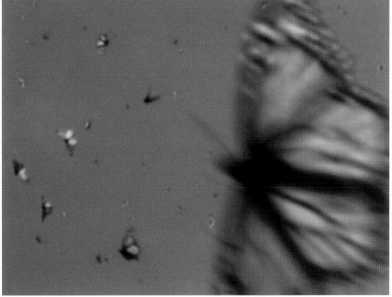

ERIKA HARRSCH · *UNTITLED, FROM* EROS-THANATOS, 2006 · VIDEO STILL

DAVID BROWN / URBAN CATHEDRAL

ARTIST: DAVID BROWN

Houston-based artist David A. Brown manages to reinterpret the world through the lens of his camera in a way that can only be described as magical. In *Urban Cathedral*, Brown has used digital photographs of the urban landscape to create an otherworldly, ephemeral environment of color, pattern, and supersaturated light. By reframing and recontextualizing the otherwise mundane trappings of urban existence—the reflection of light off a car bumper, soaring edifices of steel and glass, or water rippling in a sidewalk puddle—Brown transforms the urban environment into a place of wonder, contemplation, reverence, and awe.

Diane Barber

DAVID BROWN · *UNTITLED, FROM URBAN CATHEDRAL,* 2006 · DIGITAL PHOTOGRAPH

THE PHOTO PROJECT: AN ACT OF DEDICATION AND PERSEVERANCE

ARTISTS: YOSHI ABE, SUSAN BANK, AND PATRICIA SANDLER

This exhibition is the result of an international competition juried by Anne W. Tucker, Gus and Lyndall Wortham Curator of Photography, the Museum of Fine Arts, Houston, for the Texas Photographic Society. Tucker selected four photographic projects from hundreds of submissions. Each photographer is exhibiting fifteen images from his or her project. Yoshi Abe (San Francisco), from a series titled *At Night*, presents color photographs of small scenes or architectural elements in urban surroundings. Susan Bank (Philadelphia) presents a group of black and white photographs from Cuba titled *Campo Adentro [Deep within the Country]*. Houston's Will Michels' *Iwo Jima + 60* series documents a reenactment of that historic battle in Doss, Texas. Los Angeles photographer Patricia Sandler exhibits *Family Outcomes* where portraits of family members as children are presented with corresponding text.

Clint Willour, Curator

WILL MICHELS · *DEAD JAPANESE SOLDIER, IWO JIMA + 60, DOSS, TEXAS*, 2005 · BLEACHED AND TONED GELATIN SILVER PRINT

ROBERT LANGHAM: INTIMATE EXPANSE

ARTIST: ROBERT LANGHAM

This exhibition presents two distinct, yet related projects. Robert Langham of Tyler, Texas, has been photographing east Texas and western landscapes for more than twenty years. The *White Trees* series are photographs of trees made in and around Langham's Tyler neighborhood and surrounding Smith County. The resulting images are intimate "portraits" of blossoming trees that fill the frame.

In the *Ghosts of Shiprock* series, Langham photographed the area around Shiprock in northwestern New Mexico with the same loving care, but with the sweeping expanse of the western land as his subject. Both projects focus on the similarities of the landscapes—seasonal changes, clouds, shadow, and light.

Clint Willour, Curator

ROBERT LANGHAM · *MOONSET, SHIPROCK, NEW MEXICO,* 2001 · ENHANCED MATTE PAPER PRINT

GROUND: RECENT WORK BY FIVE HOUSTON PHOTOGRAPHERS

Beryl Striewski · *Toy Soldier, Buddha,* 2005 · Archival Inkjet Prints

WOMEN BOXERS

The New Warriors

ARTIST: DELILAH MONTOYA

Female boxers have ushered in a new generation of women who grew up with role models like Wonder Woman and Cat Woman. However, my interest is in thinking about them as *Malcriadas*. This is a woman who will not behave and is determined to do what she wants regardless of what society rules or even good sense dictates. When a family is confronted with this sort of unseemly member, they struggle to change her. Welcoming the uphill battle, the *Malcriada* remains unchanged, and in the end the family learns to accept her and even become proud of her accomplishments.

DELILAH MONTOYA · *STEPHANIE JARAMILLO, SANDIA CASINO, ALBUQUERQUE, NM.* 2003 · PIEZOGRAPH

Women boxers certainly fit the description of a *Malcriada*. By crossing the ropes and getting into the ring, they enter into the bastion of manliness to confront a brutal sport. Social convention rules that a woman is not to witness, demonstrate, or indulge in acts of violence. Many women indeed are appalled by such a violent sport and feel boxing should be banned. But the *Malcriada*, determined to box, turns her back on these opinions. Title IX, civil rights, and the feminist movement gave her the right, and she willingly takes it. The female boxer fights because she can—it is sanctioned combat.

Delilah Montoya

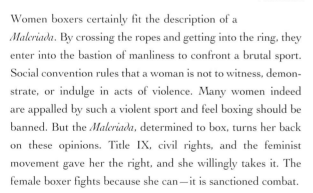

Women Boxers: The New Warriors, a collection of photographs by Delilah Montoya with an essay by Teresa Marquez, is available online at www.artepublicopress.com. This project was funded in part by the University of Houston Small Grants Program and the Cultural Arts Council of Houston and Harris County.

UNIVERSITY ART SPACES

UNIVERSITY ART SPACES

GODS OF WAR

ARTIST: MICHAEL FRY

Visually, the work in this exhibition is the digital equivalent of stained glass. I chose the subject matter specifically to confront the viewers' preconceptions about the appropriate use of the stained glass medium, and to challenge the idea that war and violence are an acceptable means to an end. Although the use of halos around the heads of the figures clearly references the religious aspect of stained glass, I feel that the visual satire is strong enough to deflect any criticism that I am making light of someone's beliefs. What I am really interested in is casting a critical eye on that aspect of faith that allows people to follow their ideology blindly and without question. I am also criticizing the acceptability of the message these icons deliver. The message is an illusion that exists on many levels: movie idols playing roles, real people playing soldier, and digital photographs pretending to be stained glass art.

Michael Fry

MICHAEL FRY · *ST. SYLVESTER*, 2005 · DIGITAL LIGHTJET PRINT ON DURATRANS

EARTH: PEOPLE, PLACES AND PLANTS

ARTISTS: BILL WRIGHT, ALICE WRIGHT AND MITCH WRIGHT

MITCH WRIGHT · *SHRINE OF THE BOOK (ISRAEL)*, 1985 · GELATIN SILVER PRINT

Work by Texas photographers Alice and Bill Wright and their son, Mitch Wright, is featured in *Earth: People, Places and Plants*. The Wrights' imagery celebrates the innate beauty of the earth and humanity's place within its cultures and environments. Their diverse approaches underscore their belief that humanity's relationship to the earth serves as a foundation for the mutual understanding that is so necessary for societies today.

Jean Caslin

Founded in 1973, North Harris College is located twenty-five minutes from downtown Houston on 200 beautiful, pine-filled acres, and serves as the educational and cultural center of North Harris County. The college, north Houston's center for the arts, has a well-established visual arts program with classes in painting, drawing, ceramics, photography, sculpture, and printmaking, as well as a state-of-the-art digital arts center. The visual arts department maintains the Fine Arts Gallery of North Harris College. The department recognizes the pivotal role its exhibition programming plays in educating not only the academic community but also the outlying community it serves.

ICELAND

ARTIST: BILL WRIGHT

I went to Iceland because I had never been there before. That is as honest as I can say it. I will admit that there were things that intrigued me about the country. I had heard that it is becoming a tourist destination for Europeans, and I wanted to photograph a bit of it before the country is overrun. I knew that Iceland has experienced an amazing florescence in the last couple of generations, moving from virtual Third World status to among the top ten in the world in per capita income. I was aware that in Iceland more books are published proportionate to its population than in any other country in the world. I knew that the geology and physical character of the land is extraordinary—with geysers and thermal areas alongside great glaciers, deserts and snow-covered mountains, waterfalls and salmon streams. The abundance of birdlife makes it an incredible paradise for birdwatchers.

In a land full of history, I didn't meet any ghosts or Vikings, but I toured the country and, in a brief eleven days, saw enough to know that I will return. There is so much to see and photograph—people, culture, and landscape. These photographs are but an introduction.

Bill Wright

BILL WRIGHT · *SODHOUSE WINDOW, ICELAND,* 2005 · INKJET PRINT

FLOWERS

ARTIST: ALICE WRIGHT

Even as a child, I was attracted to flowers. Now, as a photographer, I have begun to look at them more analytically. I am fascinated by the relationship of the parts and how they work together, joining my subjective pleasure in the flower's beauty with the discipline of form, line, texture, and pattern. Every photographer needs an ongoing project—one without end. Photographing flowers so completely engages my photographic skills and emotions that I anticipate enjoying the process for the rest of my life.

Alice Wright

ALICE WRIGHT · *BLUE IRIS*, 2005 · INKJET PRINT

DYNAMIC COMMUNITY LIVING

ARTIST: MITCH WRIGHT

I have traveled and photographed internationally since the early 1980s, seeking places that are alive with rich community spaces. As a landscape architect, community planner, and photographer, I have become deeply interested in the relationship between the built and the social community, and how community forms become alive with timeless qualities. Photography is my vehicle for exploring these relationships. This exploration is about cultural place-making, and how thoughtful planning and design can improve the quality of life in our communities.

My photographic work with sequential and mosaic studies not only helps me to explore relationships, but also adds a heightened sense of drama, accentuating the experience of a space that is ordinarily not easily conveyed. Many separate images displayed in groupings tend to draw attention to details otherwise overlooked in single-image works. These constructions express my interpretation of those aspects of place that are essential and timeless and enrich our lives.

Mitch Wright

MITCH WRIGHT · *SION MOSIAC, SWITZERLAND*, 2004 · GELATIN SILVER PRINT

RECENT WORK: BICYCLE PILGRIMAGES TO THE BASILICA OF GUADALUPE

ARTIST: BYRON BRAUCHLI

In this series of photogravure and plastic camera images, Byron Brauchli explores the religious pilgrimages that commemorate the three annunciations by the Virgin of Guadalupe to Juan Diego. While participating in the pilgrimages from the small Veracruz town of Jalacingo often since 2002, Brauchli has become familiar with not only the ride to the Basilica, but the other pilgrims as well, allowing him a closer look at this age-old tradition. This series gives the viewer an opportunity to step beyond the Virgin as a traditional religious icon and see her for the political/social entity that she is in modern Mexico.

Clint Willour

Byron Brauchli · *Mr. Ray Ban*. 2004 · Photopolymer Gravure

FOOTNOTES

ARTIST: GUENNADI MASLOV

The notion of using multiple images to convey an idea is not new in photography. Some of the best news coverage in photojournalism rests on the strong and careful juxtaposition of selected pictures. Guennadi Maslov's work, however, belongs to a completely different realm of combined imaging. His *Footnotes* offer more psychological insight than documentary fact. Deeply rooted in reality, they are also oddly enigmatic.

The artist is obviously concerned with social themes and the mysteries of growing up. Political undertones can also be discovered in some of his photographs. But these themes are neither dominant nor critical.

We notice and examine the smaller image in each pair just a second after our mental absorption of the larger one. In most cases, this "footnote" photo redirects our first impression considerably, enhancing it with an important layer of meaning, forming a new and convincing unity. And in that I see the work's strength and beauty.

Tatjana Pavlova
Kharkiv Museum of Photography

Guennadi Maslov:

MY WORK IS AN INTERPRETATION—
an attempt to translate the verse of life encounters into the poetry of photography, to catch the fluid material of the subconscious and put it on the somewhat more stable base of photographic paper.

MY WORK IS RECONCILIATION—
an effort to settle the Eastern and Western halves of my brain.

MY WORK IS AN ILLUSTRATION—
a never-ending quest to depict the fragile dualities of human nature.

GUENNADI MASLOV · *LOUISVILLE DIVE*, 2005 · ARCHIVAL DIGITAL PRINT

Guennadi Maslov · *Zarnica*, 2005 · Archival Digital Print

BELÄGRINGEN

ARTIST: HANS-JÖRGEN JOHANSEN

The beauty of the world lies in putrefaction.

Hans-Jørgen Johansen's series *Belägringen* represents this belief. In his photographs and video, Johansen beautifies the breakdown of organic material by emphasizing regrowth and a constantly changing environment. His photographs of mold signify new life, similar to that of a burned forest that struggles to rebuild itself through its own natural process.

These subtle photographs put the viewer in the perspective of an animal scavenging through the tundra. A Scandinavian sensibility is evident in Johansen's representation of a complex concept through the simplicity of the final image.

The images signify the decomposition and regeneration necessary to sustain life in nature…or on a block of cheese in a Stockholm artist's studio.

Troy Huechtker

HANS-JÖRGEN JOHANSEN · *UNTITLED,* FROM THE *BELÄGRINGEN* SERIES, 2005 · C-PRINT AND GLASS

4

COMMERCIAL ART GALLERIES

COMMERCIAL ART GALLERIES

THE ART OF WAR

ARTISTS: NANCY CHUNN, OTTO DIX, ALFRED EISENSTADT, LEON GOLUB, FRANSISCO GOYA, CHEMA MADOZ, ROBERTO MATTA, OSCAR MUÑOZ, JAMES NACHTWEY, DARIO ROBLETO, JOE ROSENTHAL, MICHAL ROVNER, SEBASTIAN SALGADO AND NICK UT
CURATORS: FERNANDO CASTRO AND FERNANDO CASAS

Together with the cosmos, the transcendent, Eros, and living organisms, war has been a recurring theme of art since humans began to make it. It should not be surprising, therefore, to put together an exhibition that confirms this art historical fact. Indeed, in a time when armed conflicts around the world abound, it would be surprising to ignore it. The ambiguity in the title of the exhibition (the objects and skill for making war, the works of art about war, and the wisdom and behavior of humans at war) does not inconvenience but inspires the selection.

The exhibition does not gather artworks for or against war, but explores many aspects of the phenomenon that artists have intelligently addressed over time. Thus, the methodological approach in building the exhibition has been

CHEMA MADOZ · *UNTITLED*, 2002 · SEPIA-TONED PHOTOGRAPH · COURTESY OF DR. JOSE LOPEZ. PHOTOGRAPHY IS ART GALLERY

twofold. On the topical side, it has been both semantic and experiential. War summons the themes of conquest, cruelty, enemies, allies, weapons, valor, discipline, desertion, treason, victory, defeat, collateral damage, MIAs, and refugees, as well as the symbols, the wounds, the blunders, the rules, the atrocities, the heroes, the war criminals, the mercenaries, and the spoils, etc., of war. Although the exhibition does not have works dealing with all of these topics, they are implicated in the general phenomenon of war.

On the artistic side, the curatorial approach has been more empirical. We set out in search of artworks that provide insight into the aforementioned topics. The search was not limited to any particular historical period, medium, or genre. We have not avoided points of views because to do so would have been contrary to the aim of understanding the phenomenon of war; however, we have passed on artworks that are overtly propagandistic.

The Art of War aims to induce the viewer to reflect upon war through art. As some works in the show are historical signposts, we would also like to instill in the viewer a sense of curiosity about what happened to the parties at war before, during, and after each conflict.

Fernando Castro

ANONYMOUS · *INSURGENT FORCES IN MORAZAN, EL SALVADOR* · INKJET PRINT · COURTESY OF THE MUSEO DE LA PALABRA Y LA IMAGEN, EL SALVADOR

BLOCO

ARTIST: STEPHEN DEAN

Stephen Dean's work, whether installation, sculpture, or video, investigates color as a crucial element in understanding objects and especially experiences. Color reigns as an essential force that links perception to understanding. Through compositions of color, Dean ascribes new meaning to ordinary common objects.

Dean presents *Bloco*, a six-minute video also exhibited at the 51st Venice Biennale in 2005. Taken from above the streets of Rio de Janeiro's Carnival, *Bloco* shows us crowds so dense that to wander by oneself would be to lose one's identity. In response, groups travel in tight, uniform packs that form highly colorful units of wild organic mass, each rubbing violently against contrasting groups. Rhythmic music complements the movement of the crowds and lends a cultural authenticity to the environment.

Scott Peveto

STEPHEN DEAN · *BLOCO*, 2005 · VIDEO STILL FROM SINGLE-CHANNEL DVD WITH AUDIO

FREUD SERIES

ARTIST: ANNE DELEPORTE

Through photography, painting, video, and installation, Anne Deleporte creates mixed-media visual "micro-situations." Her collections of images emphasize the enigmatic quality of vision while undoing photographic certitudes.

In her *Freud* series, Deleporte explores surfaces, capturing images of herself reflected in glass. Intellectually charged and challenging, the self-portraits come alive with color. Deleporte reminds us that photography, as part of the search for self-awareness, is an act of seeing distinct from everyday looking. Seeing with the camera is intentional, and by closer attention to surfaces, we can learn to see more deeply within. In the creation of these images, Deleporte demonstrates that the reality of external surfaces is just as suggestive and ironic as that of our inner worlds.

By affixing pages of newsprint to the wall, Deleporte creates photo-frescoes, painting out a majority of the information and leaving behind a celestial blue ground dotted with images. These newspaper images, detached from their context, appear in a leveled hierarchy, one inherent to different types of representations such as calligraphy, geometric shapes, objects, and historical reproductions. The floating images hang like constellations in a blue sky, pregnant with meaning but devoid of context.

McClain Gallery

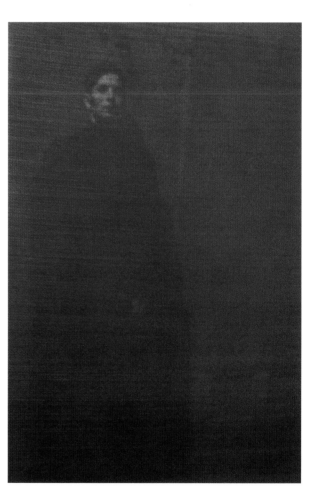

ANNE DELEPORTE · *FREUD*, 2003 · DIGITAL PRINT ON TYVEK

DIARY OF THE ARTIST AGAINST VIOLENCE

ARTIST: GOTTFRIED HELNWEIN

You can't show anyone anything he hasn't seen already on some level—anymore than you can tell anyone anything he doesn't already know. It is the function of the artist to evoke the experience of surprised recognition: to show the viewer what he knows, but does not know that he knows. Helnwein is a master of surprised recognition.

William S. Burroughs
Writer

Well, the world is a haunted house, and Gottfried Helnwein at times is our tour guide through it. I think in any art that is really relevant and emotional, there is some kind of a mirror that people experience. I don't think that you can recognize a feeling evoked by something that you look at unless it's part of yourself, and so when someone is willing to take on the sadness, the irony, the ugliness, and the beauty of the world in the kind of way that Helnwein does, the viewer is challenged to face it.

Not all of Helnwein's work is on a canvas. A lot of it is in the way he has approached life. And it doesn't take someone knowing him to know that. You take one look at the paintings and you say, "This guy has been around." You can't sit in a closet and create this. This level of work is earned.

Sean Penn
Actor and filmmaker

For Gottfried Helnwein, the child is the symbol of innocence, but also of innocence betrayed. In today's world, the malevolent forces of war, poverty, and sexual exploitation, and the numbing, predatory influence of modern media assault the virtue of children.

Helnwein's work concerning the child includes paintings, drawings, and photographs, and it ranges from subtle inscrutability to scenes of stark brutality. Of course, brutal scenes—witness Peter Paul Rubens' *The Massacre of the Innocents* (1611–12)—have been important and regularly visited motifs in the history of art. What makes Helnwein's art significant is its ability to make us reflect emotionally and intellectually on the very expressive subjects he chooses.

Many people feel that museums should be a refuge in which to experience quiet beauty divorced from the coarseness of the world. This notion sells short the purposes of art, the function of museums, and the intellectual curiosity of the public. Helnwein's work will inspire and enlighten many; it is also sure to upset some. It is not only the right but the responsibility of the museum to present art that deals with important and sometimes controversial topics in our society.

Harry S. Parker III
Director, Fine Arts Museum of San Francisco

GOTTFRIED HELNWEIN · *THE GOLDEN AGE IV / PUTTING HOLES INTO HAPPINESS,* 2004 · DIGITAL PRINT

CONVERGING TERRITORIES

ARTIST: LALLA ESSAYDI

LALLA ESSAYDI · *CONVERGING TERRITORIES #2*, 2003 · CHROMOGENIC PRINT · COURTESY OF LAURENCE MILLER GALLERY, NEW YORK, AND SCHNEIDER GALLERY, CHICAGO

My work reaches beyond Islamic culture to invoke the Western fascination with the veil and, of course, the harem, which has been expressed in Orientalist painting using the odalisque. By revisiting and reinterrogating the Arab female body, I am tracing and mapping a history often coded in misunderstanding. Through my photographs, I am able to suggest the complexity of Arab female identity, as I have known it, and the tension between hierarchy and fluidity that are at the heart of Arab culture. But I do not intend my work to be simply a critique of either Arab or Western culture. I am going beyond mere critique to a more active, even subversive, engagement with cultural patterns to convey my own experience as an Arab woman caught somewhere between past and present, East and West. In the absence of any specificity of place, the text itself becomes the world of the subjects—their thoughts, speech, work, clothing, shelter—and a nomadic home. Henna is a crucial element in the life of a Moroccan woman. It is associated with the major celebrations in her life: the passage intowomanhood, marriage, the birth of her first child. The texts, written in henna, are a diary—incomplete, of course, as the viewer and the writer become involved in a process of reading and revising, finding and losing multiple and discontinuous threads.

Lalla Essaydi

ONLY A LITTLE PLANET

ARTIST: KEITH CARTER

This exhibition of new work by Keith Carter explores the passage of time, the temporal beauty of memory, and the universal courage of the human spirit.

McMurtrey Gallery

Keith Carter · *Stairway*, 2005 · Toned Gelatin Silver Print

CYPRESS CREEK, WIMBERLY, TEXAS

David Gibson · *An Autumn Place Triptych (November 22, 2002 7:42 AM), Cypress Creek, Wimberley, Texas,* 2002 · Silver Gelatin Print

David Gibson · *An Autumn Place Triptych (November 22, 2002 7:44 AM), Cypress Creek, Wimberley, Texas,* 2002 · Silver Gelatin Print

David Gibson · *An Autumn Place Triptych (November 22, 2002 7:48 AM), Cypress Creek, Wimberley, Texas,* 2002 · Silver Gelatin Print

ARTIST: DAVID GIBSON

It is a matter of choice that I have returned to Cypress Creek in Wimberley, Texas, for nearly twenty-five years. I find the intimacy with the land along the creek calms my spirit. The overhanging cypress trees filter and change the light every season. In the fall and winter months, mist and light combine to create remarkable effects. It is a place to be quiet, listen to sounds, and experience dynamic changes of light. There I become more attuned to the events that form the moment. When back in the darkroom, I work to achieve what the Japanese call aware (ah war eh), "a poignant memory of an ephemeral moment."

At Cypress Creek I can look beyond the scars of human negligence and abuse that exist elsewhere. Photographs of the damage done to our environment are important to our awareness; however, I seek to reveal the poetry of beauty that remains in our midst.

David Gibson

FORM

**ARTISTS: BETH BLOCK, SPARKY CAMPANELLA
AND CLAUDETTE CHAMPBRUN GOUX**

SPARKY CAMPANELLA · *17TH & MISSION*, 2004 · DIGITAL PRINT

MIGUEL ANGEL ROJAS

Points of Fact

ARTIST: MIGUEL ANGEL ROJAS

Miguel Angel Rojas is one of a handful of Colombian artists who use the processes, semantics, and pragmatics of the medium of photography to expose unexpected layers of reality. These layers involve not only Rojas's sexual preferences and interests, but also the sociopolitical circumstances of his life. An early series of photographs from the Faenza cinemas in Bogotá comprises long exposures, covertly made, of scenes from a popular gay meeting place for casual sex. *Atenas c.c. [Athens Continuous Cinema]* is an installation of seventy photographs of sperm-marked floor tiles. A later installation, *Paquita compra un helado [Paquita Buys Ice Cream]*, is a cartoonlike story of the vicissitudes a little girl encounters as she goes shopping for ice cream, the images created from multiple photographs of sexual encounters reduced to confetti size.

In the work *Go On* (2001), Rojas used a similar strategy to depict a scene of the American West, using confetti dots of coca leaves. Another image, *Bratatá* (2001), also using coca-leaf dots, takes off from Roy Lichtenstein's *As I opened fire* (1964) except the cartoon strip captions Lichtenstein included in his triptych have been changed to the single phrase "Addiction Storm." Rojas appropriated a jaguar from Colombian truck iconography, which he rendered with confetti dots of U.S. dollars, in a work titled *It's Better to Be Rich Than Poor* (2001). "I tried to address the theme of drug-trafficking from several angles: the presence of empire, the acculturation caused by the influx of dollars, the war financed with that money, and the immorality and corruption that are the direct consequence of easy money," says Rojas.[1]

Fernando Castro

[1] Miguel Angel Rojas, conversation with Hans-Michael Herzog, in *Cantos Cuentos Colombianos: Contemporary Colombian Art*, exh. cat. (Zurich: Daros Latinamerica, 2004), p. 104.

MIGUEL ANGEL ROJAS · FROM THE SERIES *ANTROPOFAGIA NO. 1*, 1979–2004 ·
SILVER GELATIN PRINTS, MOUNTED ON ALUMINUM

LEWIS AND CLARK TRAIL PHOTOGRAPHIC SURVEY

ARTIST: BRENT PHELPS

The emence Seas and waves which breake on the rocks & Coasts to the S W. &

N W roars like an emence fall at a distance, and this roaring has continued ever

Since our arrival in the neighbourhood of the Sea Coast which has been 24 days

Since we arrived in Sight of the Great Western; (for I cannot Say Pacific) Ocian as

I have not Seen one pacific day Since my arrival in its vicinity. . .

Meriwether Lewis and William Clark

Excerpts from the *Journals of the Lewis and Clark Expedition*, ed. Gary E. Moulton, 13 vols, abridged (Lincoln, Neb.: The University of Nebraska Press, 1983–2001).

BRENT PHELPS · *MOUTH OF THE COLUMBIA RIVER, SOUTH JETTY, CLATSOP SPIT, FORT STEVENS STATE PARK, OREGON, DECEMBER 27, 2002*
[VIEW WEST: 46° 13' 37"N 3/4 124° 00' 51" W], 2002 · CHROMOGENIC PRINT

APPARITION

ARTIST: BILL ARMSTRONG

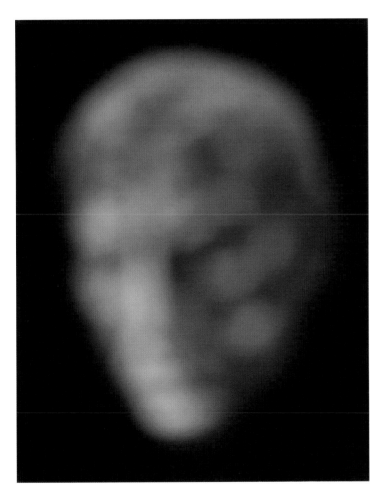

BILL ARMSTRONG · *# 913*. 2005 · C-PRINT

LOST HIGHWAY

Roadscapes from the West

ARTIST: ARTHUR MEYERSON

In the spirit of America's poets of the road, including Jack Kerouac, Robert Frank, William Least Heat Moon, and Hank Williams, I traveled west searching for images from the map's red and blue highways…the lost highways. Turn on the ignition, add some music, bring along a camera, and the ride becomes an adventure. Through a bug-splattered windshield or a rearview mirror, a scene is framed. What's up ahead on that never-ending horizon?

A landscape of raw natural beauty and the remnants of manmade structures, both interesting and strange, split by a ribbon of blacktop.

Arthur Meyerson

ARTHUR MEYERSON · *SUNRISE AT SUNSET, TEXAS*, 1988 · LIGHTJET PRINT

PELE, GODDESS OF THE VOLCANO

ARTIST: SUZANNE BANNING

Pele, goddess of the volcano:
her behavior erratic and volatile
full of fire and anger
her fury penetrates powerfully
capricious are her moods
she has many faces

SUZANNE BANNING · *PELE #1*, 2005 · LIGHTJET PRINT

Suzanne Banning · *Pele #2*, 2005 · LightJet Print

ROTATION

ARTIST: SUSANNE L. YORK

U nlike traditional landscape photography, my images address the movement and excitement of a planet orbiting the sun at 67,000 miles per hour while rotating on its own axis at slightly over 1,000 miles per hour (at the equator). Considering these forces, it no longer makes sense for me to illustrate Earth with solely static images.

Influenced by the Impressionists and the Abstract Expressionists, I strive to capture and communicate the movement, mood, and emotion that define the chaotic order of our planet.

Four elements—earth, fire, water, and wind—comprise the backdrop for life on Earth. As mere backdrops, however, they are easily overlooked. *Rotation* celebrates a planet in motion and the volatile elements acting upon it.

Susanne York

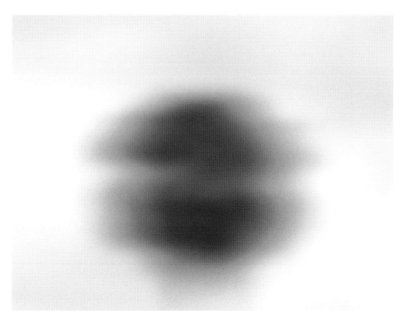

SUSANNE YORK · *PALM*, 2005 · GICLEE PRINT

Susanne York · *Azure Tide*, 2005 · Giclee Print

Susanne York · *Eruption*, 2005 · Giclee Print

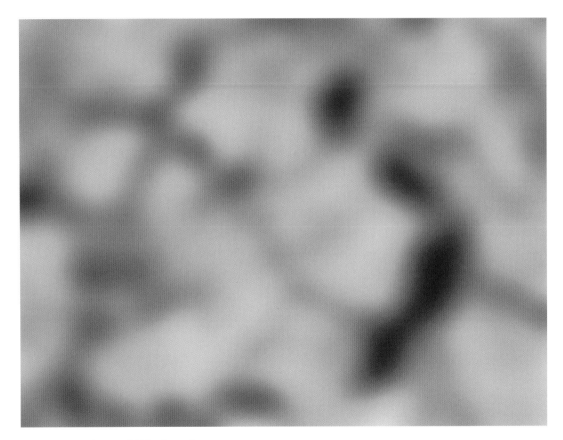

Susanne York · *Parched*, 2005 · Giclee Print

IT'S ALL PLASTIC

ARTIST: DAVID BROWN

The series *It's All Plastic* investigates the beauty hidden in the minutia of daily life. It also offers commentary on American consumerism and materialism. The enigmatic subject of these works—photographs of plastic headlights—challenges the viewer to solve the photographic riddle: What is it? The photographs also demonstrate a fundamental argument in life: one must "work" to consume beauty or luxury. Furthermore, the work explores shallow marketing ploys—purchase BLING! and be happier—and asks the question: "Where, in truth, lies value?"

By compressing multiple planes of light into the single photographic plane, the image emerges from "the real," with a single click of the shutter, and becomes surreal. As a result, the photographs create a visual conflict between organic and manufactured forms. Finally, a common thread flows through each image, narrating for the viewer the story of the surreal complexity of our superficial reality.

David Brown

DAVID BROWN · *FOCUS,* 2003 · TYPE C PRINT

IN BETWEEN

ARTIST: BETH BLOCK

Between. Transition. Movement. Respite. Stepping back, moving forward. Hesitation. Progression. Day, twilight, night. Day into night and back again. Anticipation. Possibility and hope. "Between" serves as a connection from one to another and as a comparison.

Beth Block's photographs show us all of this. It's always there to be seen, but we rarely take the time to look. That is what is so alarming about Block's work: she does take the time to look at these things, these occurrences. The seductive mystery of her work places her in the space in between these things, these occurrences. Block's work is not about slices of life; it is about the life that we, as a society, so carelessly let pass us by in continual instants without ever taking a moment to simply see what is here, there, everywhere. It is about the simplicity of the instant before the next, and that which is in between. www.bethblock.com

R. Eric Davis

BETH BLOCK · *BLUE ROAD, NEW YORK*, 2005 · CHROMOGENIC PRINT

RESISTING INVISIBILITY

ARTIST: JAWSHING ARTHUR LIOU

In *Illness as Metaphor* (New York: Doubleday, 1990), Susan Sontag wrote about typical societal responses to illness, particularly cancer, in terms of dread, mystery, taboo, and concealment. She outlined the anti-intellectual responses to this devastating disease, suggesting that they are indicative of the increasing unwillingness of advanced industrial societies to come to terms with death and serious illness. Arthur Liou's high-definition video series *Bloodwork* repudiates these obstructive responses to long-term illness by forcing himself and, by extension, the public to witness in microscopic detail an aesthetic expression of the disease.

Simultaneously horrifying and uncannily beautiful, Liou's work constitutes an ongoing constructive response to his young daughter Vivian's struggle with leukemia. Liou's series, which consists of three video installations—*CBC*, *Blasts*, and *Hairline*—not only boldly confronts the leukemia diagnosis by using it as the series' central subject, but also takes the disease's scientific structure as the basis for his work's formal language. The abstract imagery found in this series originates in Vivian's body, magnified hundreds to thousands of times. According to Liou, "The composition is based on the similarity between the cancer cells and the normal blood cells. As a metaphor for the medical process, the work refers to the terrifying effects of both the disease and its treatment."

Head of the digital media program at Indiana University's School of Fine Arts, Liou has undoubtedly achieved in *Bloodwork* his most powerful and provocative work to date, in terms of both its content and its technological prowess. In *CBC* (i.e., complete blood count), Liou poignantly interweaves sound and imagery to suggest how chemotherapy attacks both normal and cancerous cells, creating cycles of anemia that require patients to undergo blood transfusions to restore normal bodily function. While the music and sounds of running water intensify, the viewer witnesses hundreds of tiny naked babies attempting to crawl through an abstract, uneven field of organic red blood cells. The babies' energetic, Sisyphean movements begin to slow down along with the music until their bodies eventually disappear into the field of gray that overtakes the screen. Soon after, the anemic cells are replenished by an infusion of new red blood cells (and small bodies). The video's aesthetic structure reiterates the repeated cycles of attack, cell death, and regeneration experienced during cancer treatments.

Like *CBC*, Blasts takes its title from cancer terminology. Lymphoblasts, or immature white blood cells, accumulate in the bone marrow, crowding out normal blood cells until they cease to be produced. This highly abstracted video shows variously magnified representations of Liou's daughter's feet moving around the screen, while we hear the pleading voice of a young child whispering, "I'm going to get better," "Please get better," "I want to get better, please help me, please get better," and "I want it to go away." The heartbreaking refrain is coupled with a foreboding, haunting soundtrack that builds

along with the density of the images, reinforcing the tragic action of the accumulating lymphoblasts.

Hairline addresses the inevitability of hair loss, one of the most common, visible side effects of chemotherapy. It focuses on a year-long period during which Vivian first lost all of her hair, then watched it slowly replenish itself along with her health.

The video presents a bird's-eye view, looking down into a celestial, bloodlike pool, where babies appear to be leaping upwards, multiplying, and gradually moving off-screen and fading away into white light.

Lisa D. Freiman
Curator of Contemporary Art, Indianapolis

JAWSHING ARTHUR LIOU · *BLASTS*, 2003 · HIGH-DEFINITION VIDEO STILL

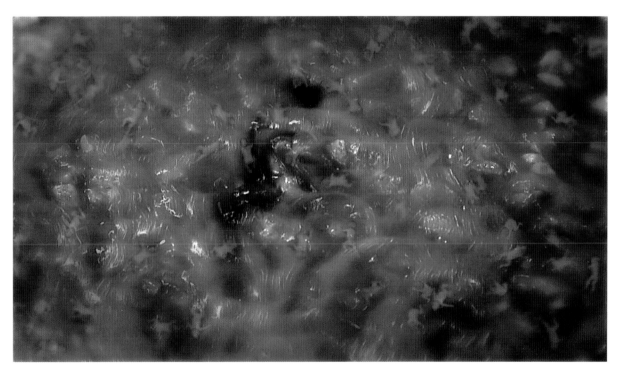

Jawshing Arthur Liou · *Blasts (detail)*, 2003 · High-definition Video Still

NO SHORTAGE HERE

ARTISTS: KELLY GALE AMEN AND SCOTT GRIESBACH

N*o Shortage Here* is a collaboration of historians who delve into the world of photography, furniture, and energy. Houstonians have long been at the forefront of the energy scene. This exhibition combines works by Houston artist Kelly Gale Amen and Los Angeles–based Scott Griesbach, who will provide us Houstonians with a little history lesson in the war of power.

Blakely Bering

SCOTT GRIESBACH · *OIL DRUM*, 2005 · DIGITAL PRINT

FROM MEMORY TO MEDITATION

ARTIST: JULIE BROOK ALEXANDER

Taking photographs creates a physical record of actual times and places. But human memory is a tricky thing. Eventually, the memory a person carries inside of herself changes from the original picture. Edges blur. Colors evolve. Thoughts of disparate moments merge.

I create images that reflect the subtleties of this experience. Because I was trained in the fine arts, pure love of the physical act of creation drives me to use the actual pencil, paintbrush, or scissors rather than their virtual counterparts in a digital toolbox. Working directly requires daring: each step is permanent, no starting over. The process mirrors what happens in my mind—floods of memories come together. Once a thought crystallizes, it doesn't go away; it shapes the way the whole scene evolves.

An original black and white photograph serves as my starting point. I layer colors not to imitate nature nor to mimic color photographs: each hue instead speaks its own expressive language, setting the poetic tone. Through the collage of found objects and other of my photographs, I weave into the work aspects of different memories.

The resulting composite vision links many different times and places to transcend traditional landscape. No longer limited to recording experience, these works reveal the thoughts that guide the collection of memories. The works exist as meditations. They invite reflection, opening the door separating the literal physical world and the lyrical inner soul.

Julie Brook Alexander

JULIE BROOK ALEXANDER · *STARTING OVER*, 2005 · MIXED MEDIA ON PHOTOGRAPH

AT A GLANCE

ARTIST: JIM FALICK

Mementos are things that serve to warn or remind, or that are souvenirs. In that spirit, I've created these images to evoke some of the anomalies of our everyday existence and to point out our separation from, as well as our longing for nature. I am concerned that we so easily accept and are seduced by the mixture of visual signals that constitute our daily environment.

Jim Falick

JIM FALICK · *POW*, FROM THE *FASHIONISTAS* SERIES, 2005 · C-PRINT · COURTESY OF HOOKS-EPSTEIN GALLERIES

MORE THAN MEETS THE EYE

ARTIST: KATHRYN DUNLEVIE

David Hockney's claims about photography and painting effectively illustrate not only Dunlevie's use of paint but also her unique representations of place and space, which might be interpreted as an intriguing new variant of analytic cubism.[1]
Don Snyder

Inspired by a space, I photograph it segment by segment from various vantage points. Next I arrange and rearrange the images until a new coherence emerges. The result—a photographic equivalent of a Cubist collage—is uneven, with visual jumps occurring wherever the edges of two photos meet. Finally I paint, blurring the borders between photos and smoothing the abrupt shifts in perspective.

This knitting together of disjunctive parts seems to coax the space into giving up its secrets. It is as if a plateau's sunken riverbed were to unfold and rise up into the viewer's line of sight, or as if a "mirror-on-a-stick" spy toy allowed a look directed straight ahead to reveal details from outside the viewer's visual scan.

The interweaving of perspectives creates a space with twists and ripples, revealing unexpected nooks and crannies, and peeks around corners. The initial photo collage is transformed, through the act of painting, into a pictorial space where weird transitions and subtle spatial anomalies emerge.

The depiction of this new space is not just a record of what we see while moving in space over time, but it includes elements that have appeared as if from beyond the customary four dimensions. Amidst the reorganization of the various perspectives, one catches sight of details not visible in the original space—details suggestive of the extra dimensions posited in contemporary theoretical physics. It offers glimpses of what may actually exist around us that we do not see.

Kathryn Dunlevie

[1] Don Snyder, "Not at First Glance," Gallery TPW Panscopic Journal [online magazine], available at http://www.photobasedart.ca/html/publications/essays/ESY0401.html [2004].

KATHRYN DUNLEVIE · *CHANGING STATION*, 2004 · C-PRINTS AND ACRYLIC ON PANEL

Kathryn Dunlevie · *Caution*, 2003 · C-prints and Acrylic on Panel

GROUP EXHIBITION FOR FOTOFEST 2006

ARTISTS: DAVE ANDERSON, WYATT GALLERY, DAVID HALLIDAY, RAYMOND MEEKS AND BOB SACHA

In conjunction with FotoFest 2006, Watermark Fine Art Photographs and Books is pleased to feature five artists' work relating to this year's Earth theme. Watermark opened in support of FotoFest 2004 in March 2004. The gallery features contemporary emerging and mid-career artists, and is dedicated to photography as an art form. In addition to original prints, Watermark has a well-stocked library of fine art photography books, including many limited edition artist books and titles.

Kevin Longino

WYATT GALLERY · *SUNKEN COAST GUARD SHIP*, 2005 · C-PRINT

AT THE CENTER OF NAPANTLA

ARTIST: DELILAH MONTOYA

Delilah Montoya · *Se Fue*, 2001 · Silver Gelatin Photograph

By recording the visible world, I observe (rather than create) the unraveling of my own unconscious or the intricate web of connection in the world around me. The photograph is the union of my "subjective" self with the "objective" world. This realism consists of more than just a reproduction of the façade: it cracks open that surface. Similarly, the photograph is more than indexical. Rather it encapsulates time by recording fleeting moments that freeze memory. The attempt is to slip into the crack that divides, so as to witness the twilight, that moment when the day moves into night, the point when the world is in opposition. This break is known by the Nahuatl/Aztecs as the sacred space of Napantla. When in Napantla, change lies dormant as a latent possibility …this is my center.

Delilah Montoya

ROAD TRIP

ARTISTS: JOAN BUELING AND JERRY HERRING

Joan Bueling and Jerry Herring travel extensively by car, often on trips that have no agreed upon destination: Houston to Fargo to Mount Rushmore, London to Edinburgh, across the U.S. southern states, or to south Texas and back. The by-product of these trips is a collection of images of roadside attractions, food, highway signs, and the visual world that people everywhere construct around themselves.

Joan Bueling and Jerry Herring

PORTRAITS

ARTIST: CHUCK RAMIREZ

Chuck Ramirez's *Portrait* series voyeuristically comments on how cultural identity can be expressed by the choices we make as consumers. He defines objects carried in a woman's purse as physical manifestations of the owner's personality—the objects giving form to interests and vices alike. The imagery of this series captivates through a provocative emotion—curiosity. Many would say it is taboo to look into a woman's purse since it holds deeply intimate possessions. Ramirez, however, not only grants permission but encourages it through the scale of work. One cannot help but be seduced into trying to dissect these portraits.

CHUCK RAMIREZ · *MFAH (CYNTHIA)*, 2005 · PIGMENTED INKJET PRINT · COURTESY OF FINESILVER GALLERY

FURIOUS COMPASSION

MAUD LIPSCOMB, JANICE RUBIN, BETSY SIEGEL AND CAROL VUCHETICH ·
COLLABORATION, 2005 · INKJET PRINT

ARTISTS: JEAN CASLIN, MAUD LIPSCOMB, JANICE RUBIN, BETSY SIEGEL, SCOTTIE STAPLETON AND CAROL VUCHETICH

Our world is upside down.
We aren't paying attention.
We haven't done the work democracy demands.
We have many Americas—white, black, brown, poor, rich ...
Some Americas do not understand other Americas.
How do we create and reconstruct?
We are all connected.

The Artists

ENDING TIME

ARTISTS: ROBERT BERLIN, LEIGH DEHANEY, BRYAN KUNTZ, BIRGIT LANGHAMMER AND ANGILEE WILKERSON
CURATORS: KEN CHRISTI AND WAYNE GILBERT

People continue to debate the duality of humankind: emerging from Nature, yet negatively altering Nature's delicate balance through our current existence. What will create an awakening great enough to redirect our desires to give life back to our planet? Perhaps capturing this dichotomy on film can begin to build an awareness that will lead to positive change.

Here, six experienced artists—three from Canada and three from Texas—record the violence impacting our sacred dwelling. Their combined work acts as a visual canary in the mine, its wellness and energy slowly drained by the actions of those who would be its caregivers. Perhaps through these works humankind will begin to admit that the bird is sick, and together we will help the world start the slow journey back to health. Maybe we can save the planet: one picture at a time.

Elisa Fink and Wayne Gilbert

ANGILEE WILKERSON · *SUBMERGED III*, 2004 · GICLEE PRINT

MYSTICAL SURROUNDINGS

ARTIST: LILY EARL

LILY EARL · *MADONNA*, 2004 · OIL PAINT ON SILVER GELATIN IRIS PRINT

ALLISON HUNTER

ARTIST: ALLISON HUNTER

Allison Hunter's most recent series comprises photographs of animals taken while in captivity, particularly in the recreated natural environment of a zoo. By removing the details of their habitats, she leaves the animals isolated within a luxurious, yet surreal landscape similar to that of a lunar or planetary surface. This forced isolation and the recontextualized environment change the way we view the animals, as their gaze becomes one of sweet vulnerability and their stance that of creatures suddenly exposed to possibility.

Julie Kinzelman

ALLISON HUNTER · *UNTITLED #1*, 2005 · LIGHTJET PRINT · COURTESY OF THE ARTIST AND 511 GALLERY, NEW YORK

MIRAGE

ARTISTS: DEBRA BOYLAN, FARRAH BRANIFF, JEROME CROWDER, JAMES DILGER, JR., LINDA GILBERT, GERALDINE GILL, RUTH HEIKKILA, ANTHONY PALASOTA, CHARLOTTE RANDOLPH, ROYCE ANN SLINE, CAROL STEVENS, DAVID VAUGHAN, LINDA WALSH, RODNEY WATERS AND DOROTHY LAM WONG

This *Mirage* show appears as our collective vision—a shared expression of individual efforts on a common theme. A mirage is sometimes viewed as just the mind "playing tricks." But should we understand such "tricks" as merely optical illusions or as newly opened doors? Are they reflections? Deeper dreams? Tied to our past or our future?

Perhaps it finally doesn't matter. Whether a Fata Morgana, or the product of heat/water/desert, or the result of our attempt to impose our own concerns on the world, the images tell myriad stories. Stories of tranquility, intimacy, adventure, simplicity, whimsy. Stories of the open road and of small rooms, of people and of nature.

Linda Walsh

[LEFT TO RIGHT, TOP TO BOTTOM] LINDA GILBERT, JAMES DILGER, JR., GERALDINE GILL, FARRAH BRANIFF, CHARLOTTE RANDOLPH, DAVID VAUGHAN, DOROTHY LAM WONG, DEBRA BOYLAN, ROYCE ANN SLINE, RODNEY WATERS, RUTH HEIKKILA, JEROME CROWDER · *MIRAGE COLLAGE*, 2006 · DIGITAL PRINT

TRANSFORMATION

ARTISTS: JOHN BERNHARD AND ROBERT A. SCHAEFER, JR.

On my first trip to China, I became fascinated with Chinese culture. I was overwhelmed by the character of a people who exhibit an incredible tolerance for the contradictions of the life in which they live. They are dealing with an outdated communist system, while capitalism dictates the evolution they are currently undergoing.

My challenge as a photographer was to develop a personal point of view. In recording my experiences and my emotional responses to China's new history in the making, I captured still images that indicate a movement through time. I worked to convey the essence of transition now defining this multi-faceted country. In doing so, I witnessed the euphoric drive and fast pace of an Asian society working to achieve its prospects in the new millennium. The Chinese have a genuine conviction that their day is coming. However, is this transformation positive if it is only an absurd reflection of the materialistic Western world?

In this body of work, reality vanishes and dissipates—intentionally or unintentionally—in an intricate process that is indispensable to the transformation of China.

John Bernhard

This project juxtaposes images conveying the Nazi element from the paternal side of my father's German heritage with those of the maternal side, which was Jewish. The room environment uses floor-to-ceiling scrims with images either printed on them or flashed on them with a projector. Six feet behind the scrims are actual prints—of the same height but totally contrasting in nature. A film of the material is shown as part of the environment. It confronts viewers with the duality of images arising from the Holocaust and its continuation in today's world.

Robert A. Schaefer, Jr.

John Bernhard · *Transformation #1* from the *China* series, 2004 · Archival Inkjet Print

Robert A. Schaefer, Jr. · *Anita, New York City*, 2004 · Silver Gelatin Print

TIBET

New Horizons for an Ancient Culture

ARTIST: LINDA DUNBAR

It's the rhythm that draws me in. It's the rhythm of the hot wind bending the tall, dry grass. It's the rhythm of two roaring lions letting the world know it is their time and place. It is the rhythm of the broken heart of a street beggar holding her infant that she knows will not live through the year. It is the rhythm of the love of a father holding the hope of the future of his country in his lap. It is the rhythm of an old country exploding with new values. It is the rhythm of the ocean reminding us how small we really are and how temporary our problems. We are a speck in time—like the butterfly that makes the most of his beauty and is gone in twenty-four hours.

As photographers, we are the ones who memorialize and document these rhythms. We see with our hearts just as much as with our eyes. As we fall into the rhythm of each new environment, we change and evolve. Each new experience becomes richer. Each photograph has more depth because of our experiences.

Linda Dunbar

LINDA DUNBAR · *PRAYER FLAGS*, 2005 · DIGITAL C-PRINT

ON THE WING IN BLACK & WHITE

ARTIST: JOHN C. DYES

John Dyes has been photographing the birds of Galveston Bay for more than thirty years. The majority of those images are in color; only recently has John turned to black and white photography. Since John is color blind and unable to make color a design element of the pictures, and since the birds of the bay (with the exception of the roseate spoonbill and the reddish egret) are primarily black and white and shades of gray, it seems a wise decision.

Additionally, John has made the artistic decision to lose the solid edge of the photograph, opting instead to apply layers of photo emulsion on Fabbriano watercolor paper, thus leaving the borders undefined. The resulting removal of boundaries gives the viewer a visual impression of the birds' freedom. Armed with his telephoto lenses, John chronicles the lives of the black skimmers, royal terns, brown pelicans, gulls, white ibises, and reddish egrets of the bay, and offers us hauntingly beautiful images of these nesting creatures.

Clint Willour
Curator, Galveston Arts Center

JOHN C. DYES · *UNTITLED*, 2005 · BLACK AND WHITE PHOTOGRAPH PRINTED ON APPLIED EMULSION ON WATERCOLOR PAPER

VISTA

ARTIST: T. MITCHELL JONES

Vista, a vision either real or perceived, a view, an outlook.
Paradise, a vision either real or perceived, a view, a dream.
Afterlife, a vision either real or perceived, a dream, a desire.
Destiny, the future, either real or perceived, awaits, unyielding.

A photograph, the image. What defines its bounds?
A document, a vision?
Trickery to make the temporal surreal;
or is it reality, the moment?
Possibly, it is somewhere between the two.
A photograph; a picture.
A picture speaks a thousand words.
Yet a photograph never lies.
Curious?
Indeed.
A photograph, like life, should be an adventure.

T. Mitchell Jones

T. Mitchell Jones · *Catrinas Descending*, 2004 · Inkjet Print

NON-PROFIT ORGANIZATIONS

5

NON-PROFIT ORGANIZATIONS

GEOFF WINNINGHAM

ARTIST: GEOFF WINNINGHAM

In 1982, a Mexican friend in San Miguel de Allende suggested that I might enjoy a trip to the nearby ghost town of Mineral de Pozos. He explained that Pozos had once been a prosperous mining city of over sixty thousand inhabitants, but that most of the men had left around 1910 to fight in the Revolution and had never returned. The mines had filled with water, and the city was abandoned. The old town was a pueblo *fantasmo*, he said, full of adobe ruins and faded glory.

My visit to Pozos, almost twenty-four years ago, remains vivid in my memory. I recall the main street through the center of town, its cobblestones dazzling in the sunlight. I found two old plazas and a bullring, all overgrown with weeds and sprouting cactus, but there was hardly a soul in sight. Occasionally, a child would appear, darting in and out of the ruins. I discovered two old churches, one of them occupied by a family, including all their livestock. There was a clock tower on the municipal building in the center of town. Though the time on the clock bore no relationship to the actual time of day, the clock nevertheless chimed each half hour. I felt as though I had fallen into a dream.

Following a road that rose to the west, I discovered the ruins of elaborate mining buildings. Wildflowers, cactus, and maguey grew all among the ruins. Huge *pirul* trees had grown up over the past century or so, their gnarled and twisted branches hanging over open mineshafts. Wandering through the mines that afternoon, I fell in love with Pozos. I returned to explore and photograph the town once or twice a year for the next sixteen years. Each trip led to new discoveries. Each road led to another old mine, to an abandoned hacienda, or to another grove of beautiful *pirul* trees.

In 1999, my wife and I purchased a piece of land in the center of Pozos and began to build our home there. I continue to live and work for most of each year in Houston, but our home is in that Mexican town. We are by no means the only ones to have discovered Pozos. The population has grown to almost three thousand people, including about twenty of us from the States. The photographs in this exhibition represent the beginning of my attempt to describe my new hometown in pictures. I have begun with my favorite things: the mines and the landscape around them, especially the *pirul* trees; the streets of the town; the crumbling ruins, which diminish in number each year as people rebuild and move in; and of course my friends and family, as we build a life in this beautiful place, *mi pueblo*.

Geoff Winningham

Geoff Winningham · *Pirul #1, Mineral de Pozos,* 2005 · Carbon Pigment Inkjet Print on Brushed Aluminum

HEALING QUALITIES OF SPIRIT

ARTIST: AMY BRADFORD UFER

Balancing the two natures of humankind, the natural and the spiritual, constantly challenges me in this lifetime. At midlife, illness violently demanded change in my narrow world! Very slowly the world of symbols began to raise serious questions as it penetrated my unconscious through dreams. The language of dreams, which is one way symbols are presented, opens us to our richest resource, the unconscious. Through the years, I've become more and more intrigued with the healing properties these images provide.

In reading the theme of FotoFest 2006, *Artists Responding to Violence*, I am reminded how the arts have always contributed to our natural healing by balancing our being and soothing the souls of both artist and beholder. I've often wondered why certain images touch our emotions so deeply by comforting, empowering, repelling, or healing us. We may find amazing insight and beauty within the connections we consciously experience through symbols pointing beyond themselves, because the invisible world of the unconscious is the source of all potentialities in existence.

Being a photographer constantly inspires me with the hope of capturing the unexpected, that which transforms and enriches our being. As I await the mysteries of the Holy, I am both challenged and excited by the symbols revealed and brought to light through the eye of the camera.

Amy Ufer

AMY BRADFORD UFER · *MANIFESTATIONS OF LIGHT*, 2002 · CHROMOGENIC IMAGE DIGITALLY FORMATTED

ON THE BRINK

ARTIST: MICHAEL MCKANN

Earth Day 1970—the Awakening. We were 3.6 billion then; today we are 6.5 billion—6.5 billion still sleepy souls. FotoFest, with its 2006 exhibition themes of *The Earth* and *Artists Responding to Violence*, is calling forth images to help evoke a Second Awakening.

Since founding Photocard International in 1993, my objective has been to capture images that emphasize the beauty, the humor, and the hope that can be drawn from our surroundings. The 2006 FotoFest exhibition has challenged me to take a look at the darker side, and so perhaps contribute to the greater good.

Michael McKann

Mother Earth has shaken our collective complacency with Hurricane Katrina. Its wave of destruction and subsequent torrent of media images have shaken the global psyche and set the stage for conscious and deliberate changes in how we treat our environment and its inhabitants. Photographers and artists must produce the images, subtle and not so subtle, to compel the sleepwalking masses to action.

MICHAEL MCKANN · *DUST TO DUST IN TIME*, 2005 · DIGITAL PHOTOGRAPH

AT PLAY

ARTISTS: AMY BLAKEMORE, KENNY BRAUN, RAY CARRINGTON III, KEITH CARTER, JEFF DEBEVEC, KAY DENTON, BEN DESOTO, STEPHEN DIRADO, DENNIS FAGAN, KIMBERLY GREMILLION, EARLIE HUDNALL, JR., MISTY KEASLER, PAULA WILLMOT KRAUS, GEORGE KRAUSE, O. RUFUS LOVETT, MINHTHU M. NGUYEN, TUONG NGUYEN, PIPO NGUYEN-DUY, MYLINH PHAM, PATRICIA RICHARDS, SAUL ROBBINS, KEN ROSENTHAL, ROBERT STRAUS, CHARLES VADOVIC, AND GEOFF WINNINGHAM
CURATOR: ANNE W. TUCKER

In Dennis Fagan's delightful image, the boy mirrors the gesture of the seal. With the glass barrier all but invisible between the two, we witness a tender moment of interspecies communication and connection.

Play is an activity that can be organized or spontaneous, solitary or group, indoors or outside, sedentary or active. To get away from regular duties and relax at play is vital to our mental and physical well-being. Play is also the wellspring of human creativity. The exhibition *At Play* presents a diverse range of photographs capturing children and grown-ups in leisure activities, games, or imaginative playacting.

The Methodist Hospital Center for Performing Arts Medicine is dedicated to the treatment and research of injuries and conditions affecting performing artists, and to providing education regarding preventive measures and healthy practices that can prolong careers. The goal of its Healing Arts exhibition series is to provide experiences for the viewer that may inspire the mind, uplift the spirit, and soothe the soul.

There is an undeniable relationship between the arts and healing, and making a connection between the mind and body aids in the healing process. Current research supports patient involvement with the healing process through art therapy, meditation, breath work, visualization, and other therapeutic modalities. Hospital staff, patients, their families, and visitors all benefit from this important visual art series.

Anne W. Tucker and Aline D. Wilson

Dennis Fagan · *Seal Boy*. 2003/2005 · Inkjet Print · Courtesy of the Museum of Fine Arts, Houston

DU MONDE DANS LE MONDE

ARTIST: BRIAN AFTANAS

Du monde dans le monde examines the transitory nature of existence: how generations come and go from within Paris and how Parisian monuments and infrastructure transcend the generations that created them. Cathedrals outlast roads, which outlast trees, which outlast graffiti, which outlasts café talk. In Paris, there are marks on the earth that are 2,000 years old.

Brian Aftanas.

BRIAN AFTANAS · *CHILD IN PARK, PARIS—MARCH 2000* · SILVER GELATIN PRINT

OPEN WINDOWS

Looking into Metaphors

ARTIST: NAN DICKSON

Great literature opens windows with words through which to view life. It achieves many of its effects by means of metaphors and other literary figures. For example, a vine and its branches, a lost coin, a shepherd, a house built on sand, or a sparrow that falls to its death all have metaphorical resonance beyond their actual being. These and other figures of speech have been highly influential in understanding aspects of human life common to all cultures. They prompt readers to create mental images. What might an artist's photographic images contribute to grasping these common metaphors? That is a question this exhibition explores.

Dorian Coover-Cox

NAN DICKSON · *IDOLS CAST AWAY*, 1994 · SILVER GELATIN PHOTOGRAPH

GROUP SHOW

**ARTISTS: TRICIA MCFARLIN, MARY MURREY,
MONIQUE RIJNKELS, AND SHEILA SHAW**

Mary Murrey · *Dinnertime with Dad*, 1998 · Selenium-toned Silver Gelatin Print

Tricia McFarlin · *Self-Portrait in Woods*,
2005 · Selenium-toned Silver Gelatin Print

Monique Rijnkels · *Untitled*, from the *Light
Within* series, 2001 · Silver Gelatin Print

SHEILA SHAW · *UNTITLED (FOUR HATS)*, 2005 · OIL-TONED SILVER GELATIN PHOTOGRAPHS

6

CORPORATE
SPACES

CORPORATE SPACES

DANGER PAY

A Female Photojournalist in the Middle East

ARTIST: CAROL SPENCER

My sister Carol Spencer wrote: "I'm anxious about how my pictures could be used by *Newsweek*, about how this conflict will be oversimplified. The more I am exposed to the complexities of the Middle East, the more I find the situations, which have been turned into media events, defying stereotypical photographic representation. I think about the connections between 'the story' and the manner in which real people are constructed or contrived in photographs; how images that purport to have captured real life can be used by the mass media to perpetuate a specific way of looking at the world; and how the lives of people seen through the camera's lens have become a commodity for the international news media. You learn to toughen up, expect less, and notice more, until one day the madness of an unpredictable moment blurs your sure-shot vision, and suddenly you ask yourself: 'What am I doing here? What the hell am I doing?' Everything's negotiable at the right price, even life. 'Danger pay,' the invoice says. Double day rate—a photographer's war zone value."

Carol's writing and photographs chronicle the refugee camps of the Gaza strip before, during, and after the *intifada*, record historic meetings between world leaders, cover the hijacking at sea of the *Achille Lauro*, and provide profiles of dignitaries such as Yassar Arafat, Anwar Sadat, and King Hussein of Jordan. The violence and turmoil Carol witnessed in the Middle East in the 1980s and 1990s has its repercussions today. After photographing a PLO training camp for children in 1986, she wrote, "Where will they be in seventeen years' time?" That time is now.

Ellen Spencer Susman

CAROL SPENCER · *DANCE TROUPE,* JORDAN, 1989 · COLOR TRANSPARENCY · COURTESY OF ELLEN SPENCER SUSMAN

COEXISTENCE

ARTISTS: MARK BAGGE AND DAVID ROMER

C*oexistence* is a two-person exhibition showcasing works by Dorian Romer and Mark Bagge that illustrate a harmonious existence between humans and nature. These photographers' quiet, contemplative, minimal compositions depict natural settings indicative of dreamscapes. Each image offers the viewer an immediate escape into what seems to be a world of dreams.

While alluding to the emotions of fleeting moments, Romer's work also references the nineteenth-century Romantic tradition of depicting the sublime in nature. She is able to capture these transcendental qualities by observing and internalizing her ephemeral experience of the outer world. Her play with focus creates a blurring effect that gives a surreal quality to her compositions, making our eyes doubt the reality she portrays. Bagge's abstracted representations of the landscape reveal a similar distortion. His soft-focus compositions are engulfed in a haze that appears to freeze the natural cycle. This body of work speaks of the fragility of nature and the importance of preserving our planet.

Catalina Montaño,
Kinzelman Art Consulting, Houston

This exhibition has been organized for FOTOFEST2006 by Kinzelman Art Consulting on behalf of Trammell Crow Company.

MARK BAGGE · *UNTITLED*, FROM THE *EARTH, KYOTO* SERIES, 2005 · GICLÉE PRINT

Dorian Romer · *Untitled*, from *Earth* series, 2005 · C-print

WORK, WATER + LAND = FOOD

ARTISTS: oliver

Oliver's work reflects a desire to see thee beauty of the world. He also enjoys playing with new tools, which he believes are part of the future of photography. This artwork started as a standard analog picture taken with an old Olympus camera. Enjoy!

Lisa Kilroy

OLIVER · *COWBARN (SV17)*, 2003 · ARCHIVAL ART CANVAS AND PIGMENT INK

RED

ARTISTS: ANGELA SNEED AND NANCY MAHLEY

After knowing each other for five years, Nancy Mahley and Angela Sneed began a collaboration based on their common perceptions and life experiences. This has been an ongoing project since 2002 in addition to their individual work. *Red* depicts the reconciliation of fears and violence with reality. Archetypal and actual violence bombards us daily, even if we only turn on our televisions or read our newspapers. There is no escape but only acts of recognizing and reconciling. The artists created the large format photographs using a studio setting and printed them in the Ilfochrome process to accentuate the saturation of red. Individual images from the series have been exhibited in group shows at the Glassell School of Art, the Museum of Fine Arts, Houston.

Angela Sneed

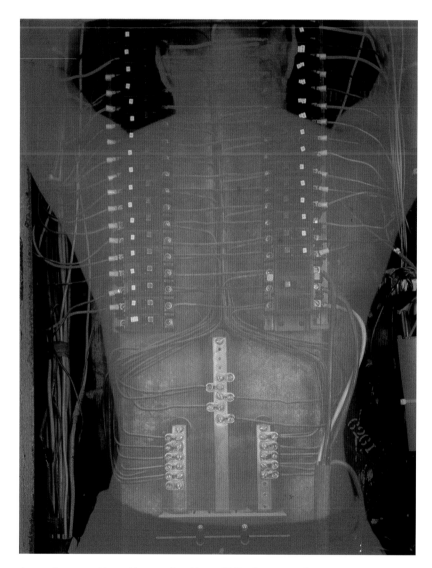

Angela Sneed and Nancy Mahley · *Raw Nerves*, 2003 · Ilfochrome Photograph

ARTIST STUDIOS

ARTIST STUDIOS

CONSCIOUSNESS AS RESPONSE TO VIOLENCE

ARTIST: MICHAEL JULIAN BERZ

As an artist and a photographer, I look at the world around me with wonder. I seek to capture the energy of my subjects in a way that dissolves all issues of rightness and wrongness.

Since 9/11, my life and my photography have identified best with the idea of living from the question. I now have the awareness that within every moment I have a choice. That choice is to live from the question instead of from the answer. I am acutely aware of the consciousness within all things that surround me. In response to the violence I perceive increasing on and against our planet, I now use my pictures as a signpost.

Could there be another choice for all of us who live on planet Earth? What if we were able to perceive how much caring we truly had to offer one another? What if we were able to perceive the consciousness in the plants, animals, and the Earth? Could we in full conscious awareness continually destroy ourselves, our neighbors, and our Earth? Is it possible to be fully aware and conscious, and still create wars, famine, and the pollution of our oceans and skies?

How much do we separate ourselves from our true being if we say: I AM American; I AM German; This is MY country; This is MY history. Does the river cease to flow when it reaches the border of another country? Does pollution in the air of one nation stop at the border because people have agreed to divide themselves in this manner?

Does Nature follow human ideas or does Nature follow a course of its own? How many rules and regulations of life have we created as our reality? How long will it take for us to become aware that life is a continuous flow of energy and matter? How can we assist the planet in recovering from the patterns of violence and overconsumption?

These are some of the ideas I wish to express with my videos and photos. What would it take to create more peace, joy and ease in our daily lives?

Michael Julian Berz

Michael Julian Berz · *B no. 1*, 2005 · Digital File

SOLVE ET COAGULA

ARTIST: SUZANNE M. MANNS

The memorial garden I planted in 1993 serves as my sanctuary, an extension of my studio, and the source of my images. I conceived the installation *Tabula Rosa* in 2003 as an antidote to the intense turmoil and sense of massive loss that had gripped us all since 9/11 and had been exacerbated by the beginning of the war in Iraq.

The opposite of a tabula rasa, or blank slate, the installation uses large-scale images to contend with these larger issues, a development from serving personal themes to addressing communal needs. To create the installation, I amassed digital photographs of the garden as murals and floor pieces. The roses in the murals had been captured at the peak of their color and form, a delightful, reassuring, even overwhelming opulence, unwittingly marking the beginning of their senescence. I placed the images of fallen leaves directly on the floor, and the two-part sky image flanked the exit, simultaneously suggesting the beginning and the end. Then I provided a single, large, color-coordinated ottoman on which viewers could contemplate the continuum of the cycle, rest, and be restored.

I created the exhibition *Solve et Coagula*, dedicated to my mother, Rose, who died in February 2005, for FotoFest 2006. Generated by *Tabula Rosa*, it combines excerpts from that installation with new elements, both visual and technical, that together continue to investigate natural cycles and the duality of permanence and evanescence.

Suzanne M. Manns

SUZANNE M. MANNS · *TABULA ROSA (DETAIL)*, 2004 · INKJET ON TYVEK, FABRIC, AND ACRYLIC

DOWN TO EARTH

ARTISTS: MEMBERS OF THE ASMP HOUSTON CHAPTER

A merican Society of Media Photographers (ASMP) is the premier organization for professional photographers whose images are largely used for publication.

ASMP Houston Chapter

HALL PUCKETT, NASH BAKER, JOHN SMALLWOOD, BRUCE SENIOR, JIM CALDWELL, BERYL STRIEWSKI AND PAM FRANCIS – ASMP HOUSTON CHAPTER MEMBERS

THE SPACE BETWEEN

ARTISTS: JEROME CROWDER, DAVID VAUGHAN AND RODNEY WATERS

The photographs of Jerome Crowder, David Vaughan, and Rodney Waters explore the beauty and meaning of ongoing relationships that affect their lives. Space exists in many forms—physical, spiritual, psychological, emotional, and cultural. It is only by reaching across these spaces that we are able to create lasting bonds with the people that share our lives and hearts. In a group of images made between 1995 and 2005, visual anthropologist Jerome Crowder has reflected upon his friendship with Alvaro Mamani Quispe, a migrant worker living in El Alto, Bolivia. Documenting his life's work, David Vaughan's photographs of personal relationships merge the mundane with the archetypal. Rodney Waters's portraits and audio recordings of HIV-positive individuals reveal their struggles with the disease that has permanently changed the space between them and the world around them.

Jerome Crowder, David Vaughan and Rodney Waters

RODNEY WATERS · *MARLENE*, 2005 · SILVER GELATIN PHOTOGRAPH · COURTESY OF AIDS FOUNDATION HOUSTON, INC.

Jerome Crowder · *Alvaro washes his newborn son*, 1997 · C-print

David Vaughan · *Lloyd said that he had been true to Linda for sixteen years....*1998 · Lambda Print

NEW WORK AND RESPONSE TO VIOLENCE

ARTISTS: MICHELE GRINSTEAD AND NANCY O'CONNOR

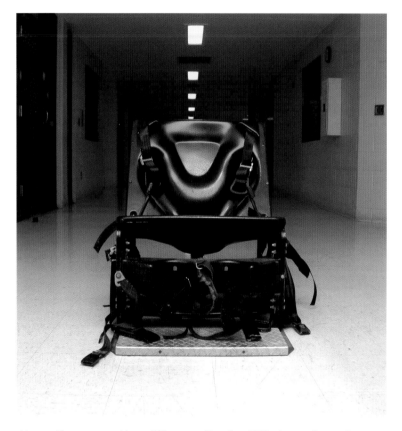

MICHELE GRINSTEAD AND NANCY O'CONNOR · *TIME OUT*, 2005 · LAMBDA PRINT · COURTESY
OF AIDS FOUNDATION HOUSTON, INC.

ELEMENTS

ARTISTS: DEBRA BOYLAN, FARRAH BRANIFF, JEROME CROWDER, JAMES DILGER, JR., LINDA GILBERT, GERALDINE GILL, RUTH HEIKKILA, ANTHONY PALASOTA, CHARLOTTE RANDOLPH, ROYCE ANN SLINE, CAROL STEVENS, DAVID VAUGHAN, LINDA WALSH, RODNEY WATERS, DAVID WILLIAMS AND DOROTHY LAM WONG

El-e-ment

1. any of the four substances (earth, air, fire, and water) believed to constitute all physical matter

2. any of these four substances thought of as a natural habitat or environment for a class of living things

3. a natural environment for a person or thing, as "being in (or out of) one's element"

4. a basic contributing part that is essential to the nature of a concept or group

Dorothy Lam Wong and Linda Gilbert

RUTH HEIKKILA, JAMES DILGER, JR., ROYCE ANN SLINE, DOROTHY LAM WONG, LINDA GILBERT, JEROME CROWDER, GERALDINE GILL, DAVID WILLIAMS, DAVID VAUGHAN · *ELEMENTS COLLAGE*, 2006 · DIGITAL PRINT

CRITICAL MASS

ARTISTS: CRAIG J. BARBER, STEVEN BENSON, F&D CARTIER, DAVID MAISEL, JONATHAN MOLLER, A. LEO NASH, MORTEN NILSSON, LORI NIX, ABBY ROBINSON AND MAGGIE TAYLOR

This extraordinary exhibition of the work of ten nationally and internationally known mid-career and established visual artists is organized by Photolucida of Portland, Oregon, and presented in Houston by Caslin Gregory & Associates. The work ranges from straight black and white photographs to platinum prints to digital color inkjet prints, and it encompasses the full range of fine art and documentary traditions. The exhibition features some of the best work being created in contemporary photography today. The featured artists include Craig J. Barber, Woodstock, New York; Steven Benson, Lake Orion, Michigan; f&d cartier, Bienne, Switzerland; David Maisel, Sausalito, California; Jonathan Moller, Denver; A. Leo Nash, Oakland, California; Morten Nilsson, Bronshoj, Denmark; Lori Nix, Brooklyn, New York; Abby Robinson, New York; and Maggie Taylor, Gainesville, Florida.

For Photolucida's first annual juried competition, fifty curators from the U.S. and abroad selected ten artists from a pool of over six hundred submissions. These final ten received the highest number of "top choice" nominations from the curators. This exhibition supports Photolucida's mission to increase our understanding of the world through photography and to promote an in-depth, informed, and supportive dialogue among photographers and nonprofit, commercial, and corporate galleries and publishers.

Jean Caslin
Caslin Gregory & Associates, Houston

Jean Caslin was among the fifty curators involved in the selection process for *Critical Mass*. For more information, contact Caslin Gregory & Associates at 713-864-1563 or email caslingregory@gmail.com.

A. Leo Nash · *Vaca Mirrorage*, from the series *The Black Rock Desert Project*, 1997 · Giclée Print

UNIVERSITY OF HOUSTON SPRING 2006 BFA CANDIDATES

ARTISTS: ADAM BAKER, SEBASTIAN BERALDI, JOHNATHAN BRUDER, CARISSA DELACERDA, JOHNNY DIBLASI, KARA DUVAL, HOPE EUGENE, MEI-MEI LIEM, JOHN LUCAS, PAIGE MAJKO, BILLIE JEAN HIGNIGHT, CONNILEE LUSK, MARCUS MEDELLIN, BRANDY STOESZ, JAKE TOLER AND FABIOLA VALENCIA

This student show invites viewers to become acquainted with a diverse body of work from sixteen talented emerging artists. Work ranges from traditional black and white photography to mixed media and video.

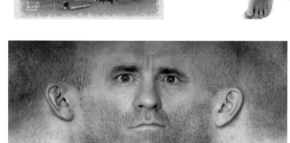

Photos by University of Houston Spring 2006 BFA Students

8

RETAIL, COMMERCIAL AND RESTAURANT SPACES

RETAIL, COMMERCIAL AND RESTAURANT SPACES

JUST VISITING

Amber Eagle, Paula Goldman, Robert Ziebell

ARTIST: AMBER EAGLE, PAULA GOLDMAN, ROBERT ZIEBELL

These three artists work with the artifice of the "real" world. Amber Eagle creates dioramas from spun sugar and other edible materials, and then photographs them. The photographs are documents of an entirely constructed environment, fabricated in natural materials. Paula Goldman examines the strange surrealism of the everyday natural world, captured in moments against artificial constructs. Robert Ziebell explores habits of mind in art-historically aware compositions: arrangements of natural elements elicite-motionally charged responses to ostensibly neutral materials. All three artists remind us that it is a very strange planet we live on—and, even then, we're only visiting.

Cecily E. Horton

AMBER EAGLE · *UNTITLED*, 2005 · C-PRINT

ROBERT ZIEBELL · *OXBOW*, 2005 · ENDURA METALLIC PRINT

PAULA GOLDMAN · *NATURE (BROMELIAD)*, 2005 · DYE SUBLIMATION PRINT

HECHO EN EL BARRIO

ARTISTS: FRANCISCO BLASCO, DANTÉ RODRIGUEZ AND ALFONSO VASQUEZ

ALFONSO VASQUEZ · *LITTLE MEXICO # 1*, 2005 · SILVER GELATIN PRINT · COURTESY OF CASA RAMIREZ, MACARIO AND CHRISSIE DICKERSON RAMIREZ

For twenty-four years, Richard Reyes, a.k.a. Pancho Claus, has worked with youth at risk of gang membership in the East End barrios, joining with Talento Bilingue de Houston (TBH) to provide performing and visual arts programs for underprivileged youth. Reyes created the Pancho Claus character, a Latino cultural icon, in 1981 for a Christmas Eve stage performance. The colorful barrio figure in a red zoot suit has delivered toys from low-rider cars for the past twelve years, while also delivering a value-based message specifically for at-risk youth.

In 2003, to the dismay of many in the community, the TBH board changed the center's course, dismissed Reyes as executive director, and dropped the programs for at-risk neighborhood youth. Reyes, however, continues to impact these youth year round through his Pancho Claus Art & Education Project, conducted in coordination with the nonprofit group Multicultural Education and Counseling through the Arts (MECA) and with Harris County Precinct 6 Constable Victor Treviño's office. Reyes is highly respected by community service providers for his persistent focus on providing opportunities for barrio youth. He has steered several to successful careers in the performing arts. A current effort provides important youth services to those from Clayton Homes housing and Little Mexico, one of Houston's poorest barrios, each within a few blocks of the TBH center.

Casa Ramirez is pleased to present *Hecho en El Barrio*, photo documentation of the community activities of Richard Reyes and the Houston barrios in which he works.

Macario and Chrissie Dickerson Ramirez

TOY JOY

ARTIST: MICHELLE BATES, CYNTHIA BATMANIS, WADE BEALS, KIMBERLY BERBA, TIMOTHY BERG, LAURA BURLTON, SUSAN BURNSTINE, LAURA BURLTON, MATT CALLOW, JEAN CASLIN, SHANTI CHANG, RYAN DANIELS, HAZEL DOONEY, GRANT EDWARDS, D. CLARKE EVANS, JOHN FULBRIGHT, TINKER GREENE, DIANE GRIFFIN GREGORY, EMILY GROSS, NICOLAI GROSSMAN, MATT HALL, WARREN HAROLD, ROBERT HOLMGREN, MIKAS KALINAUSKAS, JAN KAPOOR, CAROL SANDIN KELLY, BOB KUBIAK, JOCELYN MATHEWES, KYLE MERCER, JEREMY MOORE, CREED O'HANLON, BECKY PENDEL, VALYN PERINI, LINH PHAM, CHRICEL PORTELA, JOHN REEVES, FRANCISCO MATA ROSAS, KATIE CLARK SLICK, ROYCE ANN SLINE, EDIE STAVINOHA, GORDON STETTINIUS, RYAN STODDART, ANN TEXTER, LARRY TREADWAY, CANDICE TRIPP, BILL VACCARO, MARCO VITTUR, SHANNON WELLES, BARBARA WINDERMAN AND LU YI-CHUAN

LAURA BURLTON · *RABBIT QUEEN*, 2005 · SILVER GELATIN PRINT

Toy Joy is a juried show of work created with toy cameras by regional, national, and international artists. These toy cameras, which have names like Holga, Diana, Dorie, Snappy, and Click and Clack, are made of plastic with simple lenses and few, if any, adjustable features. The resulting images characteristically are blurry and have light leaks and other strange aberrations that most photographers would consider unacceptable. But photographers who use these cameras embrace their inherent flaws with zeal. The artistic vision of these photographers, combined with the optical properties of the toy cameras, can produce hauntingly beautiful, dreamlike images.

Laura Burlton

This show was organized by Laura Burlton and is presented in association with Green at London Hair Co. Thanks to photographer and educator Will Michels for jurying the exhibition.

YES, YOU ARE MOVING

ARTIST: MARK HIEBERT

Unlike other modes of utterance, photography is a transaction exchanging a moment in time for the expression of meaning, whether as declaration, statement, argument, or question. Among other things, we capture, through the mechanical process of image creation, a trace of being that points toward the always inexpressible notion of the whole: a fiction to stand in for the Real.

As something made unfinished, the captured instant is never the object of our desire—the Other we would like to hold, claim, or say is ours—but is the fine thread lashing us to the cause of our desire, the image that was never there.

Bringing together a series of photographs, *Yes, you are moving* explores being as the action of motion. As such, being is never encompassed within an exact or single moment: it cannot be uttered completely. As landscapes, the photographs enact a narrative about the relation between the viewer and the represented earth. In terms of analysis and rhetoric, these images seek to express the self and its relation to the world as something written in trajectories of motion and enacted in discourse—the diverse conversation the body engages in with the world outside it for the sake of existence. However, their first aim is to provide pleasure

The images presented here, made between 1990 and 2005, were captured in analog and printed digitally; however, I employed no additional modification or manipulation of the image files, except as regards color correction, burning, dodging, and other techniques that are also employed in traditional photographic printing.

Mark Hiebert

MARK HIEBERT · *HIGHWAY 99 (WEST OF HOUSTON) I.* 2004 · ARCHIVAL INKJET PRINT

TEXAS PHOTOGRAPHIC SOCIETY 21ST ANNUAL MEMBERS' ONLY SHOW

ARTISTS: JAMES B. ABBOTT, STEPHEN J. ALLEN, SUSAN BANK, LYNN BLANCHARD, GERHARD BOCK, AL BRADEN, BILL BRUZY, DOROTHY BURNS, JAY CALDERON, POLLY A.CHANDLER, RHONDA CHURCHILL, FAUSTINUS DERAET, PERRY DILBECK, JOHN EDWARDS, ROBERT L. FLAVIN, LINDA FOARD ROBERTS, PAUL FORD, JULIA FULLERTON-BATTEN, CANDACE PLUMMER GAUDIANI, JILL GEESLIN, MELODY SWANEY GOLDING, JOY GOLDKIND, PAUL A. GREENBERG, ROBERTO GUERRA, ROBIN RENEE HIX, LARRY E. JONES, SIRI KAUR, LAURIE KIDDER, KEN KONCHEL, JENNIFER LOOPER, JOYCE LOPEZ, DEDE LUSK, WILLY MACHAN, DAVE MARTINEZ, GABRIELLA NISSEN, ELIZABETH OPALENIK, WILLIE OSTERMAN, CRAIG PAYNE, KIM RIEGEL, LIZA WEEMS SAWYER, HOWARD SCHATZ, KAREN GORDON SCHULMAN, ANSEN SEALE, ROBERT SILANCE, CHAD SMITH, SHYLAH SMITHEY, ALINE SMITHSON, ROY SOTO, RITA D. SWINFORD, DEBORAH MILLS THACKREY, BECKWITH THOMPSON, CHAD WINDHAM AND JOYCE WOOLEMS

Texas Photographic Society is a nonprofit organization of amateur and professional photographers whose work reflects a broad spectrum of photographic interest and skills. It provides its members with educational, promotional, and exhibition opportunities, and creates and expands occasions for the public to experience contemporary photography. Founded in 1984, Texas Photographic Society has more than 1,300 active members who have come to Texas from forty-eight states and ten countries. Its website is www.texasphoto.org.

Richard Newman juried the 2006 show. He is an internationally known photographer and author based in Pacific Grove, California. He is also the education coordinator of Calumet Photographic Gallery. He has said, "I feel that Texas Photographic Society is the most progressive and responsible photo organization in the world, offering its membership the most information, services, and opportunities to have their work seen and appreciated by the world."

Here is an excerpt from a statement Newman wrote to photographers submitting work for the show: "When you are considering what to send in for this show, consider no further than sending me your best work. Make my responsibility as your juror really hard. Don't send images that you think will win; they won't. Send the images that you love, that keep you returning to your passion of photography, that stay in your mind, the ones that keep you up all night and torment you until you get them right. If you send those images, we will all be winners."

The show travels to Houston after its premiere in San Francisco at Calumet Photographic Gallery.

D. Clarke Evans
Texas Photographic Society President

NATALIE YOUNG · *GEORGIA & SABINE #12*, 2004 (FROM *TEXAS PHOTOGRAPHIC SOCIETY 20TH ANNUAL MEMBERS' ONLY SHOW*) · GELATIN SILVER PRINT

ELEMENTS

ON THE BEACH

ARTIST: PHILIP HAWKINS

ARTIST: REBECCA VILLARREAL

When we walk through our everyday lives, we frequently fail to see the brilliance of the earth around us. We get so sidetracked with jobs and money and activities that we don't pay attention to the complexity of the planet we inhabit. We perhaps miss seeing the natural environment that sustains us. My photography, through snapshots of simple things like moss or soil or a rock or a tree, gives the viewer an opportunity to pause and appreciate the beauty in our world. Each photograph captures a moment and a subject with the intent to draw the audience into nature. While the object focuses attention on the small and overlooked, it also hints at a more complex system. The framed images have the potential to pull the viewer into a deeper experience of the earth, instead of leaving us to focus solely on the surface of our everyday lives.

Philip Hawkins

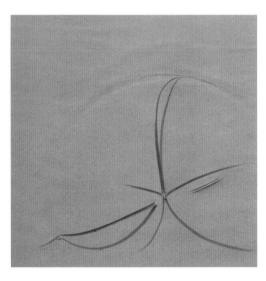

Rebecca Villarreal · *Grass in the Wind #1.* 2005 · Chromogenic Print

Philip Hawkins · *Lichen Dining on Granite at Enchanted Rock State Natural Area. Texas,* from the series *The Feast.* 2005 · Digital Photograph

LESLIE FIELDS: VISTAS

ARTIST: LESLIE FIELDS

Leslie Field · *Wonder—is not precisely knowing and not precisely knowing not*, 2005 ·
Archival Inkjet Print

FOTOFEST2006 PARTICIPATING SPACES NOT IN CATALOGUE

MUSEUMS

Contemporary Arts Museum Houston

Houston Museum of Natural Science

NON-PROFIT ART SPACES

ArtCar Museum

Buffalo Bayou Artpark

Stages Repertory Theatre

Talento Bilingüe De Houston

UNIVERSITY ART SPACES

Art Gallery at Houston Community College, Central

University of St. Thomas, Little Archaeology Gallery

The University of Texas Health Science Center
   at Houston Medical School

COMMERCIAL ART GALLERIES

DesignWorks

Fleury Gallery

Gallery Sonja Roesch

Goldesberry Gallery

Harris Gallery

Inman Gallery

Joan Wich & Co. Gallery

M² GALLERY

Peel Gallery

Rudolph Projects/Artscan Gallery

Seaside Gallery

NON-PROFIT ORGANIZATIONS

Heritage Society Museum

The Margolis Gallery, Congregation Beth Israel

Museum of Cultural Arts Houston (MOCAH)

Texas Accountants &Lawyers for the Arts (TALA)

X Nihilo

CORPORATE SPACES

Foley's

m Architects

Minnette Boesel Properties, Inc.

ARTIST STUDIOS

Art Factory

Commerce Street Artist Warehouse

RETAIL, COMMERCIAL AND RESTAURANT SPACES

6° LOUNGE

Camera Co/op

Clarks

Croissant Brioche

Dean's Credit Clothing

DesignWorks at Mod Coffee House

The Right Mix

Shutters

Tart Café

Artist & Curator Biographies

Bios Provided by Participating Spaces

ARTISTS

YOSHI ABE

Yoshi Abe received his B.F.A. from the San Francisco Art Institute in 2001. His work has been included in exhibitions throughout the U.S. as well as in Europe. He is represented by the Rena Bransten Gallery in San Francisco, where he currently resides.

BRIAN AFTANAS

Brian Aftanas is a well-traveled, documentary-style photographer. His work focuses on the aspects of modern human existence that transcend geographic location and the passage of time. His oeuvre is predominantly 35 mm, black and white street photography. Past projects have included documenting the streets of Atyrau, Kazakhstan; life in Luanda, Angola; and the shopping culture of Walnut Creek, California. He is current working on two projects: photographing the modern-day urban crush of downtown Lagos, Nigeria, and the morning commute in downtown San Francisco. He has exhibited in the U.S. and Japan, and has had photographs published in *Shutterbug, Shots*, and the *San Francisco Chronicle*. FotoFest 2006 is his sixth solo exhibition. Aftanas resides in the San Francisco Bay Area.

EIJA-LIISA AHTILA

Eija-Liisa Ahtila was born in Hämeenlinna, Finland, in 1959. She completed the Certificate Program in film, TV, theater, and multimedia studies at UCLA in 1995, and now lives and works in Helsinki. Recent solo exhibitions include shows at Berkeley Art Museum, California; Klemens Gasser & Tanja Grunert, Inc., New York; Museion, Bolzano, Italy; Dallas Museum of Contemporary Art; Tokyo Opera City Gallery; De Appel, Amsterdam; Dundee Contemporary Arts, Scotland; Kunsthalle Zurich; Tate Modern, London; Kiasma–Museum of Contemporary Art, Helsinki; the Art Gallery of Windsor, Ontario; Neue Nationalgalerie, Berlin; Salzburger Kunstverein, Austria; Museum of Contemporary Art, Chicago; Museum Fridericianum, Kassel, Germany; Kunsthaus Glarus, Switzerland; Gallery Arnolfini, Bristol, England; Klemens Gasser & Tanja Grunert, Cologne; Raum der aktuellen Kunst, Vienna; Gallery Roger Pailhas, Marseilles/Paris; Cable Gallery, Helsinki; and Gallery Index, Stockholm,. Her work was also included in Documenta 11, Kassel, Germany, and the 2002 Sydney Biennial, Australia.

JULIE BROOK ALEXANDER

Trained at Rice University, Houston, as an art teacher, combines photography with a variety of media. An original black and white photograph initiates the artistic process. She alters the photograph by hand, adding color, more of her images, and found objects. Alexander exhibits her work at Hooks-Epstein Galleries, where her solo exhibition, *Coloring Outside the Line*, was held in 2005. In addition, she participates in regional juried group shows in the Houston area, where she has received several awards.

KELLY GALE AMEN

Kelly Gale Amen, a graduate of the University of Oklahoma, Norman, started his own design business, KGA Inc., in 1974. He has been an influential participant in the Houston arts and design community for decades. He is a founding member of the American Society of Interior Designers and the American Society of Furniture Artists. In the 1990s, Kelly began creating his own art furniture to give voice to his personal vision. His furniture has been exhibited at Bering & James, Houston; GAIA, Havana; and Macon and Co, Atlanta. Kelly's *KGA Triple Benches* form a permanent installation in Houston's Shady Grove Victims Memorial at Eleanor Tinsley Park, and his *Memorial Bench* is in Houston's Bob Lanier Building.

DAVE ANDERSON

Dave Anderson has long been attracted to the undefined, almost uncanny feeling that can emanate from isolated objects and remote places. Though currently living in Little Rock, Arkansas, Anderson is a native of East Lansing, Michigan, and formerly a resident of New York City. His silver gelatin prints are in the collections of the Museum of Fine Arts, Houston, the Worcester Art Museum, Massachusetts, and private collector Todd Oldham.

BILL ARMSTRONG

Bill Armstrong is a New York–based fine art photographer who is well-known for his Infinity series, an extended body of blurred imagery that he has been working on since 1997. Armstrong is represented by galleries across the country and in Europe. His work has been exhibited in numerous museum shows, including exhibitions at the Smithsonian Institution, Washington, D.C.; Fogg Art Museum, Cambridge, Massachusetts; Southeast Museum of Photography, Daytona Beach, Florida; and DeCordova Museum and Sculpture Park, Lincoln, Massachusetts. His work is in many museum collections, including those of the Museum of Fine Arts, Houston; Brooklyn Museum, New York; Santa Barbara Museum of Art, California; Musée de l'Elysée, Lausanne, Switzerland; and Bibliothèque nationale de France, Paris. Armstrong's work is published in many venues, including *Exploring Color Photography* by Robert Hirsch (Dubuque: Wm. C. Brown Co., 1988). Armstrong was the photographer chosen to be featured in *House and Garden's* color issue for 2005. www.billarmstrongphotography.com/index.html.

MIKE BAGGE (no bio provided)

SUSAN BANK

Born in Portsmouth, New Hampshire, in 1938, Susan Bank received a B.A. from Barnard College and a M.A. from Villanova University. In addition, she studied with Mary Ellen Mark in Oaxaca, Mexico. She has exhibited extensively in the U.S., as well as in Cuba. She is currently living in Philadelphia.

SUZANNE BANNING

Suzanne Banning was born in 1973 in Hengelo, Overijssel, The Netherlands. Since 2000, she has lived and worked in Houston. In 1998, she graduated from the Hogeschool voor de kunsten Arnhem [Academy of Art Arnhem], The Netherlands, with a B.F.A. in photography and printmaking. Banning's award-winning work is very experimental. Among other things, she plays with the unlimited possibilities of her camera in combination with movement. A crucial element in her process is her habit of fueling herself through her favorite music, mostly Tori Amos, while shooting pictures. She dances and sings and bathes herself in waves of sound that take her to her creative source. Banning's work has been featured in many shows in Houston, the U.S., and internationally. Jurors who have selected her work include Dan Cameron, Gus and Sharon Kopriva, Dominic Molon, James Rondeau, Jackson Rushing, and Clint Willour. Her work was recently acquired by the Art Museum of South Texas, Corpus Christi.

CRAIG BARBER

Craig Barber, known for his provocative landscape photographs and recognized as one of today's premier platinum printers, has shown his work in more than sixty solo exhibitions. His work is represented in numerous public and private collections, including the George Eastman House, Rochester, New York; Museum of Fine Arts, Houston; Victoria & Albert Museum, London; Chrysler Museum, Norfolk, Virginia; Museum of New Mexico, Santa Fe; Minneapolis Institute of Arts; Portland Art Museum, Portland, Maine; Brooklyn Museum of Art, New York; and Bibliothèque Nationale de France, Paris. Barber lives in New York's Hudson Valley and teaches at photography workshops throughout the U.S. and Europe.

DEBORAH BAY

Deborah Bay of Houston is a photographer whose work is based on the imagined realities she constructs from the detritus of Cyber culture. She has studied with Peter Brown, Keith Carter, and the faculty at the Glassell School of Art, Museum of Fine Arts, Houston. Her work is in the collection of the Museum of Fine Arts, Houston. She has a background in public affairs and is a former university administrator.

STEVEN BENSON

Steven Benson received his B.F.A. from the College for Creative Studies in Detroit and an M.F.A. from Cranbrook Academy of Art in Bloomfield Hills, Michigan. His work has been exhibited internationally, including a solo exhibition at the Centre Georges Pompidou in Paris. He is a recipient of three Creative Artists Grants from the Michigan Council for the Arts and a National Endowment for the Arts/Arts Midwest Regional Fellowship. His photographs are represented in numerous permanent collections, including those of the Detroit Institute of Art; Bibliothèque nationale de France, Paris; and Centre Georges Pompidou, Paris. He has presented many lectures at venues that include the People's University of China in Beijing and the 1988 and 2000 national conferences of the Society for Photographic Education. In November 2004, his work was the subject of a thirty-year retrospective, *Steven Benson: Thirty Years in Black and White*, in Paris during Le Mois de al Photo. He has been a freelance photographer and teacher for twenty-five years.

ROBERT BERLIN

In her book *On Photography*, Susan Sontag suggested that reality is fundamentally "unclassifiable casual fragments." [Susan Sontag, *On Photography* (New York: Farrar, Straus and Giroux, 1977].This sense of the indefinable is central to Robert Berlin's

current body of work. Here nature, both urban and rural, exists as fragmented cultural spheres, where personal moments and public spaces intertwine, sometimes violently. Viewers are encouraged to examine the depicted scene as a series of events rather than as a fixed moment in time and space. Berlin's work, which is rapidly gaining the attention of an international audience, is an extension of the already blurred relationship between photography and painting. The unique technique he has developed allows him to transfer the dyes of color photography directly onto aluminum sheets. He maintains the integrity of the original image, but can combine the glow and luminosity of the aluminum with the transparency of the photo dyes. Toronto-based Berlin has a background as a painter, sculptor, and photographer. He lives and works in Canada, the U.S., Singapore, Malaysia, and Spain.

JOHN BERNHARD

John Bernhard has been pursuing the art of photography for more than twenty years. His work has won numerous awards and has been exhibited and published throughout the U.S. and Europe. In addition, his photographs are in museums and private collections. Bernhard's work was included in *Body Work* (2001) a 120-year survey of photographs of the nude that focused on the work of twelve photographers from the permanent collection of the Minneapolis Institute of Arts. He has published six books, including *Nudes Metamorphs* (Houston: Emco Press, 2000), a compilation of seven years' work focusing on nude bodies and transformations using elements of the earth; *Polo Watercolor Series* (Houston: DeFrog Gallery, 2002), a compilation of thirteen years' work from when he was the official photographer of polo tournaments in Houston; and *Nicaragua—A Journey to Remember* (Houston: The Nicaraguan Children Texas Benefit Fund, 2002), a reflection of his travels to Nicaragua that expresses his strong social concerns. His most recent book, *Diptych* (Houston: Elite Editions, 2004), emphasizes the correlation of two images with the visual duplicity of resembling forms. He recently had a retrospective exhibition of his work at the Musée des Suisses dans le Monde in his native city of Geneva. Bernhard resides in Houston, where he has designed and built his studio and art gallery.

MICHAEL JULIAN BERZ

Born in 1969 in Ontario, Canada, Michael Julian Berz grew up with his brother. They and their mother split their time between Austria and Germany. At twenty, he attended Universität Wien, where he studied journalism as well as political science. In August 2001, he became a correspondent for Austrian televi-

sion, reporting and filming arts and culture programs from New York City. Berz began documenting the 9/11 attack on the Twin Towers within hours of the event. He worked with filmmaker Deborah Shaffer, who directed the film *From The Ashes—Ten Artists* and co-directed the film *From The Ashes—Epilogue*, both presenting a profile of ten downtown artists and their experiences on September 11. The films were presented at many sites in America and Europe, including Robert Redford's Sundance Film Festival, Park City, Utah; Global Peace Film Festival 2002, Orlando, Florida; Diagonale 2002, Graz, Austria; Robert De Niro's Tribeca Film Festival 2002 and 2003, New York; and *Unplugged: Art as the Scene of Global Conflicts*, Ars Electronica 2002, Linz, Austria. HBO/Cinemax purchased the films for distribution in the U.S. Berz also worked closely with artist Nancy Burson, assisting her in the filming of certain unnatural and unexplainable phenomenon while she was compiling her first book, *Focus: How Your Energy Can Change the World* (New York: Simon and Schuster, 2004).

FRANCISCO BLASCO

Francisco Blasco has extensive experience in photography and the visual arts, both as an instructor and as an artist. He received his B.F.A. from The School of the Art Institute of Chicago and currently works for the Houston Independent School District.

BETH BLOCK

Beth Block was born in Houston and received her B.A. from Sarah Lawrence College, Bronxville, New York, and her M.F.A. from the School of Visual Arts, New York City. She currently lives and works in New York. Her work was recently exhibited at the Harry Ransom Center Galleries at The University of Texas at Austin. Block has exhibited in New York, Los Angeles, Germany, and Houston. She has been included in the Print Collector's Program at the Houston Center for Photography and her work has appeared in several international publications. Her photographs are included in the collections of the Museum of Fine Arts, Houston, The University of Texas at Austin's Harry Ransom Center, and private collectors.

DEBRA BOYLAN

Debra Boylan, a seven-year resident of Houston, has studied photography at Rice University, Houston, with Carol Vuchetich and Fraser Stables. She has exhibited in numerous local shows and travels extensively in search of new images. This is her first time exhibiting during FotoFest.

FARRAH BRANIFF

Professional portrait photographer Farrah Braniff received her B.F.A. in photography from the San Francisco Art Institute and a M.Ed. in counseling from the University of Houston. She has taught photography at the High School for the Performing and Visual Arts, Episcopal High School, and Emery Weiner School, all in Houston. Braniff's current project is a photo documentary about sexual assault, inspired by her volunteer counseling of domestic violence and sexual assault survivors at the Houston Area Women's Center. She maintains a professional photography studio in Houston, focusing on portraits of families, children, and babies. She has two boys, Sayer, two, and Finnian, six months.

BYRON BRAUCHLI

In his series of photogravure and plastic camera imagery, Byron Brauchli explores the religious pilgrimages undertaken in commemoration of the three annunciations by the Virgin of Guadalupe to Juan Diego. Participating in the pilgrimages from the small Veracruz town of Jalacingo on numerous occasions since 2002, Brauchli has become familiar with not only the ride but the participants as well, allowing him a closer look at this age-old tradition. This series gives the viewer an opportunity to step beyond the Virgin as traditional religious iconography and see her for the representation of present-day political/social reality that she is in modern Mexico.

ELINA BROTHERUS

Elina Brotherus was born in Helsinki in 1972. She received her M.A. in photography from the University of Art and Design Helsinki in 2000 and a M.S. in analytic chemistry from the University of Helsinki in 1997. She lives and works in Helsinki and in France. She has had solo exhibitions at The Wapping Project, London; Galleri Stefan Andersson, Umeå, Sweden; Photography Gallery Hippolyte, Helsinki; Fotografisk Center, Copenhagen; Chateau d'eau, Toulouse, France; Kunsthalle Lophem, Bruges, Belgium; Festival Foto-Encuentros, Murcia, Spain; Hämeenlinna Art Museum, Finland; Västeras Art Museum, Sweden; Lund Art Hall, Sweden; Botanical Gardens, Madrid; INOVA (Institute of Visual Art), Milwaukee; gb agency, Paris; Encontros de Fotografia, Coimbra, Portugal; and Finnish Museum of Photography, Helsinki.

DAVID BROWN

David Brown resides with his family in Houston, where he works as an artist and as the founding director of Spacetaker.Org /Culture Arts Guide. A graduate of the University of Houston with a B.F.A. in sculpture and digital media, he is best recognized for his innovative work in photography. Brown has shown his work in Houston at the Axiom, Commerce Street Artist's Warehouse, and the FotoFest exhibition *Photography in Houston Galleries*. During FotoFest 2006, Brown will show his work in the solo exhibition *It's All Plastic* at the Deborah Colton Gallery and in the group exhibition *Urban Cathedral* at DiverseWorks Art Space. Brown's works are in many major private collections.

PETER BROWN

Peter Brown is an award-winning photographer based in Houston, where he teaches at Rice University. His career, spanning more than thirty years, has led to numerous monographs, exhibitions, and awards. His work is collected throughout the U.S., including The Museum of Modern Art, New York; the Museum of Fine Arts, Houston; the San Francisco Museum of Modern Art; and the Amon Carter Museum, Fort Worth, among others. Brown has published monographs that include *Seasons of Light* (Houston: Rice University Press, 1988), winner of an Imogen Cunningham Award, and *On the Plains* (New York: W. W. Norton, 1999), the result of a twelve-year journey across the Dakotas, Nebraska, Kansas, Oklahoma, Wyoming, Montana, Colorado, New Mexico, and Texas. He was recently awarded the 2005 Dorothea Lange–Paul Taylor Prize by the Center for Documentary Studies at Duke University, Durham, North Carolina, to complete *High Plains*, a collaboration with writer Kent Haruf.

JOAN BUELING

Joan Bueling, raised in North Dakota, and Jerry Herring, from Iowa, have been taking photographic road trips together for the past six years. Bueling is an accomplished photographer who manages Dakota Framing and Photography, where she consults with corporate art collectors and provides turnkey framing services. Herring is a graphic designer and publisher by trade, having established Herring Design in 1973 and Herring Press in 1984. Their work is in many private and corporate collections, and has been widely published.

SPARKY CAMPANELLA

Sparky Campanella has been a photographer all of his life, creating images with a refined absence of content that leave room for interpretation and expansion. His work reflects a dichotomous life, notably a career switch from software marketing to fine art photography. He has exhibited in galleries across the country and his images are in the homes of many private collectors. Campanella has also been commissioned for several public art installations, including a large-scale exhibition of his conceptual portraits made at Burning Man 2003, Gerlach, Nevada. Campanella is represented by Gallery 825 in Los Angeles and maintains studio space in New York City. His work can be seen online at www.campanella.com.

KEITH CARTER

Keith Carter is an internationally recognized photographer and educator. He is the recipient of the Lange-Taylor Prize from The Center for Documentary Studies at Duke University in Durham, North Carolina, and two Regional Survey Grants from the National Endowment for the Arts. He holds the endowed Walles Chair of Art at Lamar University in Beaumont, Texas. In 1998, he received the two highest honors given to faculty there: The University Professor Award and The Distinguished Faculty Lecturer Award. He has been the subject of a profile on "CBS Sunday Morning." Carter's haunting and enigmatic photographs have appeared in over ninety solo exhibitions in thirteen countries around the world. Eight monographs of his work have been published to date. His photographs are in many permanent collections, including those of the George Eastman House, Rochester, New York; The Art institute of Chicago; Smithsonian American Art Museum, Washington, D.C.; San Francisco Museum of Modern Art; and the Wittliff Collection at Texas State University, San Marcos.

FRANÇOISE AND DANIEL CARTIER (F&D CARTIER)

Françoise and Daniel Cartier (f&d cartier) work without a camera, creating one-of-a-kind photograms by placing an object directly on light-sensitive paper and exposing it to natural light. While developing the gelatin silver paper, they consciously mishandle the chemistry to produce their signature rose-toned work. Symbolizing the "absent body," f&d cartier's photograms both reflect on gender roles and conjure thoughts of intimacy. By recording feminine objects, such as Barbie clothes in the series *Someday*, f&d cartier investigate the emphasis that commercial culture places on exterior beauty, the idealization of the female image, and the role of dress as a social indicator. In another series, *Boys Do Not Cry*, images of delicate handkerchiefs bring to mind the societal restrictions of gender. Their work was featured at the Houston Center for Photography during FotoFest 2004, through a Creativity Grant from the National Endowment for the Arts. Their work is in public and private collections, such as those of the Museum of Fine Arts Houston; Musée de l'Elysée, Lausanne, Switzerland; Swiss Foundation of Photography, Winterthur; Kunstsammlung F. Hoffmann–La Roche AG, Basel, Switzerland; and Museet for Fotokunst Odense, Denmark. Their work has been exhibited throughout the U.S., Mexico, and Europe. Yossi Milo Gallery, New York, represents them in the U.S. Roses, a book illustrating their work from the past ten years, will be published in 2006 by Niggli Editions, Niederteufen, Switzerland. They live and work in Bienne, Switzerland. www.fdcartier.fr.st

JEAN CASLIN (bio in Curator section)

NANCY CHUNN (no bio provided)

JEROME CROWDER

Jerome Crowder: "Although categories seem arbitrary, I call myself a visual anthropologist, one who studies culture through still images or video. I work with photography. Over the past decade, I have focused my research on the processes of urbanization and migration in the Americas, particularly among Aymara-speaking migrants living in the Andean cities of La Paz, Bolivia, and Puno, Perú, with whom I have lived, often for extended periods (six months to a year). While I consider myself a serious photographer, I use photography in research as a methodological tool: not as documentation, but as a subject for discussion and reciprocal gift giving. Photography gives me glimpses of Aymara migrants' lives—aspects of their personalities, families, and issues of urban survival—that I would not otherwise have. As a photographer and ethnographer, I believe that my goal is to explore and demonstrate the similarities we share as people from different cultures, not to sensationalize our differences."

AYA DORIT CYPIS

Aya Dorit Cypis was born in Tel Aviv in 1951. She received her M.F.A. from the California Institute of the Arts, Valencia, in 1977 and a M.A. in conflict resolution from Pepperdine University, Malibu, California, in 2004. She lives and works in Los Angeles. Recent solo exhibitions include shows at Galerie Optica, Montreal; Storage, Los Angeles; Sweeney Art Gallery, University of California, Riverside; Galerie de l'Université du Quebec, Montreal; Krannert Art Museum, University of Illinois at Urbana-Champaign; Isabella Stewart Gardner Museum, Boston; Catherine G. Murphy Gallery, College of Saint Catherine, St. Paul, Minnesota; Roy Boyd Gallery, Santa Monica, California; Walker Art Center and Southern Theater, Minneapolis; Intermedia Arts and First Bank System, Minneapolis; Anderson Gallery, Virginia Commonwealth University, Richmond; International Center of Photography, New York; Whitney Museum of American Art, New York; Space AD 2000, Tokyo; Anna Leonowens Gallery, Nova Scotia College of Art and Design, Halifax; De Zaak, Groningen, The Netherlands; Grande Theater, Groningen, The Netherlands; Apollohuis, Eindhoven, The Netherlands; T'Hoogt, Utrecht, The Netherlands; A Space, Toronto; Vehicule Galerie, Montreal; and Los Angeles Contemporary Exhibitions.

STEPHEN DEAN

Stephen Dean was born in 1968 in Paris, and now lives and works in New York City. He has exhibited extensively in the U.S. and Europe. His work is in many private, corporate, and public collections, including those of Yale University Art Gallery, New Haven, Connecticut; Fonds National d'Art Contemporain, Paris; and Banque Société Générale, Paris.

LEIGH DEHANEY

Leigh Dehaney's background is a mixture of fine arts and technology. He is currently attending the Alberta College of Art & Design, Calgary, Canada, on a full-time basis, and he plans to major in media arts and digital technologies with a studio-based emphasis in printmaking. He seems to have a predisposition toward anything quirky, and is drawn to Constructivist architecture, industrial sites, ruins, painted dumpsters, old technology, and machines. Dehaney's documentation of murals records human factors within a guarded world. To him, the term *graffiti* brings to mind personal imagery, much of which just happens to be within an urban environment. Remarking on graffiti's ever-changing ideas and influences, and its presentation in environments that may shape the outcome of the images, Dehaney said, "I find the idea of temporary imagery that can never be recreated uneasy and somewhat affecting. That's probably what draws me toward [the murals]. They're not necessarily meant to last forever, but I think [about] how many layers of paint hide so many here-and-nows." For Dehaney, taking a snapshot of a mural is like being able to save a bit of visual information that is in danger of becoming secondhand information years from now.

ANNE DELEPORTE

Anne Deleporte was born in France in 1960. She lives in Brooklyn, New York, and in Paris with her husband, artist Stephen Dean. Deleporte has exhibited at Musee d'Art Moderne de la Ville de Paris; The Drawing Center, New York; The New Museum, New York; Paco Imperial, Rio de Janeiro; Galerie Xippas, Paris; and Hales Gallery, London. Her work was recently included in the exhibition *From Paris to Shanghai: Fifty Years of French Photography* at the Shanghai Art Museum, China. The Santa Monica Museum, California, will feature her work in its upcoming exhibition *Dark Places*.

NAN DICKSON

Nan Dickson is a fourth-generation Texan educated at universities in Tennessee and Texas. Her photographic career began in 1979 and included years of continuing interest in photojournalism. The training she received from David Clanton and Don Rutledge, a photographer with Black Star, had early and lasting impact. She combines a trained eye with technical skills, experience in public relations, and her growing knowledge of people and life. She has recently begun to exhibit her black and white fine art photography at locations in Texas.

RINEKE DIJKSTRA

Rineke Dijkstra was born in Sittard, The Netherlands, in 1959. She graduated from the Gerrit Rietveld Academie, Amsterdam, in 1986. She still lives and works in Amsterdam. She has had solo exhibitions at ABN AMRO Plaza, LaSalle Bank, Chicago; Marian Goodman Gallery, New York; Art & Public, Geneva; Frans Halsmuseum (De Hallen), Haarlem, The Netherlands; Sommer Contemporary Art, Tel Aviv; Galerie Max Hetzler, Berlin; The Art Institute of Chicago; Anthony d'Offay Gallery, London; DAAD Galerie, Berlin; Museu d'Art Contemporani de Barcelona; Museum Boymans-van Beuningen, Rotterdam; Sprengel Museum, Hannover, Germany; Photographers' Gallery, London; Galerie Mot & van den Boogaard, Brussels; and Le Consortium, Dijon, France. Her work was also included in the Venice Biennale in 1997.

JAMES DILGER, JR.

James Dilger, Jr., is a native Houstonian. He started working with a camera in 1988 and began attending continuing education photography classes at Rice University, Houston, in 2001. Current interests include night photography and landscapes in black and white.

RICK DINGUS

Rick Dingus is a professor of photography at Texas Tech University in Lubbock. He received his B.F.A. from the University of California, Santa Barbara, and his M.F.A. from the University of New Mexico, Albuquerque. He is an author and photographer who has received funding for projects from the National Endowment for the Arts, Polaroid Corporation, Art Matters, Inc., and the Arizona Commission on the Arts. The last provided funding for the Rephotographic Survey Project that resulted in the book *Marks in Place: Contemporary Responses to Rock Art* (Albuquerque: University of New Mexico Press, 1988). His work reflects an ongoing exploration of the landscape as not limited to traditional subjects and documentary as not limited to straight photography.

LINDA DUNBAR

Linda Dunbar: "I was born in North Carolina into a society of white gloves and party manners. Then came college and

Vietnam. I married a musician, and we opened a high fashion shoe store while I continued my education in psychology. I did my master's work in New Orleans, where I was the director of the Toulouse Street Theatre. After a year of travel in Europe and North Africa with my camera in tow, I entered the health care market, purchasing several medical equipment companies and clinics. I still traveled extensively and seem to have stored up more than forty years of photographs. Dunbar Galleries opened last year, featuring artists from around the world as well as local artists."

KATHRYN DUNLEVIE
Two-time recipient of the Visual Artist Fellowship in Photography awarded by the Arts Council Silicon Valley in Santa Clara, California, Kathryn Dunlevie lives and works in Palo Alto, California. She is a fine arts graduate of Rice University, Houston. Dunlevie also studied film at the Université Paris, photography at Taller de Artes Creativas in Madrid, and painting at the California College of Arts and Crafts, Oakland. Dunlevie's recent works—fusions of photography and painting—both *de*construct and *re*construct urban spaces, creating mysterious passages not visible in reality. She has exhibited her work at San Francisco Camerawork, San Francisco Museum of Modern Art Artists Gallery, Houston Center for Photography, Hooks-Epstein Galleries in Houston, San Jose Institute of Contemporary Art in California, Society for Contemporary Photography in Kansas City, Missouri, Southeast Museum of Photography in Daytona Beach, Florida, Gallery TPW in Toronto, Burnes Institute in Stuttgart, Germany, and Vertigo in London.

JOHN CLIFTON DYES
John Clifton Dyes acquired his first camera, a twin lens Rolleiflex, in Puerto Rico while serving with the U.S. Air Force. After the four-year Air Force stint, he finished his B.S. in chemical engineering at the University of Houston and worked as a tech service engineer at a refinery in Texas City. While working as an engineer, he spent many hours photographing the coastal landscapes and the water birds residing on the Gulf Coast. Dyes took an early retirement from the refinery in 1986 and went to Rice University, where he earned a B.A. in photography. He then attended the University of Houston, where he received his M.A. in photography. He also taught photography as a graduate fellow at the University of Houston. After graduating, he taught photography at the College of the Mainland, Texas City, and at continuing education workshops at Rice University. In 1993, he published a book, *Nesting Birds of the Coastal Islands* (Austin: University of Texas Press, 1993). Dyes participated in 1992

FotoFest and has exhibited at the Blaffer Gallery, University of Houston; Houston Center of Photography; Odessa College, Texas; Galveston Arts Center, Texas; SF Camerawork, San Francisco; and Allen Street Gallery, Dallas.

AMBER EAGLE
Upon finishing a Core Fellowship at the Glassell School of Art, Museum of Fine Arts, Houston, Amber Eagle received a Cultural Arts Council of Houston/Harris County travel grant to study sugacraft and fiestas in Mexico, where she has lived ever since. This year her exhibition *Golpe de Vista* was on view at Kerrigan Campbell Fine Arts and Projects in New York. She is currently an artist-in-residence at the McColl Center for Visual Art in her hometown of Charlotte, North Carolina. She received her B.F.A. from the Rhode Island School of Design and her M.F.A. from California College of the Arts. Her work is a reflection on the ways our environment shapes us, as seen through eyes of a southern U.S. consumerist living in colonial Mexican culture. Her work explores themes of Mexican saints, global communications, and Maya cave culture through the mixed-media dioramas she constructs mainly of cake icing. www.ambereagle.org.

LILY EARL
Lily Earl was born in Danville, Illinois, and raised in the San Francisco Bay Area. She studied film and television production at Solano College in Fairfield, California. After several years' working in radio broadcasting, Earl returned to photography by completing an internship at Moya Photography in West Palm Beach, Florida. There she gained hands-on experience in all phases of studio and lab production. Earl also worked at the Academy of Art University School of Photography in San Francisco for ten years, learning valuable photographic skills in an academic environment. She is at present working as a black and white custom printer in San Francisco. Earl just completed the *Holy Water-Madonna* series of photographs, which visually explore religious icons as they relate to spirituality. She is currently working on her next photography project: *Paris*.

LALLA ESSAYDI
Lalla Essaydi grew up in Morocco and lived in Saudi Arabia for many years. She at present lives in Boston, where she received her M.F.A. from the School of the Museum of Fine Arts, Boston/Tufts University in May 2003. She has exhibited throughout the U.S. and Europe, and her work is found in a number of public collections, including those of Williams College Museum of Art, Williamstown, Massachusetts; The Art Institute of Chicago; Fries Museum, Leeuwarden, The Netherlands;

Museum of Fine Arts, Houston; Columbus Museum of Art; Museum of Fine Arts, Boston; and DeCordova Museum and Sculpture Park, Lincoln, Massachusetts. Her art, which often combines Islamic calligraphy with representations of the female body, addresses the complex reality of Arab female identity from the unique perspective of personal experience. In much of her work, she returns to her Moroccan girlhood, looking back on it as an adult woman, caught somewhere between past and present, and as an artist, exploring the language in which to "speak" from this uncertain space. She works in numerous media, including painting, video, film, installation, and analog photography. "In my art, I wish to present myself through multiple lenses—as an artist, as Moroccan, as traditionalist, as liberal, as Muslim. In short, I invite viewers to resist stereotypes."

JIM FALICK

Born in New York in 1936, Jim Falick has lived in Houston since 1966. He has undergraduate and graduate degrees in architecture from Columbia University, New York, and is a fellow of the American Institute of Architects. He feels lucky to have learned about photography while he was young from photography exhibitions at The Museum of Modern Art, New York. An inveterate traveler, he gathers impressions and images that make him smile or that lead him in less than obvious directions. He has had several solo exhibitions and has been in a number of group shows in Texas.

LESLIE FIELD

A photographer and mixed-media artist Leslie Field has been active as an artist since 1990. She works in alternative processes, photo-sculpture, and installation. Her work has been exhibited throughout Texas, Vermont, and New York, and has been acquired by numerous private collections. Field's work is also in the permanent collections of Congregation Emanu-El, Houston; Congregation Beth Israel, Houston; and the Museum of Fine Arts, Houston.

STEVE FITCH

Steve Fitch's photographs have been exhibited throughout the U.S., Australia, and New Zealand. His work is in the collection of The Museum of Modern Art, New York, among others. Fitch's primary subject matter is the architecture of the Midwestern Great Plains. He has published a number of articles and has been the recipient of several awards. Fitch has taught around the country, including at the University of Colorado, Boulder; The University of Texas, Austin; Princeton University, New Jersey;

and for the past number of years, the College of Santa Fe, New Mexico.

TONI FRISSELL

Toni Frissell was born Antoinette Frissell in 1907 and raised in a privileged family in New York City. She received her initial training in photographic techniques from her older brother, Varick, who was a documentary filmmaker. After his sudden death while shooting a film in Newfoundland, Frissell, who was in her twenties at the time, determined that she would make photography her life. She was hired as a caption writer for *Vogue* and soon after took on small photographic assignments at the magazine. Frissell was one of the first to abandon the studio and position her subjects outdoors, thereby revolutionizing fashion photography. She went on to photograph for *Collier's* and *Harper's Bazaar*, among other magazines, and she became the first woman sports photographer for *Sports Illustrated* in the early 1950s. Over the course of her forty-year career, Frissell learned from Edward Steichen (1879–1973) and briefly apprenticed with Cecil Beaton (1904–1980). From 1939 to 1944, she was commissioned to document King Ranch in South Texas, which resulted in her most well-known photographic essay. During World War II, she served as a photojournalist and war correspondent. Her work was included in a number of exhibitions during her lifetime, including Edward Steichen's *Family of Man* exhibition at The Museum of Modern Art, New York, in 1955.

MICHAEL FRY

Michael Fry grew up in a military family, traveling and living in the U.S. and Europe. He has spent most of his adult life in Texas. He earned his B.F.A. in 1984 and began making a living as a professional photographer. In 2002 he graduated from The University of Texas at San Antonio with a M.F.A. and began teaching. He taught photography and digital imaging in Austin and San Antonio before moving to Houston, where he currently resides, teaching photography, drawing, design, and art appreciation. He also continues to practice professional photography. In his work, he explores every facet of the medium, from traditional black and white photography to pinhole camera experiments to digitally manipulated imagery.

WYATT GALLERY

Wyatt Gallery, a New York photographer, has traveled in the Caribbean since 1997 on a Rosenberg Grant and a Fulbright Fellowship. At the age of twenty-nine, Wyatt was selected as one of the top thirty emerging photographers in the world by *Photo*

District News magazine, and he is featured in the book *25-Under-25, Up-And-Coming American Photographers* (New York: powerHouse Books, 2003). Gallery currently teaches color photography at the University of Pennsylvania, Philadelphia, and his photographs appear in publications such as *Mother Jones, The New York Times, Sophisticated Traveler, Architectural Record, VIBE,* and *Budget Travel.*

MIGUEL GANDERT
Miguel Gandert was born and raised in the northern New Mexico town of Española. Gandert considers himself an Indo-Hispanic and has spent the last twenty years documenting this culture through his photography. He photographs people on the fringes of American society, including cholos, bikers, low-riders, boxers, teenage mothers, and Mexican immigrants. Gandert recently received a Southwest Book Award for *Nuevo Mexico Profundo: Rituals of an Indo-Hispano Homeland* (Santa Fe: Museum of New Mexico Press, 2000). The book documents the Rio Grande corridor from northern New Mexico to the Mexican border and the annual pilgrimages to Chimayó, New Mexico, as well as historical Matachines dances. Gandert's work has been exhibited at the National Museum of American Art, Washington, D.C.; Whitney Museum of American Art, New York; San Francisco Museum of Modern Art; and Denver Art Museum, as well as at other venues. He is a professor in the department of communication and journalism at the University of New Mexico, Albuquerque. He recently traveled to Bolivia as a Fulbright Scholar, where he photographed the Indo-Hispano feast day celebrations.

DAVID GIBSON (no bio provided)

LINDA GILBERT
Linda Gilbert performs regularly with the Houston Ballet and Grand Opera orchestras. As a Fulbright Scholar, Gilbert studied in Amsterdam before receiving her Ph.D. from the University of Southern California, Los Angeles. She maintains a teaching studio in Houston and is the photographer for Mercury Baroque Ensemble. An author and editor, Gilbert provides professional editing services to individuals and is writing her second book, on safe stretching for musicians. Her articles and photographs have appeared in various journals. Certified nationally as a yoga therapist, instructor, and rehabilitative specialist, she teaches yoga privately and at Rice University's Shepherd School of Music in Houston. As a photographer, Gilbert is drawn to the interaction between living beings and the environment. She finds beauty in the subtleties within open landscapes, most recently in southeastern Idaho. Her FotoFest contributions include images that reflect the light, color, and use of land in this part of the country.

GERALDINE GILL
Geraldine Gill was born and raised in New York City. Several years ago, with encouragement from her family and a brand new Nikon, she began to pursue in earnest her longtime interest in photography. Gill travels extensively worldwide and is particularly interested in documenting people in the countries that she visits, capturing them in portraits within their natural environment. She has studied with Joe Englander and Fraser Stables. Her work was accepted in the Houston Center for Photography 2004 Juried Member Show and currently hangs in private and international corporate collections. She works predominantly with black and white film and uses traditional printing methods.

TONY GLEATON
Tony Gleaton is currently a visiting professor of photography at Texas Tech University in Lubbock. Gleaton has exhibited throughout the U.S. and Mexico, including at the National Museum of American Art, Washington, D.C.; Los Angeles County Museum of Art; and Smithsonian Institution, Washington, D.C., where his work was featured in a traveling exhibition that toured the U.S., Mexico, and Cuba. Gleaton has lived and traveled extensively in the American West, Mexico, and South America, chronicling *mestizaje*, the assimilation of Asian, African, and European immigrants with indigenous Americans. Gleaton explores his own cultural identity in his work, an archetypal American quest to understand and explore one's sense of self while paying homage to a largely unrecognized culture. Gleaton has started a multiyear project on the African diaspora in the Trans-Mississippi West in collaboration with the Southwest Collection of Texas Tech University and the Denver and Oakland public libraries.

PAULA GOLDMAN
Paula Goldman's work has always involved an intensive look at cultural interpretations of natural or emotional phenomena. Her most recent work centers on still lifes that examine natural objects past their prime. Educated at the University of Michigan and the California Institute of the Arts, she has exhibited her work at the LACE Annual, Los Angeles; *The World From Here*, UCLA Hammer Museum, Los Angeles; *Time Capsule*, Creative Time, New York; and at Women and Their Work, Austin, Texas. Her work is in various private collections and those of the Museum of Fine Arts, Houston, and Metro Art/MTA, Los Angeles.

CLAUDETTE CHAMPRUN GOUX
Born in 1951, Claudette Goux now lives in the Los Angeles area. She completed her bachelor's degree in photography in 1998 at Rice University, Houston, following study at the New York Institute of Photography, New York. Prior degrees include a bachelor's degree in philosophy and one in sociology from the

University of Nancy, France. In 2005 she received a master's degree in art history from the University of California, Riverside. Her work has been exhibited in several group and solo shows, and published in the 1996 *Houston Area Exhibition Catalogue* and the spring 1997 issue of *Heritage Magazine*; she received mention in exhibition reviews in *Public News*, *The Press Enterprise*, and *The Highlander*. She was awarded the California Museum of Photography fellowship, the Christine Croneis Sayres Memorial Award in Studio Art, and a prize from the Texas Historical Foundation for a photograph from her series *Places of Worship*. Her work is represented in numerous collections in America and Europe, including that of the Blaffer Museum of the University of Houston.

KATY GRANNAN

Katy Grannan was born in Arlington, Massachusetts, in 1969. She received her B.A. from the University of Pennsylvania in 1991 and her M.F.A. from Yale University in 1999. She lives and works in Brooklyn. Solo exhibitions include shows at 51 Fine Art, Antwerp, Belgium; Greenberg Van Doren Gallery, New York; Emily Tsingou Gallery, London; Jackson Fine Art, Atlanta; Michael Kohn Gallery, Los Angeles; Artemis Greenberg Van Doren Gallery, New York; Salon 94, New York; Lawrence Rubin Greenberg Van Doren, New York; and Kohn Turner Gallery, Los Angeles.

SCOTT GRIESBACH

Scott Griesbach, a native of Wisconsin, splits his time between Santa Monica and Joshua Tree, California. He is a master of philosophical journeys, which he explores through digital compositions. His expanding body of work, *Portraits* and *Social Practice*, is highly acclaimed and has captured the attention of some of America's most prestigious institutions, including the Museum of Fine Arts, Houston. Scott continues to exhibit domestically and internationally.

MICHELE GRINSTEAD

Born in Houston, Michele Grinstead received a M.F.A. from the University of Houston. She began her work as a commercial photographer in Chicago. She returned to Houston in 1993 and began a dual career in fine art and commercial photography. She has exhibited her work at the Blaffer Gallery, Houston; Galveston Arts Center; FotoFest, Houston; Houston Center for Photography; Women and Their Work, Austin; Woman Made Gallery, Chicago; and The Print Center, Philadelphia. Grinstead currently resides in Houston and teaches photography.

DAVID HALLIDAY

David Halliday was born in Glen Cove, New York, and studied at both Syracuse University, New York, and The Maine Photographic Workshops in Rockport. Halliday's attention to detail, strength of composition, and exquisite printing make his photographs widely sought after. His work is featured in many collections, including those of the Banana Republic; Philip Morris Corporation; Hunter Museum, Chattanooga, Tennessee; New Orleans Museum of Art; and Museum of Fine Arts, Houston. He has lived and worked in New Orleans since 1991.

ERIKA HARRSCH

Erika Harrsch was born in Mexico City in 1970. She studied art at Scuola di Arte Visive-Art'e, Florence; Fine Arts School, Universidad Autónoma de Querétaro, Mexico; and Centro Cultural El Nigromante and Instituto Allende, both in San Miguel de Allende, Mexico. Her work has been the subject of solo exhibitions at the Göteborgs Konstmuseum-Hasselblad Center, Gothenburg, Sweden, Alternativa Once, Monterrey, Mexico; Hopper House Art Center, Nyack, New York; and Kunsthaus Santa Fe, San Miguel de Allende, Guanajuato, Mexico, among others. Harrsch has been included in group exhibitions and festivals in the United States, Mexico, Germany, Sweden, Turkey, and Spain. Her work is also included in the collections of Lehigh University Art Gallery, Bethlehem, Pennsylvania: Museo de Arte de Querétaro, Mexico; Museo Universitario Contemporáneo de Arte, Mexico City; Homenaje Luis Donaldo Colosio, Mexico City; and Televisa, Dirección Administrativa, Mexico City. Harrsch currently lives and works in New York City.

PHILIP HAWKINS

Philip Hawkins is a photographer and web developer originally from Houston. He began to experiment with basic black and white photography while a student at Lamar High School, continued with studio classes throughout his studies at Texas Christian University, Fort Worth, and has worked on personal photography projects since graduation. Hawkins has devoted a significant portion of the past twelve years to photography. Images of his work are available at happymeadows.com. His portfolio explores a wide range of subject matter, including landscape, still life, architectural photography, and photo mosaic. The artist's interests include chemical-based photography (35 mm, medium and large format, and pinhole) as well as digital photography in all its versatile glory. Hawkins now lives with his girlfriend and two cats in Austin. Aside from photography, his interests include Internet technology, cooking, lively political discussion, and camping in the beautiful Texas Hill Country.

MARK HIEBERT

A native of Wichita, Mark Hiebert now lives in Katy, Texas. Born in 1971, he works as a photographer, editor, and writer. He is a graduate of Wichita State University and earned his M.F.A. from Old Dominion University, where he studied poetry, poetics, rhetoric, and English and American literature.

RUTH HEIKKILA

Originally from Austin, Ruth Heikkila has lived in Sugar Land, Texas, for more than thirty years. She studied traditional photography at the Glassell School, Museum of Fine Arts, Houston, and has been taking photographs since the 1970s. Heikkila is drawn to a variety of subjects, from portraits to intimate landscapes. She views landscapes as art pieces, discovering their abstract qualities as captured through the camera lens. Heikkila is married and has three grown children and three grandchildren.

GOTTFRIED HELNWEIN

(born October 8, 1948 in Vienna) An Austrian-Irish fine artist, photographer, and performance artist, Gottfried Helnwein studied at the University of Visual Art in Vienna (Akademie der Bildenden Künste, Wien). He was awarded the Master-class prize (Meisterschulpreis) of the University of Visual Art, Vienna, the Kardinal-König prize and the Theodor-Körner prize. His early work consists mainly of hyper-realistic watercolors, depicting wounded children, as well as performances—often with children—in public spaces. Often considered provocative and controversial, Helnwein is a conceptual artist, concerned primarily with psychological and sociological anxiety, historical issues and political topics. He has worked as a painter, draftsman, photographer, muralist, sculptor and performance artist, using a wide variety of techniques and media. Helnwein is also known for his stage and costume designs of theater, ballet and opera productions; amongst them Staatsoper Hamburg, Volksbühne Berlin and the Los Angeles Opera.

JERRY HERRING

Joan Bueling, raised in North Dakota, and Jerry Herring, from Iowa, have been taking photographic road trips together for the past six years. Bueling is an accomplished photographer who manages Dakota Framing and Photography, where she consults with corporate art collectors and provides turnkey framing services. Herring is a graphic designer and publisher by trade, having established Herring Design in 1973 and Herring Press in 1984. Their work is in many private and corporate collections, and has been widely published.

ALLISON HUNTER

Allison Hunter is executive director of the Houston Center for Photography. Previously, she served as artistic director of De Santos Gallery in Houston. She was a curatorial assistant for the Tang Teaching Museum and Art Gallery in Saratoga Springs, New York, and worked for other commercial galleries in New York and Lausanne, Switzerland. Hunter taught university-level visual arts courses (in computer art, cyber art, and web design) for several years after completing her M.F.A. in electronic art at Rensselaer Polytechnic Institute. Hunter writes about art for national publications such as *HOW design, Sculpture*, and *electronicbookreview*. She has edited *SPOT* magazine for the past three years. Hunter is most interested in reviewing work that redefines photography through experimental or conceptual strategies. She welcomes multimedia work and installation, as well as traditional media. At the Houston Center for Photography, Hunter responds to artwork with a contemporary eye, advises artists on sequencing images in their portfolio, and suggests appropriate venues in the U.S. and Europe (particularly Houston and New York).

HANS-JÖRGEN JOHANSEN

Hans-Jörgen Johansen is an artist living and working in Stockholm. His work includes photography, sculpture, multimedia, and installation. Johansen has shown his work throughout Sweden as well as in Helsinki, Amsterdam, and London. He has most recently been included in a group exhibition in Wilmington, Delaware.

SARAH JONES

Sarah Jones was born in London in 1959. She received her M.A. from Goldsmiths College, University of London, in 1996. She lives and works in London. Jones has had solo exhibitions at Maureen Paley Interim Art, London; Anton Kern Gallery, New York; Huis Marseille – Foundation for Photography, Amsterdam; Folkwang Museum, Essen, Germany; Centro de Fotografia, Universidad de Salamanca, Spain; Museo Nacional Centro de Arte Reina Sofia, Madrid; Galerie Anne de Villepoix, Paris; L'Ecole supérieure des Beaux-Arts, Tours, France; Sabine Knust Galerie & Edition Maximilian Verlag, Munich; Le Consortium, Dijon, France; Camerawork Gallery, London; Hales Gallery, London; Watershed Arts Centre, Bristol, England; and F Stop Gallery, Bath, England. Her work was also included in *Another Girl Another Planet* (1999, Lawrence Rubin Greenberg Van Doren Fine Art, New York) and the *Third International Tokyo Photo Biennial* (Tokyo Metropolitan Museum of Photography).

T. MITCHELL JONES

Twenty-seven years ago, T. Mitchell Jones created his first graphic image, a photogram. Since that time, he has had the pleasure of exhibiting his work in Houston at the Museum of Printing History, Art Car Museum, and various art spaces, as well as through guerilla art actions. Jones's art actions have covered a span of twenty years and scores of images, none of which he retains. More recently, he has been working in the digital medium while continuing to produce black and white silver prints. His philosophy of art has remained unchanged since he was a student at Sam Houston State University in Huntsville, Texas: to create an image that presents the familiar in a new and interesting way.

HELEN C. KLEBERG

A self-taught photographer, Helen C. Kleberg was born Helen Mary Campbell in Pittsburg, Kansas, in 1902 and grew up primarily in Arlington, Virginia. As a teenager, she took snapshots of things, places, and events that interested her. In 1926, she married Robert J. Kleberg, Jr., soon to be manager and president of King Ranch whose founder, Richard King, was his grandfather. During the war, Helen Kleberg became involved with the American Red Cross. She served as a director of the Volunteer Service Committee and organized the Camp-Hospital Council in South Texas. Although Kleberg extensively photographed the property of King Ranch from the 1930s until her death in 1963, and produced a noteworthy body of work, her photographs were never exhibited during her lifetime. Her work was reproduced in the December 15, 1947, issue of *Time* magazine, which focused on the achievements of King Ranch, and one of her photographs appeared in the 1975 exhibition catalogue *The King Ranch: 1939-1944*, a photographic series by Toni Frissell presented at the Amon Carter Museum, Fort Worth.

BRYAN KUNTZ

Bryan Kuntz was born in San Antonio in 1955 and now resides in Richmond, Texas. He graduated from Texas A&M University, Commerce, in 1979 with a B.A. in photography. He worked with photographers in Dallas and New York City before moving to Houston in 1982 to open his own photography studio. Kuntz's photography has been published in *Communication Arts Photography Annual, Print Magazine Regional Design Annual, Photo Design Magazine*, and *Creativity Annual*, and has received awards from the Houston Advertising Federation, Dallas Society of Visual Communications, and the Art Directors Club of Houston. His subject matter and style have varied widely over the years. He is currently working on a series of black and white tree photographs, as well as a series of Polaroid emulsion transfers on Plexiglas.

ROBERT LANGHAM

Robert Langham was born in Tyler, Texas in 1952. He received his undergraduate degree from Sam Houston State University in Huntsville and did graduate work at the University of Texas-Austin. He currently lives in Tyler and has been photographing East Texas and the Western Landscape since 1971. He has had numerous exhibitions throughout the United States and his work is represented in a number of museum collections including the Museum of Fine Arts, Houston and the Amon Carter Museum, Fort Worth.

BIRGIT LANGHAMMER

Birgit Langhammer was born in Magdeburg, Germany, in 1968. In 2000, she moved to Houston. She studied at universities in Erfurt and Jena, Germany, earning her M.A. in visual arts and German language and literature in 1993. From 1993 to 2000, she taught visual arts/photography and German literature at a high school in Weimar, Germany. After Langhammer moved to Houston, she resumed her passion for photography. She works with black and white negative film, and tones her prints in sepia and selenium. She takes her photos with a 35 mm SLR camera. Mostly comprising details of natural elements or man-made objects, her photographs appeal to the eye in a more abstract way at first. The texture, lines, and forms that time creates on the surfaces of things are what catches her interest.

DAVID LEVINTHAL

Born in San Francisco in 1949, David Levinthal studied art at Stanford University and Yale University, completing his M.F.A. at the latter in 1973. He is the co-author, with Garry Trudeau, of *Hitler Moves East* (New York: Lawrence Miller Gallery, 1977). *Dark Light*, a ten-year survey exhibition of his work, was organized in 1994 by The Photographers' Gallery in London and traveled throughout the UK. In 1997 the International Center of Photography in New York presented his first retrospective, *David Levinthal Work from 1977 to 1996*. He has received a National Endowment for the Arts Fellowship and a Guggenheim Fellowship. His work is exhibited widely and is part of the permanent collections of The Museum of Modern Art, New York; the Whitney Museum of American Art, New York; The Menil Collection, Houston; and the Metropolitan Museum of Art, New York. Writing in T*he New York Times*, Charles Hagen remarked, "What distinguishes Mr. Levinthal's work is his interest in emotionally charged historical material. But the real force of his images comes not from his choice of subjects but from the way he tells their stories." (Charles Hagen, "Treating Nazis in Art, Even Seriously, Is Risky," *The New York Times*, November 25, 1994.)

ANDREW JOHN LICCARDO

Andrew John Liccardo is a photographer and educator who teaches photography at Northern Illinois University, DeKalb, Illinois. Liccardo received his B.A. from Loyola University of Chicago and his M.F.A. from Texas Tech University, in Lubbock, Texas. His work has been exhibited in Texas, Louisiana, Florida, Georgia, Michigan, and New York. He was awarded a fellowship to the Photography Institute's National Graduate Seminar at Columbia University and received the Mitchell A. Wilder Award from the Texas Association of Museums.

ARTHUR LIOU

Arthur Liou worked as a video journalist in Taiwan before coming to the U.S. in the early 1990s. During the past decade, his work has gravitated toward the increasingly personal issues of media experience, ethnicity, food, and illness. To explore these themes, he has worked with a variety of media, from digital prints to high-definition video installation. Liou is the recipient of the 2006 Garry B. Fritz Award from the Society for Photographic Education and the 2004 Rising Star Award at FOTOfusion, Palm Beach Photographic Centre, Florida. His work is in private and public collections, including the *Blood Work* series recently acquired by the Indianapolis Museum of Art. He has exhibited his work nationally and internationally, at venues that include the Asian American Arts Center, New York; Schopf Gallery, Chicago; Poissant Gallery, Houston; Atlanta Contemporary Art Center; Society for Contemporary Photography, Kansas City; Gothenburg New Media Art Festival, Sweden; and numerous film festivals in Italy, Argentina, and Brazil. Liou received his M.F.A. in electronic intermedia and photography from the University of Florida. He is currently an associate professor of digital art at Indiana University, Bloomington.

MAUD LIPSCOMB

Maud Lipscomb is a visual artist who studied photography in the Continuing Studies program at Rice University, Houston, as well as photography and art at the Glassell School of Art, the Museum of Fine Arts, Houston. Her collages, which utilize the transfer process, employ both original and found images. Lipscomb has exhibited her work in numerous photography and mixed-media exhibitions in Houston, including Mama Said at FotoFest 2000 and shows at the Houston Center for Photography and the Foundry.

DEBORAH LUSTER

Deborah Luster is a photographer based in Monroe, Louisiana. She has received numerous awards, including the Anonymous Was a Woman, John Gutmann Fellowship; Buchsbaum Family Award for American Photography from the Friends of Photography, San Francisco; Louisiana Endowment for the Humanities Publication Award; Dorothea Lange–Paul Taylor Prize, Center for Documentary Studies, Duke University, Durham, North Carolina (with writer C.D. Wright); and a Louisiana Division of the Arts Fellowship. Her work is in the collections of numerous museums throughout the country, including the Whitney Museum of American Art, New York; Museum of Fine Arts, Houston; San Francisco Museum of Modern Art; Los Angeles County Museum of Art; and National Archives, Washington, D.C. Her series *One Big Self: Prisoners of Louisiana* was selected by both *The New York Times* and *The Village Voice* as one of the best photography books of 2003.

NANCY MAHLEY

Nancy Mahley, born at Fort Sam Houston in San Antonio, currently resides in Houston. She became interested in photography as a teenager and photographed her travels and family until her children started school. Her recent individual work includes a self-portrait series.

DAVID MAISEL

In David Maisel's series *Black Maps*, the artist used aerial photography to make surreal images of adversely impacted landscapes. The photographs of these environmentally damaged sites are spectacular, sublime, and horrifying. They transcribe the devastation of the natural world even as they limn similarly desolate psychic landscapes. As otherworldly as the images appear, they nonetheless depict shattered realities of our own making. Maisel received a B.A. from Princeton University and studied at the Graduate School of Design at Harvard University. His worked is represented in the permanent collections of the Metropolitan Museum of Art, New York; Los Angeles County Museum of Art; Museum of Fine Arts, Houston; and many others. His recent monograph, *The Lake Project* (Tucson: Nazraeli Press, 2004), was named one of the Top 25 Photography Books of 2004 by the critic Vince Aletti in the *Village Voice*. His work was recently exhibited at the *Beijing Off Biennial*.

SUZANNE M. MANNS

Born in Pittsburgh in 1950, Suzanne M. Manns has lived and worked in Houston since 1973. She earned her B.F.A. in painting and printmaking from Carnegie-Mellon University, Pittsburgh, and undertook graduate work at Rhode Island School of Design, Providence. She has lived in France and Switzerland, and traveled extensively in Germany, Italy, Spain, and Austria. Her work encompasses all forms of printmaking, including photosensitive media and digital processes. Since 1975, she has

been the head of printmaking at the Glassell School of Art, Museum of Fine Arts, Houston, where she is also the chair of studio and art history. Her work is included in numerous public and private collections.

GUENNADI MASLOV

Guennadi Maslov began his career in photography at the end of the 1980s. A founding member of the Contact group, he represented the documentary school of Kharkiv State University at the Soviet Union's last big photo festival in Moscow in 1989. In 1991, after exhibiting at the Contemporary Arts Center in Cincinnati, Maslov started teaching photography on both sides of the globe, at the University of Cincinnati and at Kharkiv State University. Since 1994 the artist has lived and worked in the U.S. Having established himself as a successful portrait photographer, Maslov continues to teach photography part-time, and he exhibits his work locally, nationally, and internationally. Almost every year he makes a trip to his native Ukraine where, as the photographer puts it, "common nostalgia often leads to personal artistic discoveries." This year, his exhibition at FotoFest coincides with the upcoming publication of his first book of selected works.

TRICIA MCFARLIN

Tricia McFarlin's longtime study of self-portraiture took a marked turn when she began composing portraits in the woods of Houston where she walks her dog. In these photographs, she focuses as much on the mood created by the fall of light on natural things as on where she places herself in the forest scene. McFarlin has been a student of photography at the Glassell School of Art, Museum of Fine Arts, Houston, since 2002. She has been in two student shows at the Glassell and was a recipient of the Carol Crow Memorial Scholarship in 2004.

MICHAEL MCKANN

Michael McKann was born in Hampton, Virginia, in 1946 and spent his boyhood on the Chesapeake Bay. The NASA migration brought his family to Texas, settling near Galveston Bay in the early 1960s. College studies in architecture, landscape architecture, and park planning and management led to his appreciation of the visual arts and a desire to find beauty and relationships in all environments. Throughout his career in land management and planning, McKann pursued his lifelong interest in photography. McKann began his professional photographic career with the founding of Photocard International in 1993. His images have been disseminated worldwide in the form of greeting cards, and his photography has appeared in magazines, books, websites, and numerous other publications. His unique sensitivity to his subject matter, which includes portraits,

landscapes, and imagery from the urban environment and his travels abroad, sets his work apart. Enlargements of his photographs, both traditional prints and Giclée prints, have been exhibited widely.

RAYMOND MEEKS

Raymond Meeks's first book, *Sound of Summer Running* (Tucson: Nazraeli Press, 2005), enjoyed many weeks on the *Photoeye* best-seller list and quickly sold through the edition. As the book's marketing copy states, "Whether his lens is focused on children playing or adults in contemplation, flora and fauna or simply beautiful landscapes, the pleasure never waivers [*sic*]." Meeks developed a deep passion for photography and the visual arts in his twenties, and it led to editorial assignments for *The New York Times, Esquire, GQ,* and *Audubon,* to name a few. His work has become part of the collections of Sir Elton John and the Museum of Fine Arts, Houston. Meeks makes his home in the Bitterroot Mountains of Montana.

ARTHUR MEYERSON

Meyerson is recognized as one of America's finest photographers. For over 30 years, this native Texan has traveled throughout the world photographing for corporate, advertising, and editorial clients. Feature articles about Meyerson and his work have appeared in books and magazines in the United States and abroad. A highly respected photography workshop leader, he is on the board of advisors for the Santa Fe Photographic Workshops, New Mexico and the Center for Photographic Arts, Carmel, California. His work is in many public and private collections including the Museum of Fine Arts, Houston and the Harry Ransom Center, University of Texas, Austin.

WILL MICHELS

Will Michels, a native Houstonian, earned his B.Arch. with honors from Pratt Institute, Brooklyn, New York. In 2000 he was awarded two separate grants from The Summerlee Foundation and Houston Endowment Inc. to photograph the former crew of the *Battleship Texas.* In 2004 he was nominated for the Louis Comfort Tiffany Award. Known primarily for taking portraits, he teaches photography at the Glassell School of Art, Museum of Fine Arts, Houston. Michels's work is represented in numerous collections, including that of the Museum of Fine Arts, Houston. His web address is www.madebywill.com.

JONATHAN MOLLER

Jonathan Moller is a fine art and documentary photographer and a human rights activist. He spent eight of the past fourteen years in Central America, primarily in Guatemala, where he worked as a human rights advocate and freelance photographer. His photo-

graphs have been widely exhibited and published in the U.S., Europe, and Latin America. Moller's book, *Our Culture Is Our Resistance: Repression, Refuge and Healing in Guatemala*, was published by powerHouse Books, New York, in September 2004, with a Spanish language edition by Turner Libros of Madrid and Mexico City. Moller has received many awards, including the 2005 Center for Photographic Art Award and the 2003 Golden Light Award. His work is in the permanent collections of numerous museums and institutions, including the San Francisco Museum of Modern Art; George Eastman House, Rochester, New York; Museum of Fine Arts, Houston; Brooklyn Museum of Art, New York; Baltimore Museum of Art; Minneapolis Institute of Arts; Polaroid Corporation, Waltham, Massachusetts; University of California, Berkeley Art Museum; Centro de la Imagen, Mexico City; and Casa de Las Americas, Havana. See his work at: www.jonathanmoller.org

CARMEN MONTOYA

Digital video, chamber music, and dance are woven into multimedia performances in the work of Carmen Montoya. Countering the aesthetics of power with the aesthetics of vulnerability, her work serves as a visual metaphor for the inherent irony of the human condition—that we are the boldest and the most intelligent beings on earth at the same time that we are hairless, upright engineers of our own disasters. She has been honored in Houston with a Creative Capital Artist Grant and a DiverseWorks Performance Arts Residency. Montoya has collaborated and partnered with local Houston artists and arts organizations. Her work has been exhibited and performed at Texas A&M University, College Station; the Center for Experimental Music and Intermedia, University of North Texas, Dallas–Fort Worth; and the State X: New Forms Festival, The Hague, The Netherlands.

DELILAH MONTOYA

Born in Texas and raised in the Midwest, Delilah Montoya eventually settled in New Mexico, the ancestral home of her mother's family. Her work, grounded in the experiences of the Southwest, brings together a multiplicity of syncretic forms and practices drawn from Aztec Mexico and Spain, as well as the vernacular traditions of the U.S.–Mexico border, all shaded by contemporary American customs and values. She explores the unusual relationships that result from negotiating different ways of understanding and representing life found in the region. Montoya's many projects investigate cultural phenomena, always addressing (and often confronting) viewers' assumptions. Her work is included in the collections of the Los Angeles County Museum of Art; Smithsonian Institution, Washington, D.C.; and Museum of Fine Arts, Houston. She is affiliated with the Andrew

Smith Gallery, Santa Fe; Photographs Do Not Bend, Dallas; and Redbud Gallery, Houston. Delilah Montoya is a professor of photography and digital imaging at the University of Houston.

ROBERTO MORÁN

Roberto Morán was born in El Salvador in 1972. He still lives and works in El Salvador Morán has had thirteen solo exhibitions in different countries in Central America as well as in Mexico, Colombia, Italy, and the U.S. He has participated in numerous international group shows in Europe, Asia, and the Americas. In 2004, Morán received recognition in the Art Statement category at Art Basel Miami. The Society of French Artists in Paris gave him the Bronze Medal. His work is represented in the collections of the Museo de Arte y Diseño Contemporáneo (MADC), San Jose, Costa Rica; Fundación Teoretica, San Jose, Costa Rica; The Margulies Collection, Miami; Darrell and Suzette Betts; and Lester Marks.

MARY MURREY

Mary Murrey is a photographer, fiction writer, passionate reader, cook, and mother of three. Her photographs have been selected for the national Krappy Kamera Competition and for juried shows at the Houston Center for Photography, Texas Photography Society, and Glassell School of Art, Museum of Fine Arts, Houston.

A. LEO NASH

A. Leo Nash was born in the Berkshires of western Massachusetts in 1964. A college career that began with a major in geography at Clark University, Worcester, Massachusetts, in 1982 ended with a degree in photography from Rochester Institute of Technology, New York, in 1989. Nash documents people who live at the edges of mainstream culture, photographing temporary artistic communities and endeavors, often in remote areas. The media has found the gathering in the Nevada desert called Burning Man, but has largely missed the soul of the event. Seduced by the spectacle, most observers lose the profound subtlety of the experience. Nash's wish is that, through this expanding body of work, viewers will see the nuances that he sees. Nash received the Carol Crow Memorial Fellowship for Photography from the Houston Center for Photography in 2001. At FotoFest 2004, he was one of the Discoveries of the Meeting Place. The Prague House of Photography, Czech Republic, was the venue for his solo exhibition in 2005. He resides in Oakland, California, and makes his living as a gaffer/lighting director in the film industry in both the San Francisco Bay Area and Los Angeles.

MORTEN NILSSON

Morten Nilsson studied at Fatamorgana, The Danish School of Art Photography, in Copenhagen from 1989 to 1990. He went on to study at the Danish School of Journalism in 1991–1994. His Dancers series has been shown in solo exhibitions at Tom Blau Gallery, London; Turner House Gallery, Penarth, Wales, in association with Ffotogallery, Cardiff, Wales; Clamp Art Gallery, New York; Stalke Galleri, Copenhagen; Ingrid Hansen Gallery, Washington, D.C.; Musée de la Photographie de Charleroi, Belgium; and Griffin Museum of Photography, Winchester, Massachusetts. His work also has been exhibited in group shows at Gallery Ujazdowskie Street, Warsaw; Photographs Do Not Bend, Dallas; Houston Center for Photography; National Portrait Gallery, London (Schweppes Photographic Portrait Prize 2004); and Discoveries of the Meeting Place, FotoFest 2006, Houston. Nilsson's work has been published in a variety of journals and magazines, including *British Journal of Photography, Head Magazine, Blue Eyes Magazine, Pozytyw Magazine, Photoworks Magazine, Contemporary Magazine*, and *Katalog*. His work is represented by Photographs Do Not Bend, Dallas.

KELLY NIPPER

Kelly Nipper was born in Edina, Minnesota, in 1971. She received her B.F.A. from the Minneapolis College of Art and Design, and her M.F.A. from the California Institute of the Arts, Valencia, in 1995. She lives and works in Los Angeles. Recent solo exhibitions include shows at Galleria Francesca Kaufmann, Milan; Shoshana Wayne Gallery, Santa Monica, California; and Plains Art Museum, Fargo, North Dakota.

LORI NIX

Lori Nix lived most of her life in the rural Midwest before moving to Brooklyn, New York, where she currently resides. Her solo exhibition *Lori Nix: The Banality of Terror* was shown at DiverseWorks in Houston during FotoFest 2004. She received a New York Foundation for the Arts Individual Artist Grant in 2004. In 2001 she was an artist-in-residence at Light Work in Syracuse, New York. Nix also received a Greater Columbus Ohio Arts Grant (1998) and an Ohio Arts Council Individual Artist Grant (1999). She has exhibited at numerous venues, including George Eastman House, Rochester, New York; Kagan Martos Gallery, New York; White Columns, New York; SF Camerawork, San Francisco; Houston Center for Photography; California Museum of Photography, Riverside; Light Work, Syracuse, New York; Miller Block Gallery, Boston; G. Gibson Gallery, Seattle; and Jenkins Johnson Gallery, New York and San Francisco.

NANCY O'CONNOR

Nancy O'Connor is a mixed-media artist who has exhibited and worked extensively in installation for over twenty years. She was born in Victoria, Texas, in 1957 and earned a B.A. in journalism from The University of Texas, Austin. Her work focuses on creating sites of experience that involve the use of photography, sound, objects, film, and video. O'Connor has exhibited at the Blaffer Gallery, Houston; Lefevere Gallery, London; Sculpture Center, Long Island City, New York; and Contemporary Arts Museum Houston. She has lived in San Francisco and New York City, and currently resides in Houston.

OLIVER

Born in New Orleans, Louisiana, in 1958, oliver has always been an artist, but he has also been an attorney, computer programmer, and small home builder. He started his photography at Phillips-Andover Academy, Massachusetts and returned to it as his underlying passion after his surgery for the installation of two artificial hips.

ANTHONY PALASOTA

Anthony Palasota directs the Center for Legal Pedagogy at Texas Southern University, Houston, where he also teaches at the Thurgood Marshall School of Law. He is active in community projects and has a personal interest in art, literature, hiking, cooking, and photography. He also publishes *Some Art & Other Events*—a weekly electronic newsletter about art shows, talks, performances, and other art-related matters. His interest in photography comes from his fascination with how the nexus of light and lens captures what we may be seeing with our eyes in time and space.

BRENT PHELPS

Brent Phelps is a professor of art and photography at the University of North Texas (UNT) in Denton. He received a B.S. in communication from Southern Illinois University in 1971 and a M.F.A. with a concentration in photography from Arizona State University in 1973. From 1973 to 1974, he taught English and photography on the Navajo and Hopi Indian reservations. Before joining UNT's School of Visual Arts in 1980, Phelps taught photography at Sam Houston State University and Northern Arizona University. Phelps received a National Endowment for the Arts Fellowship in 1980 to produce *Housescapes*, a series of portraits of rural Texas farmhouses. Throughout the 1980s and 1990s, the artist developed a love for the Montana landscape while depicting the region for numerous wilderness and sporting publications.

CHUCK RAMIREZ

Born in 1962, Chuck Ramirez lives and works as an artist in San Antonio. Primarily working in large-scale photography, he investigates the rituals and forms of everyday life in works that are charged with metaphors of ethnicity, gender, sexuality, and religion. Ramirez has shown extensively throughout Texas and the U.S. Solo and group exhibitions include shows at the Bronx Museum of Contemporary Art, New York; Arlington Museum of Contemporary Art, Texas; Austin Museum of Art at Laguna Gloria, Texas; North Texas State University Gallery, Denton; Lawndale Art Center, Houston; Finesilver Gallery, San Antonio; and Elizabeth Dee Gallery, New York. In 1999 in San Antonio, the artist exhibited a photo installation entitled *Long-Term Survivor* in ArtPace's Hudson (Show) Room. He was selected for an ArtPace residency in 2001 by Jerome Sans, independent curator and co-director of the Palais de Tokyo, Paris. He has participated in recent international exhibitions, including Arcaute Arte Contemporaneo, Monterrey, Mexico; Centro de La Imagine, Mexico City; and Galerie Khadrberlin, Berlin.

CHARLOTTE RANDOLPH

Charlotte Randolph has found fulfillment in the liberal arts throughout her life. She studied piano as a child in Oakland, California, and continues to play today. After her children entered school, she completed her B.A. in art history and M.A. in English at the University of Houston. Afterwards, she briefly taught writing. She worked awhile in the business world, and since her retirement in 1993, she has enhanced her interest in the visual arts by taking photography classes at Rice University, Houston; the Glassell School of Art, the Museum of Fine Arts, Houston; and the Southwest School of Art & Craft, San Antonio. Randolph photographs primarily landscapes and her images are shot fairly close up. Through her images, she hopes to convey affection and respect for her surroundings. Some of the photographers she admires are Harry Callahan, Annie Liebowitz, and Richard Kline. Her photos have appeared in American Orchid Society publications and she has won awards in juried exhibitions.

DEBORAH RIDDLE

Deborah Riddle creates photographic spaces and objects by using double and triple exposures to transform the known into the unknown. She further manipulates the images chemically and by retouching the inks by hand to adjust, enhance, or mimic shapes and patterns. A Houston native, Riddle received her undergraduate degree from Pratt Institute, Brooklyn, New York. Her work can be found in public, private, and corporate collec-

tions. Recent exhibitions include shows at Negative Space, Houston; Williams Tower, Houston; and the Museum of Contemporary Art, Los Angeles.

MONIQUE RIJNKELS

Ever since Monique Rijnkels bought her first camera with the money she earned from a summer job in eighth grade, she has been in love with photography. She sees black and white photography as the best outlet for expressing feelings in the printed image. Her work is about the essence of photography: *light*. She has been participating in photography classes at the Glassell School of Art, Museum of Fine Arts, Houston, since 2000, and received the Carol Crow Memorial Scholarship in 2001. Her work has been part of the Texas Photographic Society's Annual Members' Only Shows and group exhibitions at the Glassell School of Art.

ABBY ROBINSON

Abby Robinson came to New York City for school and never left. After receiving an undergraduate degree in architectural history, she went to art school to study interior design. Instead she wound up a photographer. After earning her M.F.A., she worked for a private investigator, wrote a novel—*The Dick and Jane* (New York: Delacorte Press, 1985)—based on her detective experiences, and began teaching photography at the School of Visual Arts in New York. She soon got itchy feet and started to travel; her exposure to different cultures and aesthetics made her head spin. She began her current work on an Asian Cultural Council grant that took her to Vietnam and continued it through a Fulbright Fellowship to India and Sri Lanka, with additional trips to Asia on her own. Most recently she received a fellowship from the American Institute of Sri Lankan Studies, as well as a Siskind Grant in 2005. Her work is in the collections of the Whitney Museum of American Art, New York, and the Museum of Fine Arts, Houston.

DANTÉ RODRÍGUEZ

Danté Rodríguez, an artist for as long as he can remember, explores the use of many media in his art to express ideas of culture and identity. Once attracted to gang life, he reversed his path and is now the proud father of a toddler, Frida Sophia. He and Frida's mother, Cindy, live in northwest Houston.

MIGUEL ANGEL ROJAS

Miguel Angel Rojas, one of the most important Latin American photographers from Bogotá, has shown his work in exhibitions

throughout the world, including shows at Museo Daros Latinamerica, Zurich; Museo de Arte Moderno, Buenos Aires; Whitney Museum of American Art, New York; Miami Art Museum; Museo de Art Moderno, Bogotá; Museo de Arte Contemporaneo (MARCO), Monterrey, Mexico; Museum of Modern Art, New York; and Museum Ludwig, Cologne. His work is found in many permanent collections, including those of The Museum of Modern Art, New York; Museo Daros Latinamerica, Zurich; Casa de las Americas, Havana; Museo de Bellas Artes, Caracas; and the Museo de Arte Moderno, Bogotá.

DAVID ROMER (no bio provided)

DANIELA ROSSELL

Daniela Rossell was born in Mexico City in 1973. In 1989 she began theater studies in Mexico City. Rossell completed her undergraduate studies at the National School of Visual Arts, Universidad Nacional Autónoma de México, Mexico City, in 1994. She lives and works in Mexico City. Recent solo exhibitions include shows at Blaffer Gallery, The Art Museum of the University of Houston; Nikolaj, Copenhagen Contemporary Art Center; Produzentengalerie Hamburg; Artpace, San Antonio; Greene Naftali Inc., New York; Casa de America, Madrid; and Galeria OMR, Mexico City.

JANICE RUBIN

Janice Rubin is a Houston-based photographer and teacher. Her work has been exhibited in the U.S., Canada, and Europe. Her photographs are included in several museum and private collections. Her exhibition on the ritual bath of Jewish tradition, entitled *The Mikvah Project*, is currently touring twenty-one cities in North America through 2007. She was a recipient of a National Endowment for the Arts Group Fellowship for her participation in the traveling exhibition *The Ties That Bind: Photographers Look at the American Family*. Since 1976, her work has appeared in publications in the U.S. and Europe, including *Smithsonian, Newsweek, Town and Country, Fortune, Rolling Stone*, and *The New York Times*. Her 1986 exhibition *Survival of the Spirit: Jewish Lives in the Soviet Union* toured seventeen cities in the U.S. and Canada.

PATRICIA SANDLER

Los Angeles photographer Patricia Sandler received her B.A. from UCLA and a M.A. from Loyola Marymount University, Los Angeles. She has exhibited on the West Coast and in Texas, and has won a number of awards in juried competitions.

ROBERT A. SCHAEFER, JR.

Robert A. Schaefer, Jr., was born and raised in Cullman, Alabama. After living in Munich in the late 1970s, he moved to New York City in 1981, where he continues to live and work. He is an adjunct professor of photography at New York University and teaches at The New School as well as at Pratt Institute. In the late 1990s, Apple, Inc. invited him to set up a series of seminars instructing fine art photographers in different ways they can employ Macintosh computers in their work. Apple was also one of the sponsors of Schaefer's twenty-five-year retrospective, *RASJR25* (1999), held at the Huntsville Museum of Fine Arts in Alabama. One of his more recent exhibitions was held last year at the Silver Eye Center for Photography, Pittsburgh.

MARK SELIGER

Mark Seliger is an editorial photographer who was born in Amarillo, Texas, and moved to Houston when he was five years old. He attended the High School for Performing and Visual Arts, and later graduated from East Texas State University. Seliger was the chief photographer for *Rolling Stone* for more than ten years, covering stories on the world's top musicians and actors. He currently lives and works in New York City, where he is under contract to Conde Nast Publications, working for *GQ* and *Vanity Fair*.

SHIRANA SHAHBAZI

Shirana Shahbazi was born in Teheran, Iran, in 1974. She graduated from the Hochschule für Kunst und Gestaltung, Zurich, in 2000. Shahbazi lives and works in Zurich. Selected solo exhibitions include shows at Centre d'Art Contemporain, Geneva; Galerie Bob van Orsouw, Zurich; Silk Road Gallery, Teheran; Salon 94, New York; The Wrong Gallery, New York; Trans Area, New York; Planet 22, Geneva; ICA Chicago; Bonner Kunstverein am August Macke Platz, Bonn, Germany; and The Photographers' Gallery, London.

SOODY SHARIFI

Through her photography, Soody Sharifi attempts to question the role of women under Islam as well as her own position as an Iranian-American woman. She usually stages the scenes pictured in her images to emphasize the delicate fictions underpinning them. By combining a fictive strategy and a documentary style, she explores the tension between public and private spaces through images that undo the Islamic stereotypes presented by the narrowly focused daily media. Sharifi has been honored as a National Graduate Seminar Nominee at Columbia University, New York, and she was given a residency at the

Houston Center for Photography. Her work has been shown nationally, with exhibitions in Texas, New York, and Oregon, and internationally, with shows in China, Iran, and Slovakia.

SHEILA SHAW

Sheila Shaw's love of black and white photography dates back to early childhood, when she first discovered the hundreds of family photographs taken by her father and others. He had collected the images, going back to the very early 1900s, from his parents and older sisters. Shaw has participated in silver gelatin photography classes at the Glassell School of Art, Museum of Fine Arts, Houston, for the past six years and has been a member of the museum's Photo Forum since 2001. Her work has been included in several group shows at the Houston Center for Photography, the Glassell School of Art, and the Havens Center. Shaw lives and works in Houston.

BETSY SIEGEL

Betsy Siegel earned her M.F.A. in film at Brandeis University, Waltham, Massachusetts. A working photographer and installation artist, she is known for her documentary work. Siegel has exhibited in numerous group shows in Houston, including FotoFest, and in New Mexico. Her work has been published regionally and nationally.

JOHN SMALLWOOD

John Smallwood has been a commercial photographer since 1986, and his assignments have taken him to sixteen foreign countries and forty-nine of the fifty states in the U.S. This extensive travel has given Smallwood an uncanny ability to provide the perfect photographic solution for any situation. His energy and creativity are evident in his work, as is his ability to feel at home both in the studio and on location. Smallwood is a member of ASMP.

ANGELA SNEED

Angela Sneed, a Texas native residing in San Antonio, is currently working in large-format studio photography. Her work includes an ongoing series of photos taken primarily in the streets of Mexico.

CAROL SPENCER

Carol Spencer began her career in photojournalism in 1975, working in the U.S., the Caribbean, and Central and South America. She moved to Jerusalem in 1984 as a member of the foreign press corps and spent the next decade covering the Middle East and North Africa. Her photographs have appeared on the covers of *Time* and *Newsweek*, both of which she worked for extensively. She also traveled on special assignment for *U.S. News & World Report, Look, The New York Times, The Washington Post, The Los Angeles Times, Newsday, The Philadelphia Inquirer*, and numerous European publications. From 1987 through 1990, she spent months traveling between the West Bank and the Gaza Strip documenting how the foreign press corps covered the *intifada*. The diary she created became the basis of her book *Danger Pay*, which is being put together for publication. Carol passed away from cancer in 2004 at the age of fifty.

SCOTTIE STAPLETON

Scottie Stapleton is a photographer and writer who was born in Houston. She studied photography at the Art Institute of Houston and Rice University before receiving a B.A. in art and photography from the University of Houston. In 1990, she was awarded a fellowship from the Houston Center for Photography. Her work has been included in group exhibitions at the Art Institute of Houston; Blaffer Gallery, University of Houston; Houston Center for Photography; Women and Their Work, Austin, Texas; Galveston Arts Center, Texas; Moreau Galleries, St. Mary's College, Notre Dame, Indiana; and FotoFest 2000. Her work is represented in the permanent collection of the Museum of Fine Arts, Houston. She is currently writing a screenplay in collaboration with her daughter, a New York independent filmmaker.

CAROL STEVENS

Carol Stevens has spent the last twenty years photographing urban and rural landscapes in the U.S. She uses many types of film cameras. As the digital world encroaches on the organic film world, Carol makes a point of shooting with Kodak Browning 127s and Holga 120 cameras to recreate the pictorial view of the great masters of the nineteenth century. Carol has participated in numerous art shows in Houston, Galveston, Texas, and Eureka Springs, Arkansas.

BERYL STRIEWSKI

Beryl Striewski is a photographer who shoots environmental and studio portraits as well as black and white, panorama, and photo-illustration works. Her current focus is a visual foray into the many archetypes and unconscious identities that mingle in our inner lives. Her metaphysical exploration is fueled by a personal desire to reveal and discover the essence of the "soul." She received her master's degree from East Texas State University. Striewski has received meritorious awards for her work from the Art Directors Club of Houston and *Communication*

Arts. She regularly shows her photography in exhibitions at venues that include Fotofest and Glum Rumsey Gallery in Houston, and Compton Union Gallery in Pullman, Washington.

MAGGIE TAYLOR

Maggie Taylor received a B.A. from Yale University and a M.F.A. from the University of Florida, Gainesville. After more than ten years as a still-life photographer, she began to use the computer to create images in 1996. Taylor's work has been exhibited in solo exhibitions throughout the U.S. and in Europe. In 1996 and 2001, she received a State of Florida Individual Artist's Fellowship. In 2004 she won the Santa Fe Center for Photography's Project Competition. Taylor's work is in the collections of the Princeton University Art Museum; Center for Creative Photography, Tucson; Fogg Art Museum, Harvard University; Mobile Museum of Art, Alabama; Musée de la Photographie, Charleroi, Belgium; Museet For Fotokunst, Odense, Denmark; Museum of Fine Arts, Houston; and High Museum of Art, Atlanta, among others. She lives in Gainesville, Florida.

SALLA TYKKÄ

Salla Tykkä was born in 1973 in Helsinki, where she later graduated from the Academy of Fine Arts. She continues to live and work in Helsinki. She has had solo exhibitions at Collection Lambert, Avignon, France; Statens Museum for Kunst, Copenhagen; Bethanien, Berlin; Tramway, Glasgow; Herbert F. Johnson Museum of Art, Ithaca, New York; Kontti, Kiasma –Museum of Contemporary Art, Helsinki; BAWAG–Foundation, Vienna; Kunsthalle Bern, Switzerland; Galerie Yvon Lambert, Paris; Delfina Project Space, London; and Studio Mezzo, Helsinki. Her work was included in the Venice Biennale in 2001.

AMY BRADFORD UFER

Born in Kentucky in 1938, Amy Bradford Ufer and her husband of forty-five years raised their four children in Houston, where today they enjoy nine grandchildren. Her love for photography began in her father's homemade darkroom when she was six. This love continued as she recorded the life events of her family and her activities at Christ Church Cathedral. While wrestling with a midlife illness, she came to value the inner world's language of dreams. Through the years, as she engaged in a process of guided practice translating dream images into symbolic language, Ufer became curious about the mysterious connection to her images and the healing qualities they hold. She opened a photography business, Eye Wonder, in 1999, intent on capturing images that in some way touch the soul. This is her response to the violence within and outside all of us.

ALFONSO VASQUEZ

Alfonso Vasquez, former president of the Houston Professional Photographers Guild and owner of Braeswood Vasquez Photography, is also a dedicated and proud advocate for Latino youth, supporting education and providing encouragement. A longtime civil rights supporter, he is known for his political cartoons from the 1960s that addressed the emerging political power and equality issues of Hispanics. Vasquez is a lifelong Democrat and lives in Houston's East End.

DAVID VAUGHAN

David Vaughan's path in the fine arts has been an alternate one of documenting his own life. His autobiographical work focuses on real-life relationships, presented with archetypal overtones that transcend the mundane. Various themes characterizing different aspects of the human experience find expression in photographs of a friend in the Texas Hill Country, partners in the construction business, and women shown in the intimate space of their dressing tables. His very personal life chronicle speaks to the universal with which humans collectively identify.

REBECCA VILLARREAL (no bio provided)

CAROL VUCHETICH

Carol Vuchetich received her M.F.A. from the University of Houston and has exhibited her photographs in the U.S. and abroad. For her work documenting life in the inner city, she received grants from the Texas Council on the Humanities, the National Endowment for the Arts through the Cultural Arts Council of Houston/Harris County, and the Houston Center for Photography. Her work is in the collections of the Museum of Fine Arts, Houston; the Harry Ransom Humanities Research Center, The University of Texas, Austin; and the Blaffer Gallery, the Art Museum of the University of Houston, as well as private collections. She currently teaches photography at Galveston College, Texas.

LINDA WALSH

Linda Walsh's photographs for FotoFest come from two ongoing projects. Her photographs of the Arctic National Wildlife Refuge, taken over the past two summers, extend her work on America's last wilderness. Although the Arctic Refuge has been a hotly contested landscape since its inception in 1960, the fight to maintain its integrity as an essential, intact ecosystem has accelerated greatly in recent years. Walsh's photographs depict the fragility of this landscape as well as its beauty. Her second project documents the work being done by farmers and ranchers in Texas who use sustainable agricultural practices to enhance

the health of the land and the food they raise. Walsh lives and works in Houston. She has had solo exhibitions in Houston at the Koelsch Gallery, Women's Institute of Houston, and Houston Center for Photography. Her work is in many private collections as well as the Museum of Fine Arts, Houston.

RODNEY WATERS

Pianist and photographer Rodney Waters is the artistic director of Mukuru: Arts for AIDS, a concert and art series launched by AIDS Foundation Houston to raise money for HIV prevention programs in the Houston area. A longtime advocate of using the arts to raise money and awareness for social causes, he presented the series *Seeking Refuge*, which featured portraits of refugees resettled by Interfaith Ministries for Greater Houston, at FotoFest 2004. His contributions to FotoFest 2006 explore the issues facing people living with HIV/AIDS. As a pianist, Waters has toured internationally and performs regularly with the Houston Symphony and numerous chamber music organizations. His recording of Charles Ives's Sonatas for Violin and Piano (with Curt Thompson on violin) was released worldwide by Naxos and greeted with critical acclaim by *The New York Times, Strad Magazine*, and *Gramophone*. More information about Mukuru and AIDS Foundation Houston can be found at www.mukuru.org.

ANGILEE WILKERSON

Angilee Wilkerson lives and works in the Dallas-Fort Worth metroplex. She is an artist, university instructor, and professional editorial photographer. She has participated in more than thirty national and regional exhibitions since 2002, including five solo shows. Wilkerson has also been recognized and honored by the Dallas Museum of Art; New Museum of Contemporary Art, New York; Solomon R. Guggenheim Museum, New York; George Eastman Museum of Photography and Film, Rochester, New York; Temple University, Philadelphia; SOHO Photo Gallery, New York; Society for Photographic Education; *Aperture*; and many others. Her photographs have been featured in fine art journals, editorial magazines, and newspapers, including *The Photo Review, Photographer's Forum, Harper's, Queen—London, The Wall Street Journal*, and countless others. Wilkerson is active in her community, leading workshops for institutions such as the Dallas Museum of Art and the Girl Scouts of America. She has also worked with students in local universities, colleges, high schools, and cultural centers. In 2001, she was voted the Best of Southwest Photographers in Higher Education by the Council for the Advancement and Support of Education (CASE). In 2005, Wilkerson curated *Works on Water*, an international exhibition of multimedia artists celebrating the art, science, and philosophy of water-related issues, as part of the 2005 WaterWays Symposium at the University of North Texas, Denton. Wilkerson's work frequently examines memory and identity, family narratives, and the nature of alterity through landscapes.

GEOFF WINNINGHAM

Geoff Winningham is best known for his seven books and three documentary films relating to Texas and Mexican culture, including *Rites of Fall* (Austin: University of Texas Press, 1979), his now classic book on high school football in Texas and *A Place of Dreams* (Houston: Rice University Press, 1986) a look at the city of Houston at the time of its 150th anniversary. His most recent book, *Along Forgotten River* (Austin: Texas State Historical Association, 2003), is a visual study of the landscape along Buffalo Bayou, with historical accounts of the earliest travelers to Texas. He is presently at work on a book about the landscape and cultures of the Gulf Coast of Texas and Mexico.

DOROTHY LAM WONG

Dorothy Lam Wong's interest in photography began in 1998, when she picked up a camera at the urging of her husband, also an avid photographer. Her interest soon became a passion as she discovered that she could convey the beauty and sensuality of simple, everyday objects, including flowers, fruits, a favorite corner in her home, the interplay of light and shadow, even gummi bears. Her photographs often evoke feelings of tranquility, peacefulness, and warmth. Wong's work has been featured in exhibitions organized by the Photographic Society of America; Houston Center for Photography; Beaumont Art League, Texas; Texas Art Museum, Port Arthur; Houston Chinese Photographic Society; and 4W, Houston. Her photographs have been published in *Houston Press* (2003) and in the tenth anniversary album of the Houston Chinese Photographic Society. She has exhibited in Houston at Michaeline's Restaurant, Crossline Galleries, and currently at the Houston Potters Guild/Gallery in Rice Village. A recently retired psychologist, Wong now devotes much of her time to photography.

ALICE WRIGHT

Alice Wright began her professional career as a portraitist, specializing in families and children in outdoor settings. Widely traveled, she forms a trusting relationship with the people she meets, which is reflected in her environmental portraits. Her intimate floral images further express her respect for nature. Wright has exhibited at Abilene Christian University, Texas, and her

work is in many private collections, including those of the Harry Ransom Humanities Research Center, The University of Texas at Austin, and the Center for Contemporary Art, Abilene, Texas. Her series *Bhutan: Land of Shangri-La* recently joined the permanent collection of The Grace Museum, Abilene, Texas. Wright has lectured on her photography at the Sultan Quboos University in Oman, The Grace Museum, and other locations. She is a member of the Texas Photographic Society and has studied at the Santa Fe Photographic Workshops with Nevada Wier, Joyce Tennyson, and Arthur Meyerson. Visit the website www.wrightworld.com for further information about the Bill, Alice and Mitch Wright and their work.

BILL WRIGHT

Bill Wright, a well-known lecturer on landscape and documentary photography, has published five books, including *The Tigua: Pueblo Indians of Texas* (El Paso: Texas Western Press, 1993), winner of the Border Book Award. His newest book, *The Last of the Last Frontier*, with photographer June Van Cleef, was released by Texas A&M University Press in 2005. His work appeared in the traveling exhibition *People's Lives: A Celebration of the Human Spirit (2001)*, on view at over a dozen venues. Wright has exhibited throughout Texas and the U.S. as well as in England, Scotland, Peru, Mexico, Russia, Chile, and Cape Verde. His photographs are in numerous public and private collections, including those of the British Library, London; National Museum of American Art, Washington, D.C.; Princeton Collections of Western Americana; Harry Ransom Humanities Research Center, The University of Texas, Austin; Amon Carter Museum, Ft. Worth; Witliff Gallery of Southwestern & Mexican Photography, Texas State University, San Marcos; and Museum of Fine Arts, Houston. Visit the website www.wrightworld.com for further information about the Bill, Alice and Mitch Wright and their work.

MITCH WRIGHT

Throughout high school and college, Mitch Wright photographed landscapes and architecture, leading to early exhibitions and competition awards. After completing his undergraduate degree in landscape architecture at Texas A&M University, Wright finished a M.A. in the same discipline at Harvard Graduate School of Design, approaching photography and design as a method of comprehensive study for the built environment. Currently, Wright practices as a landscape architect and planner in Austin. His

exhibition history includes solo shows at the Artist League of Texas, Abilene; Texas Photographic Society & Execucom Gallery, Austin; Riverfront Gallery, Willington, North Carolina; Arts Council of the Lower Cape Fear, Wilmington, North Carolina; and Harvard Graduate School of Design. His series Guatemala: Ten Years of Friendship traveled to the Center for International Studies, Texas Tech University, Lubbock; Center for Contemporary Art, Abilene, Texas; and Harvard Graduate School of Design. Visit the website www.wrightworld.com for further information about the Bill, Alice and Mitch Wright and their work.

SUSANNE YORK

Susanne York's fine art photography has been exhibited in many solo and group exhibitions throughout Texas, including Fotofest 2004. Her exhibition *Rapture of the Deep* appeared at the New Gallery (2004). Recent exhibitions include *Pongos Helping Pongos*, Houston Zoo; a group show in Spain; and most recently the 2005 Florence Biennale, Italy. Recent publications include *Carousel Kids*, a children's book published by Houston Zoo, Inc. York's images have appeared in books, magazines, newspapers, and commercial publications. Her successful children's photography workshops have inspired many budding artists.

ROBERT ZIEBELL

Robert Ziebell is a photographer and filmmaker who resides in Texas. His work was recently featured in *Grand Street* magazine. Ziebell's most recent solo exhibition was at Artscan in Houston. He was featured in a solo exhibition at Arthouse, Austin, in conjunction with the Society of Photographic Educators. His work also appeared in *Perspectives @ 25*, a review of twenty-five years of exhibitions in the *Perspectives* series at the Contemporary Arts Museum Houston. In addition to his pursuits in photography, Ziebell is currently working on a feature film project titled *Radio Bravo*. He is in the post-production phase of a film that conducts a virtual tour of Las Pozas, a surrealist garden in the rainforest of the Sierra Madre Mountains in Mexico, which he made for ARTpix, a multimedia nonprofit organization that integrates contemporary art with new technologies.

CURATORS

DIANE BARBER
DIVERSEWORKS ARTSPACE

Diane Barber has been the visual arts director of DiverseWorks Artspace since 1997. She is responsible for developing and implementing the organization's season of Visual Arts Programs, curating exhibitions, and organizing related educational projects. During her tenure, Barber has arranged more than forty exhibitions for DiverseWorks, including *Thought Crimes: The Art of Subversion*, which received Best Art Show honors in the *Houston Press* 2005 Best of Houston awards, and *William Pope.L: eRacism*, which was named Best Art Show in an Alternative Space by the International Association of Art Critics in 2003. Barber has served as guest curator for the Houston Center for Photography; McNeese State University, Lake Charles, Louisiana; Oklahoma Visual Arts Coalition; Hallwalls Contemporary Art Center , Buffalo, New York; and most recently Estudio Abierto, Buenos Aires, Argentina. Prior to coming to DiverseWorks, Barber served as exhibitions and publications coordinator for FotoFest, Houston. She is past board president of the National Association of Art Organizations, former chairman of the Houston Coalition for the Visual Arts, and a member of FotoFest's Art Advisory Board, and she has served as guest portfolio reviewer at various regional and national conferences.

FERNANDO CASAS
GREMILLION & CO. FINE ART, INC.

Fernando Casas is a philosopher and an artist. In 1978, after obtaining his Ph.D. in philosophy at Rice University, Houston, Casas dedicated himself full-time to painting; experimenting with alternative systems of depiction that he called "polar" and "flat-sphere" perspectives. This philosophical/artistic project led to the publication of seminal papers in Leonardo, an international journal exploring the application of contemporary science and technology to the arts and music. For the past twenty-five years, Casas has shown his work in individual and group exhibitions at private galleries, museums, and public institutions in North and South America, Europe, and Asia. He has published articles in various journals and his work has been widely discussed in numerous articles and books. Since 1985, Casas has been a professor of philosophy and the humanities at Rice University.

JEAN CASLIN
THE FOUNDRY
NORTH HARRIS COLLEGE

Jean Caslin received a B.A. in English literature and fine arts from Boston University. She then studied photography and pho-tographic history while pursuing an M.A. in art history at Stanford University, California. Caslin began her arts administration career as assistant director of the Photographic Resource Center at Boston University in 1979. She became the executive director/curator of Houston Center for Photography in 1988. Under the name Caslin Gregory & Associates, she and Diane Griffin Gregory now consult with nonprofit organizations and visual artists. Caslin's photographic work has been exhibited at FotoFest 2000, 2002, and 2004, and in Houston area shows at venues that include the Texas Photographic Society; Rice University; Glassell School of Art, Museum of Fine Arts, Houston; Koelsch Gallery; and Studio E.

FERNANDO CASTRO
GREMILLION & CO. FINE ART, INC.

Fernando Castro is an artist and a philosopher. After studying philosophy at Rice University, Houston, under a Fulbright Fellowship, he began a career as a critic in 1988, writing for *El Comercio* (Lima, Peru). Since then he has contributed to numerous periodicals around the world and is a contributing editor for *Aperture* magazine. In 1997 his photographic work took a political turn with the series *Reasons of State*. His most recent solo exhibition, *The Ideology of Color* (2004), was shown at the Centro Cultural Borges, Buenos Aires, and is currently an online exhibition at the website of Lehigh University Art Galleries. His work is in the collections of the Museum of Fine Arts, Houston; The Dancing Bear Collection, New York; Lehigh University, Bethlehem, Pennsylvania; Museo de Arte de Lima; and the Harry Ransom Research Center Collection, The University of Texas, Austin. Castro lives and works in Houston.

KEN CHRISTI
DIG 101 GALLERY

Ken Christi was born in Canada. He currently spends most of his time in Houston, where he works in the offshore oil and gas industry. Christi has lived, worked, and traveled in over thirty-five different countries. He is a passionate collector and supporter of the arts.

WAYNE GILBERT
DIG 101 GALLERY

Wayne Gilbert is the director of DIG101 Gallery in Houston. He has been putting on exhibitions for fifteen years. Gilbert graduated from the University of Houston with a B.F.A. in painting. An active artist who shows extensively, Gilbert is a partner with Digital Imaging Group (DIG).

SCOTT PEVETO (no bio provided)
MCCLAIN GALLERY

MARISA S. SÁNCHEZ (no bio provided)
MUSEUM OF FINE ARTS, HOUSTON

ANNE WILKES TUCKER
THE MUSEUM OF FINE ARTS, HOUSTON
THE METHODIST HOSPITAL CENTER
Anne Wilkes Tucker was born in Baton Rouge, Louisiana. She received undergraduate degrees from Randolph-Macon Woman's College, Lynchburg, Virginia, and Rochester Institute of Technology, New York, and a graduate degree from the Visual Studies Workshop, a division of the State University of New York. While in graduate school, she worked at the George Eastman House in Rochester, New York, and at the Gernsheim Collection of The University of Texas, Austin. From 1970 to 1971, she was a curatorial intern in the photography department of The Museum of Modern Art, New York. She is currently the Gus and Lyndall Wortham Curator of Photography at the Museum of Fine Arts, Houston, where she has worked since 1976. She founded the photography department at the museum, which now has a collection of over 20,000 photographs. She has curated over forty exhibitions, including retrospectives for Robert Frank, Ray K. Metzker, Brassaï, George Krause, Louis Faurer, and Richard Misrach, as well as surveys of the Czech avant-garde, the Allan Chasanoff Collection, and the history of Japanese photography. Most these exhibitions were accompanied by a catalogue. She has published many articles and lectured throughout the U.S., Europe, Asia, and Latin America. She has been awarded fellowships by the National Endowment for the Arts, the John Simon Guggenheim Memorial Foundation, and The Getty Center, and she received an alumnae chievement award from Randolph-Macon Woman's College. In 2001, in an issue devoted to "America's Best," *Time* magazine honored her as "America's Best Curator."

CARLOS VIGUERAS
MECA
Carlos Vigueras, curator of *Lincoln: The American Dream*, is a staff writer, contributor, editor, and photographer for several Mexico City–based periodicals, including *Unomásuno, La Jornada, El Financiero, Proceso*, and *Milenio*, as well as for *El Continental* in San Antonio. He has worked as an independent field producer for CNN, CBS, ABC, NBC, BBC, and Univision. Recently, he has worked as an independent filmmaker and cameraman, producing cultural and historical documentaries. He was the photography coordinator for *Juarez: Laboratory of Our Future* (New York: Aperture Books, 1998). Since 2000, Vigueras has curated exhibitions for the Casa de Las Américas Project, El Paso; New York Museum of the Américas, El Paso and New York; Charas Gallery, New York; City University of New York (CUNY); Museum of the Américas, University of New Mexico, Las Cruces; Casasola Museum, El Paso; and Peace Museum of the Américas, El Paso.

CLINT WILLOUR
GALVESTON ARTS CENTER
Clint Willour has been curator of the Galveston Arts Center, Texas, for the past sixteen years, serving as its executive director for ten years. From 1973 to 1989, he was director of the Tibor deNagy Gallery in Houston, later called Watson de/Nagy & Company and the Watson Gallery. A founding member and president of the Houston Art Dealers Association, he was the originator of the popular *Introductions* exhibitions held by the association each summer. Willour has served on a number of peer panels for the Cultural Arts Council of Houston/Harris County, Texas Commission on the Arts, Louisiana Council on the Arts, and San Antonio Department of Arts and Cultural Affairs, and he has been a reviewer for the Institute of Museum and Library Services. He currently serves in Houston on the program committee of the Houston Center for Photography (where he is a past president of the board), the Art Board of Houston FotoFest, the changing exhibitions committee and travelling exhibitions committee of the Holocaust Museum, the exhibitions committee of the Houston Center for Contemporary Craft, the system-wide art accessions committee of the University of Houston, and the prints and drawings subcommittee and modern and contemporary accessions subcommittee of the Museum of Fine Arts, Houston, where he is also chair of the photography accessions subcommittee and a member of the collections committee and the board of the Museum Collectors. Willour has served on the board of the Texas Association of Museums and received a Legend Award from the Dallas Center for Contemporary Art, as well as being named Texas Patron of the Year by the Art League of Houston. He curates twenty-four exhibitions per year in Galveston and serves regularly as a guest curator for institutions throughout the state of Texas. He also writes for institutional catalogues and brochures, as well as for the publications *Artlies* and *Spot*.